Asian American Politics

Asian American Politics

ANDREW L. AOKI AND
OKIYOSHI TAKEDA

polity

The right of Andrew L. Aoki and Okiyoshi Takeda to be identified as
Authors of this Work has been asserted in accordance with the UK
Copyright, Designs and Patents Act 1988.

First published in 2008 by Polity Press
Reprinted in 2013, 2014 (twice), 2015, 2016

Polity Press
65 Bridge Street
Cambridge CB2 1UR, UK

Polity Press
350 Main Street
Malden, MA 02148, USA

ISBN-13: 978-0-7456-3446-3
ISBN-13: 978-0-7456-3447-0(pb)

A catalogue record for this book is available from the British Library.

Typeset in 9.5 on 13 pt Swift Light
by Servis Filmsetting Ltd, Stockport, Cheshire
Printed and bound in the United States by RR Donnelley

Text design by Peter Ducker MISTD

The publisher has used its best endeavours to ensure that the URLs for
external websites referred to in this book are correct and active at the time
of going to press. However, the publisher has no responsibility for the
websites and can make no guarantee that a site will remain live or that the
content is or will remain appropriate.

Every effort has been made to trace all copyright holders, but if any have
been inadvertently overlooked the publisher will be pleased to include any
necessary credits in any subsequent reprint or edition.

For further information on Polity, visit our website: www.politybooks.com

Contents

Asian Americans and the Politics of Identity

This book tells a story. Unlike most stories, however, ours has no ending, because the struggles for equal rights and full political incorporation continue to this day. Although our story takes the form of a straightforward account of Asian American politics, we have tried to convey some of the ways that this politics has powerfully shaped the lives of many human beings.

This translates into two goals for the book. One is to give a summary of Asian American politics that will be accessible to undergraduates taking courses in race and ethnicity. A second is to sketch out larger themes that run through the politics of Asian Americans and other racialized groups. These larger themes help suggest responses to critics who claim that courses in race and politics are not needed. Throughout the larger themes, the common thread is the politics of identity, but we stress that we mean something somewhat different from what is usually thought of as "identity politics."

The "politics of identity," as we use the phrase, refers to the basic question of how Asian Americans are defined – including *who* gets to define them. Scholarship on race has shown how racial categories are social creations that have shifted over time. We believe that a persistent issue in Asian American politics has been where Asian Americans are to be placed in the American ethnoracial universe.

Classifications have serious consequences. Racial classification has played a critical role in denying opportunity to generations of Americans.

The first nineteenth-century immigrants from Asia did not fit well within the widely understood racial categories, but, within a short period of time, they were being classified as nonwhite. Given the enormous advantages for those classified as "white," it is no surprise that Asian immigrants resisted being identified as nonwhite.

Many things have changed over the past century and a half, but the question of identity continues to be a central issue. Today, rather than fighting against classification as "nonwhite," Asian Americans are more likely to be criticizing their depiction as a "model minority," or fighting against the "forever foreigner" stereotype. What has not changed over all these decades is the attempt of Asian Americans to define themselves, and to be accepted on their own terms.

Terms have had powerful consequences in the politics of race, and so it is important to explain the ones we use. Perhaps most important is the reason why we usually write "Asian Americans" rather than "Asian and Pacific

Islander Americans" or one of its variants. We do so because this book focuses primarily on Asian Americans. Although we discuss Native Hawaiians and other Pacific Islander Americans (NHOPI) on occasion, they are not included in our primary focus.

We exclude NHOPIs not because we think their politics is less important but because we think it deserves *more* attention than it often receives. We agree with the argument that NHOPI politics is distinctive, and should not be treated as an extension of Asian American politics. While there continue to be extremely valuable alliances between Asian Americans and NHOPIs, the history and central issues of the two groups are very different. Hawaiians, numerically dominant in the NHOPI category, face many challenges typical of indigenous peoples – ones that are often very different from the concerns of immigrant groups. Asian American politics, in contrast, is strongly influenced by the fact that the Asian American population currently includes a high percentage of immigrants. Issues of paramount importance to Native Hawaiians are little known to most Asian Americans, at least those outside of Hawai'i. Sovereignty (control over a territory), for example, is a primary concern for many Native Hawaiian activists, but would make no sense as a concern for immigrants. Incorporating Pacific Islander (some have suggested that it should be called Oceania) studies in a text on Asian Americans can too easily lead to a serious understudy of NHOPI concerns (Diaz 2004).[1]

Our usage also reflects changes made in census categories. In 1990, Native Hawaiians and Other Pacific Islanders were placed in the same category as Asian Americans, but, in response to NHOPI requests, the groups were split apart in Census 2000. Activists did not necessarily favor a new racial listing, as some seemed to feel that they would fit best in the "AIAN" category – American Indian and Alaskan Native, the other indigenous peoples of the United States. However, the unique legal status of American Indian and Alaskan Native tribes made them concerned about adding new groups to their category, so a compromise was to move NHOPIs out of the category they shared with Asian Americans and into one of their own (Espiritu and Omi 2000).

We have also followed the preference of many native Hawaiians in spelling Hawai'i with the *okina* (similar to an upside-down apostrophe) between the last two letters. "Hawai'i" is considered to be the proper spelling in the Hawaiian language.

Because alliances between Asian Americans and NHOPIs are common, we refer to both groups at times. Indeed, most panethnic organized groups refer to both in their names, which often include APA (Asian Pacific Americans), APIA (Asian and Pacific Island Americans), AAPI (Asian Americans and Pacific Islanders), or AAPIA (Asian American and Pacific Islander Americans) in their names. When referring to both subpopulations, we use one of the broader designations (e.g. AAPIA). We understand that there are some strong preferences about which term is to be used, and we have tried to balance that against a recognition of terms that are actually being used today.

When we do refer to Asian Americans, we are referring to all living in the United States with the intention to stay. Tourists would not meet our definition, nor do we usually consider temporary workers to be Asian Americans (e.g. Japanese corporate executives stationed in the U.S. for a few years). However, immigrants – including those who have proper authorization and those who do not – are counted by us as Asian Americans. Given past efforts to prevent Asian immigrants from naturalizing, we are sensitive to the need to be inclusive in our definition of the Asian American community.

In addition, we follow the widespread (although not universal) preference of Asian Americans to write the term without a hyphen. Many are concerned that the hyphenated version – "Asian-American" – implies a less-than-complete belonging, implying that Asians in America are not full members of society. The unhyphenated term, "Asian American," more clearly implies that the modifier is meant to identify only region of origin. We follow the same approach with Asian American subgroups, so we write "Chinese American" rather than "Chinese-American." We realize that some style manuals call for hyphenating these terms, but we prefer to follow usage that is more sensitive to the preferences of the people being named.

We have tried to be sensitive to the preferences of other groups in our terminology as well. However, it is impossible to be completely successful at this, since it is rare that everyone in a group agrees. In addition, our goal is to help readers understand the constructed nature of these terms, so we want to be careful how we use them.

This becomes a challenge immediately when we try to describe the broad categories that we use. While it is conventional to refer to these categories as "racial," that still begs the question of which categories are defined as racial ones. The problem, of course, is that the Census Bureau and Office of Management and Budget (OMB) categories are at odds with the way that many people understand racial categories. "Hispanic" presents the primary problem. The Census Bureau and OMB give "Hispanic" a unique status, which has resulted in many scholars referring to "Hispanic" as an "ethnic group," rather than a racial one. However, evidence suggests that many Latinos think of themselves as comprising a separate racial group, which is reflected in the fact that Latinos were by far the dominant group selecting the "Other race" category in the 2000 census (Wright 1994).

In an effort to reflect these different realities, we use the term "ethnoracial" to refer to the categories that include African American, American Indian, Asian American, Latino, Native Hawaiian and Other Pacific Islander, and White.

We should note that we also use the term "politics" in a broad sense. While some political scientists might limit "politics" to activities connected closely to governmental actions, we prefer a more expansive meaning. Indeed, a major development in the study of politics has been a growing realization that "politics" can encompass a broad range of activities, perhaps most famously expressed in the feminist declaration that "the personal is political." In the case of Asian Americans, we might say that "the perceptions are political," as images of Asian Americans can have important political consequences, a topic we explore in some depth in chapter 7.

Historically, the political consequences have usually been negative for those seen as nonwhite, a topic we explore in chapter 1. Ethnoracial minorities share a history of disadvantage, pushed to the margins of society and defined as outside the mainstream. Although their exclusion was often justified by references to physiological differences, in reality race was a social creation. We explain how political decisions helped to create and maintain racial categories, to the disadvantage of those defined as nonwhite. For Asian Americans, this process of racialization helped to define them as foreign as well as nonwhite.

Racial classification is only one way of identifying social groups, as we explain in chapter 2. A less restrictive concept is that of ethnicity, which is often conceived as something much less deterministic than race. Ethnicity is sometimes seen as a way of subdividing racial groups. For example, while Asians are often defined as a separate racial group, Asian subgroups such as Chinese Americans or Vietnamese Americans are seen as ethnic groups. Although racial classification implies uniformity, the reality is that racial groups are very diverse, and Asian Americans may be the most diverse racialized group. That diversity presents substantial challenges, since political influence is much more likely if Asian American subgroups are able to join together, but a common effort requires overcoming considerable differences.

Even if they are able to bridge their differences, political influence is not guaranteed. Because substantial numbers are immigrants, they are not eligible to vote until they are naturalized. Research suggests that voting registration requirements present another obstacle. However, other avenues for participation exist, and Asian Americans have long utilized them, contrary to the stereotype which suggests that they have been politically inactive. In chapter 3, we explore Asian American political participation and attitudes.

While chapter 3 focuses on individual participation, chapter 4 examines participation in groups. Political effectiveness usually requires collective action, so we describe some of the many groups working to advance the interests of Asian Americans. We note how these efforts may be helping to develop a stronger sense of a pan-Asian American identity.

Achieving full political equality requires not just participation but representation in government. In chapter 5, we look at Asian American representation in the legislative, executive, and judicial branches. Although our focus is primarily on the federal government, we also describe representation in California, where large numbers of Asian Americans reside.

In chapter 6, we turn to a rapidly developing issue in American politics: relations between communities of color. Although racialized groups have confronted similar challenges, they also have considerable differences, and tensions have sometimes exploded into violence. Conflict has often received more attention in the media, but we also consider prospects for cooperation, and we look at examples in alliances between ethnoracial groups.

Prospects for conflict or cooperation can be influenced by how each group is perceived. In chapter 7 we look at perceptions of Asian Americans. In particular, we explore what appear to be two powerful and contrasting images: that of Asian Americans as perpetual foreigners, and those of Asian Americans as model minorities. We explain how both those images promote the common theme that Asian Americans are somehow fundamentally different, and we look at efforts to challenge these stereotypes.

Chapter 8 looks at Asian Americans and public policy. We focus primarily on two policies: education and immigration. We note how educational attainment is often cited as evidence for the model minority image of Asian Americans, but we explain how the reality is somewhat different. In addition, we explore the important question of *transnationalism*: how connections with countries of origin can influence the public policy efforts of Asian Americans.

In our brief concluding chapter, we return to the question of Asian American identity. Where Asian Americans "fit" into the larger society has important political consequences. We note that there is some evidence that many Asian Americans may be able to gain greater acceptance for themselves, but possibly at the expense of other communities of color. The Asian American struggle to control their own identity can progress in ways that connect or separate them from other groups seeking a more just society. Young adults, such as those reading this book, are likely to play an important role in determining which path is taken.

Acknowledgments

This book is a collective effort of far more people than the authors listed on the cover. We have been fortunate to be part of a remarkably collegial and mutually supportive group of scholars who have worked in many ways to advance the study of Asian American politics. This book would not be possible without the efforts of these colleagues. Our citations give an indication of our scholarly debts, but we also want to thank many individuals who provided direct assistance to us in the writing of this book: Chuck Aoki, Lars Christiansen, Kim Geron, James Lai, Taeku Lee, Pei-te Lien, Don Nakanishi, Jennifer Nelson, Karthick Ramakrishnan, and Janelle Wong.

Aoki would also like to thank the Augsburg College Center for Teaching and Learning, which provided a grant giving him more time to devote to this manuscript, and Laurie Knox, who generously took the time to give the manuscript a much-needed final review. Takeda wants to thank the schools (and people there) which gave him an opportunity to teach a course specially focused on Asian American politics. He thanks the University of Pennsylvania (Rosane Rocher and Grace Kao), New York University (Jack Tchen), Columbia University (Gary Okihiro), and Japan Women's University (Kaz Oshio and Noriko Shimada). He also wants to thank Yasuko Takezawa for her continuing encouragement, and Masako Iino for providing her study meeting as an opportunity to present work which became the basis of parts of this book.

We have been fortunate to have very understanding, supportive, and capable editorial guidance from Louise Knight and Emma Hutchinson at Polity, and we are extremely grateful for all they have done for us. This book would never have seen the light of day without them.

In addition, we would like to thank the three anonymous reviewers of the book proposal and two anonymous reviewers of the manuscript draft for their very helpful comments. All shortcomings of this book are, of course, our responsibility.

Finally, Aoki would like to dedicate this book to his mother. She lived through some of the most searing injustices described in these pages, and what merits this book may possess owe much to the inspiration provided by the grace, courage, and dedication to justice which has defined her life. Takeda wants to dedicate this book to his friends and colleagues who have taught him who Asian Americans really are. Since the 1995 sit-in for Asian American

Studies courses at Princeton University president's office, many friends answered his questions or shared their Asian American experience. Without their personal insights, this book would not have been written, although their testimonies are not quoted.

CHAPTER ONE

Why Study Asian American Politics?
Racialization and its Consequences

Introduction

Why should you read a book about Asian American politics? Why not just cover it in a general American politics text, or in a book on the politics of multiple minority groups? To put it briefly, there are two central arguments for the separate study of Asian American politics. First, the political struggles of Asian Americans have contributed significantly to a larger struggle important to the entire United States, the struggle for equal opportunity and access. Second, Asian Americans have experienced politics in unique ways. In this chapter, we explain these justifications for a separate study of Asian American politics as well as the theoretical framework that underlies this book.

After reading this chapter, you should have a better understanding of these topics:

1 How racial and ethnic minorities have struggled for equal treatment, and how that struggle has helped to define the kind of country America would be.
2 How the politics of Asian Americans are different than those of other peoples of color.
3 How racial categories are a creation of sociopolitical factors in a society.
4 What is meant by *racialization*.
5 How Asian Americans have been racialized in the past.

The underlying theme of this book is the struggle to define Asian Americans. As we explain in the coming chapters, the struggle over an Asian American identity is also very much a struggle over the identity of all of America.

Asian American Politics and the Struggle to Define America

Throughout American history, keen observers have argued that the United States was "the first new nation," one founded not on ancestry but on a shared set of ideals. Others have doubted this, suggesting that an inherent part of the American political tradition has been a deep commitment to the idea that people are not equal – that some are inferior to others (e.g. Smith 1997). The issue, in its simplest form, is "who are Americans?" Can anyone become an

American, or does the country confer full rights only on those considered to be white?

"Identity politics" usually refers to efforts of groups to achieve recognition and respect for their existence, but we have a broader idea in mind. When we refer to "the politics of identity," we mean the struggles to define the American identity. Is the United States a society which offers equal opportunity to anyone, or do the promises of opportunity apply only to those of certain ancestries?

The battle over the American identity is therefore part of a larger struggle over access to opportunities. Throughout the history of the United States, large numbers of people have struggled for basic political rights. Many of those in power have resisted these efforts, trying to deny a majority of the population the opportunity to participate in the political process.

The founding documents of the United States promise equal rights for all, but the reality has often made a mockery of those promises. In the Declaration of Independence, for instance, Thomas Jefferson declared that the Founders found it "self-evident" that "all men are created equal" and that they are "endowed by their Creator with certain unalienable rights," among them "life, liberty, and the pursuit of happiness." And yet we know that many Americans have been denied many basic rights. African Americans were enslaved, and even after the Thirteenth Amendment to the Constitution ended slavery, many other schemes were developed to deny blacks basic civil rights. American Indians were forced off their lands, and their children were taken from them and placed in schools that sought to destroy the heritage of the many Native American tribes. The Fifth Amendment to the Constitution guarantees that "no person shall . . . be deprived of life, liberty, or property, without due process of law," and yet, during World War II, over 100,000 Japanese Americans were imprisoned without trial or even charges. We could easily fill a book with more examples.

The story of minority politics in the United States, including the politics of African Americans, American Indians, Hispanic Americans, Asian Americans, and Pacific Islanders, is the story of people fighting to hold the United States to the ideals expressed in documents such as the Declaration of Independence and the Constitution. Despite great odds, many people have struggled against violations of those political ideals. Today, schools routinely teach about epic efforts such as the civil rights movement of the 1950s and 1960s, when black Americans braved police brutality and state-sanctioned terrorism to fight for basic rights. Much less well known is the story of Asian Americans' broad effort to win these rights.

How Asian American Politics is Different

But why not just learn about these struggles in a book that covers minority politics more broadly? The reason is that the Asian American political experience differs in important ways from that of other minority groups.

For instance, although both African Americans and Asians are usually considered to be "nonwhite," Black Americans confronted slavery – a far greater denial of freedom than ever experienced by Asian Americans. Yet after the Civil War, African Americans later found it far easier to claim American citizenship than Asian Americans, whose citizenship rights were not secured until the 1950s.

One key characteristic that distinguishes Asian Americans from African Americans is that Asian Americans have been defined as foreigners. Although African Americans are as visually distinct as Asian Americans, most Americans are likely to assume that someone with dark skin is a native to the United States, while someone with "Asian" features is assumed to be a foreigner, even though many Asian American families have been here for three generations or more, and third- or fourth-generation Asian Americans may speak no language other than English.

Like Asian Americans, Latinos also are often perceived as foreigners, but they have not faced the same array of legal discrimination that confronted Asian Americans. This is probably due to treaty agreements that gave Mexicans equal rights when America acquired what had been the northern portion of Mexico, in the nineteenth century. Although these agreements were often violated – most notably in parts of Texas – they created legal protections for Mexican Americans, protections that the first-wave Asian immigrants never enjoyed.

Asian Americans also differ from Latinos and African Americans in their much greater diversity. Whereas over 50 per cent of all Latinos are of Mexican ancestry, no single nationality group comprises even 30 per cent of Asian Americans. Also, although both groups have large numbers of recent immigrants, Asian Americans are considerably fewer in number, creating different political challenges.

Asian Americans share with American Indians a history of political oppression, but the origins of the oppression differ significantly. Perhaps most importantly, American Indians have struggled as indigenous peoples (people whose ancestors lived here long before anyone else), while most Asian Americans are either immigrants or the descendants of people who immigrated within the past century or so. All these distinctions explain why we need a book on Asian American politics separate from one on minority politics in general.

But isn't the struggle of Asian Americans for equal political rights and opportunity really just a historical issue? As we will demonstrate in this book, it most certainly is *not* just history. The struggle continues. Racial discrimination continues – a point we will discuss later in this book – and the legacy of past racism has not yet been eradicated.

As we explain below, the very fact that "whites" are seen as different from other "races" is something that needs to be explained. Although most people today assume that racial difference is based in nature, the ways we understand race does not have any genetic or other scientific basis. To understand this, it helps to look more closely at how race divides us.

The Color Line and its Consequences

Political systems distinguish between "insiders" and "outsiders," giving benefits to the former that are denied the latter. In the United States, insiders have often been defined as "white." Outsiders, whatever their physical or genetic characteristics, have often been defined as nonwhite. And for much of the country's history, to be defined as "nonwhite" was to be placed at considerable economic, political, and social disadvantage.

The division between white and nonwhite is sometimes referred to as the "color line." As we will explain later in this chapter, the very notion of "white" or "nonwhite" is based only superficially on perceptions of physical appearance; in fact, these designations have derived from efforts to establish and maintain economic, political, and social advantage. The idea of race is not rooted in genetic studies of humankind, but rather in the efforts of some groups of people to gain advantages over others. The idea of race was created to make discrimination easier. The use of race to discriminate against others can be traced back at least to the earliest colonial times, but we will focus on discrimination that has occurred since the United States gained its independence.

Racial discrimination was present at the birth of the USA. In 1787, the new Constitution protected slavery, in a glaring contradiction to its claim to "secure the blessings of liberty." Only a few years later, in 1790, Congress passed an act limiting naturalization (the process of becoming a citizen) to "free white persons." Immigrants could become citizens, but only as long as they were of the proper race.

Citizenship promised its recipients important constitutional protections. Racial restrictions on naturalization – the opportunity to become a citizen – left individuals vulnerable to a wide range of discriminatory measures. One important example is the ownership of property. The United States Constitution includes important protections for property rights, but non-citizens have not always enjoyed those protections. In the past, preventing immigrants from becoming citizens could allow governments to prevent those immigrants from owning property. Not being able to own property could make it much harder for immigrants to escape poverty and enjoy other opportunities.

But how was the color line created? To answer that, we need to explain the nature of racial categories.

The Political and Social Construction of Race

Most people probably think of race as something with biological roots. Careful examination, however, shows race is something that people have invented with little or no help from nature. Racial categories are politically and socially constructed.

For example, how do we determine who is considered to be of the "white" race? Superficially, "white" refers to skin tone, but it is clear that skin tone is an insufficient means of determining who is white, who nonwhite. Many of southern European ancestry have skin tones much darker than those of Asian ancestry, yet the latter are never considered today to be "white." Some believe that the scientific term for "white" is "Caucasian," but that only begs the question of what "Caucasian" means. Presumably, Caucasians are descendants of peoples who originated in the Caucasus Mountains region, but this category includes some of the peoples of India, who are generally not considered to be white. Furthermore, only about a century ago, many considered native Hawaiians, Maoris (the aboriginal people of New Zealand), Samoans, and other Pacific Islanders to be Caucasian (Haney López 1996, 70–1). Our current understanding that "Caucasian" means "European" only developed in the twentieth century.

Even equating "white" with "European" does not solve the problem of racial definitions. Using this approach, Greeks and Bulgarians are white, while most of their neighboring Turks are not, since they live in what geographers consider to be western Asia. Turks and Bulgarians unquestionably have more in common than Turks and Japanese, yet Bulgarians are considered to be Europeans, while most Turks are considered to be Asian. Even more ludicrously, a Turk living in Istanbul, on the European side of Turkey, would be white, while a fellow Turk living just across the Bosporus Strait would be nonwhite, if we equate "white" with "European." One might reply with the common sense suggestion that Turks should be considered to be white, but that then raises the question of Syrians, Armenians, Iranians, and others in western Asia. So, defining "white" as "European" does not solve the problem of racial definition, in large part because "Europe" is also a cultural creation. The boundaries of whiteness must be set arbitrarily, because there is no obvious geographical line where people on one side are unquestionably white, while those on the other are not.

Whiteness, it turns out, is a cultural creation. This means that racial categories are not based on biological differences, but rather have been created because of the way that some people view other people. The racial categories we use today have no more basis in biology than do other social groupings – for example, book groups or baseball fans. Individuals we consider to be of different races are no more biologically different than, say, New York Yankees fans are biologically different from New York Mets fans.[1]

Evidence for the constructed nature of race can be found in the way that the "white" category has been expanded. People we assume today to be white – such as Irish and Italians – were often not viewed that way when they first immigrated to the United States. Their acceptance as "whites" occurred over time, and often after considerable effort (Ignatiev 1995; Jacobson 1998).

Further examination of our Alice-in-Wonderland world of race only emphasizes the curious way that racial categories are constructed. It has often been noted that white women can give birth to black children, but black women cannot give birth to white children. Biologically, that is nonsense. But race is not about biology; rather, it is about power and what is often called "social construction."

Racial Formation, Racialization, and Inequality

Our underlying theoretical framework here – and throughout this book – is the concept of *racial formation*. Sociologists Michael Omi and Howard Winant, who developed the idea of racial formation, define it as "the sociohistorical processes by which racial categories are created, inhabited, transformed, and destroyed" (Omi and Winant 1994, 55). Racial formation is developed through "racial projects," which Omi and Winant define as "an interpretation, representation, or explanation of racial dynamics, and an effort to reorganize and redistribute resources along particular racial lines" (Omi and Winant 1994, 56). To put it somewhat more simply, a racial project is a way of portraying race and the way race works, with the result that some so-called "racial" groups get more resources, and others get less. If someone writes opinion columns about the influence of race on crime, that person can be part of a racial project. People who argue about affirmative action are often participating in racial projects. A racial project is usually not a formal effort, although there may be some coordination between participants. At any given time, many racial projects may be underway, and the effects of some may work against the effects of others. Racial formation takes place through the interaction of racial projects. Some racial projects may be more successful than others and therefore have a greater influence on racial formation. In short, racial formation happens as a result of both the way people think about racial categories and the way that they behave based on that thinking.

One possible consequence of racial formation can be *racialization*: the portrayal of a large group of people as inferior. For instance, in the nineteenth century, many Americans cited supposedly scientific evidence that "proved" Europeans were superior to Chinese and Japanese. As George Yancey has noted, "racialization in the United States has been historically assessed by a standard of 'whiteness'" (Yancey 2003,125) Those seen as inferior were defined as nonwhite. "If a group was considered white, then that group was accepted in mainstream American society. The more white a group was considered, the more social prestige and legal rights members of this group would have" (Yancey 2003, 125). For much of the history of the United States, racial categories were created to divide humans into different groups, with one usually receiving favored treatment, while most or all of the others have usually been at a disadvantage (Kobayashi 1992). The greatest opportunities have usually been reserved for those considered to be white.

One of the challenges of racialization is that it can be difficult to maintain. Those not blinded by prejudices can see that claims of racial inferiority are false, if they get to know members of the so-called inferior race. Because of this, those seeking to discriminate against others have turned to politics to aid their efforts.

By passing a wide range of discriminatory laws, proponents of racialization can serve their cause two ways. First, they can limit contact which would enable some people to see that the claims of racial difference are false. Those seeking to racialize others have often worked for statutes ("laws") and ordinances requiring segregation of housing, schools, and other spheres. Second, discriminatory laws and rules can place the targets of racialization at a tremendous disadvantage. By cutting off easy access to education, by drastically limiting job prospects or by denying credit, those seeking to discriminate can greatly increase the chance that the victims of these policies will have low educational attainment and live in poverty. Racializers can then use these outcomes as evidence that a category of people is inherently inferior. A vicious cycle begins, which can be summarized as follows:

1 Supporters of racialization claim that a category of people are inferior.
2 That category of people are the targets of discriminatory treatment (often justified on the grounds that the people are inferior), making it difficult for them to get a good education, access to good jobs or access to other ways to build wealth.
3 Many of the people who are the targets of these discriminatory laws achieve lower levels of education and live in poverty, because of the discrimination.
4 Supporters of racialization point to low levels of education and high poverty rates to support their claims that the people are inferior.

The history of Asian Americans helps to highlight the process of racialization. Because very few Asians lived in the United States in the late eighteenth century, American racial categories originally did not even take Asians into account. This seems hard to believe today because an "Asian" racial category has since been created, and we have come to accept it so readily that it is difficult to imagine a time before it existed. However, when Asians began immigrating to the United States in large numbers, the American racial hierarchy tended to label only "black" and "white": African Americans and European Americans. Much of the early history of Asian American politics is the story of efforts by immigrants to counter others' efforts to racialize them in ways that shut them out from the opportunities available to the so-called white.

To finish our explanation of why Asian American politics is a subject worthy of separate study, we will give a brief history of the process by which Asian Americans were racialized. This story of racialization dramatically counters the mythical image of American democracy, according to which individuals can use civil rights granted to them by the Constitution to defend their own interests. The political experience of Asian Americans has instead been shaped critically by racialization and its accompanying denial of political rights, leaving them with very little political power for many years.

Racialization and the Early Years of Asian American Politics

From the start of large-scale immigration to the United States, Asian immigrants encountered forces of racialization.[2] Although some Americans have always held prejudiced views toward Asians, a critical step toward racialization was the enactment of discriminatory laws and ordinances that institutionalized those views.

Asians appear to have come to what is now the United States by the late eighteenth century (Espina 1988), but substantial Asian immigration did not begin until the mid-nineteenth century, when large numbers of Chinese headed to California to seek their fortune in "Gold Mountain."[3] Although discrimination and the natural challenges of gold mining left most disappointed, other economic factors continued to attract Chinese immigrants (Tsai 1986; Takaki 1998).

Chinese immigrants faced legal challenges almost immediately. In 1852 a committee in the California state legislature issued a report warning about "the concentration . . . of vast numbers of the Asiatic races . . . and of many others dissimilar from ourselves in customs, language, and education" (McClain 1994, 10). A week later, the California governor, John Bigler, called for action to "check [the] tide of Asiatic immigration," including measures to stop or discourage immigration from China (McClain 1994, 11). So began the racialization of the Chinese, just as they began immigrating in significant numbers. In the California legislature, anti-immigrant sentiment helped to pass the Foreign Miners' License Tax, which required foreign miners to obtain a license costing $3 per month. Although ostensibly targeting all foreigners, the tax seemed aimed primarily at the Chinese, who were working in mines in large numbers. Other taxes and fees followed, including a measure which had the effect of adding a $5 fee to the price of passage for immigrants arriving from overseas, and a statute which placed a tax of $2.50 on each Chinese resident of the state (McClain 1994, 12–13; Takaki 1998, 81–2).

Chinese immigrants fought back against these discriminatory measures. In China, merchants had created social organizations to advance their interests, and similar associations emerged among Chinese immigrants in the United States. Eventually, there were six of these associations, which came to be known as the Chinese Six Companies (or Six Chinese Companies, or just Six Companies). The Six Companies became leaders in opposing anti-Chinese measures, not only urging state and local authorities to reject such proposals, but also appealing to federal authorities, such as the president (Takaki 1998, 113; McClain 1994, 14–16; L.E.A Ma 1991, 149–56; Tsai 1986, 45–50). They and other groups, and individual Chinese, repeatedly mounted legal challenges to discriminatory laws. Although such laws continued to be enacted, Asian Americans managed to win some significant victories, such as when the California Supreme Court ruled that the tax on Chinese residents was a violation of the U.S. Constitution (*Lin Sing* v. *Washburn* 20 Cal. 534 [1862]; Takaki 1998, 113; H. Kim 1994, 49; McClain 1994, 27).

Hawai'i was also the location of important struggles.[4] Asian Americans in Hawai'i faced fewer overtly political conflicts than those on the mainland, but they engaged in coalition-building and protests that carried considerable political significance. Asian immigrants to Hawai'i usually worked on the sugar cane plantations, where they faced harsh conditions and few other opportunities. Efforts to restrict Asian immigration were less successful in Hawai'i than on the mainland, however, in large part because powerful plantation owners, who relied heavily on Asian immigrant labor, opposed the restrictions (Takaki, 1998, ch. 4; Tsai 1986, 28–30; Melendy 1984, 23–6). "Over 300,000 Asians entered the islands between 1850 and 1920," resulting in a diverse population where Japanese were the most numerous ethnic group by 1920, with 42.7 per cent of the islands' population (Takaki 1998, 133). The ethnic diversity within the Asian-worker population served plantation owners well, since workers generally organized by ethnicity, and the ethnically based worker organizations usually did not form alliances with each other. Chinese, Filipino, Japanese, Korean, and other workers staged periodic strikes and other protests against unfair and violent treatment, but their efforts were weakened by the absence of a coalition uniting the different worker groups. In 1920, though, "Filipinos and Japanese, joined by Spanish, Portuguese, and Chinese laborers . . . participated in the first major interethnic working-class struggle in Hawaii" (Takaki 1998, 154). Although the strike was eventually broken with the use of Hawaiian, Korean, and Portuguese strikebreakers, it demonstrated the potential for interethnic cooperation, a possibility that continues to be of great importance today. An important practical development was the decision of the Japanese Federation of Labor "to become an interracial union and to call the organization the Hawaii Laborers' Association," reflecting its new multiethnic composition (Takaki 1998, 155). To this day, the ability of Asian American groups to form larger coalitions is critical to their chances for political success.

To escape conditions on the plantations, many Asians migrated to the mainland as soon as they had saved enough to do so. In the latter half of the 1860s, many Chinese found work with the Central Pacific, building the transcontinental railroad. Lucrative economic incentives encouraged the Southern and Union Pacific railroads to build as fast as they could, and they needed a large supply of workers to do so. Chinese immigrants did much of the work constructing the western stretch of track, and many lost their lives as they extended the railroad across the treacherous Sierra Nevada in the horrific winter of 1866–7.[5] The accomplishments of the Chinese helped some gain work on railroad crews after the completion of the railway, but for many, work ran out when the golden spike was driven at Promontory Point, Utah, on May 10, 1869.

Although exposed to racial discrimination from the beginning, Chinese immigrants had powerful defenders among businesses who wanted their labor. With the completion of the transcontinental railroad, demand for Chinese labor decreased considerably, and anti-immigration forces gained in strength.

Excluding Immigrants

The first efforts at limiting Chinese immigration began in 1875, with the Page Act, whose stated purpose was to exclude Chinese prostitutes, but which often was applied to prevent the immigration of Chinese women in general. A more comprehensive immigration restriction law was passed in 1882.[6] Nicknamed the Chinese Exclusion Act, the law forbade the immigration of Chinese laborers for ten years. Chinese exclusion was extended for another ten years in 1892 with the passage of the Geary Act, and again for another decade in 1902. In 1904 the ban was extended indefinitely.

In recent years scholars have debated the causes of the Chinese Exclusion Act. The traditional view has been that the law was pushed largely by organized labor, which was aided greatly by widespread prejudice against the Chinese (e.g. Saxton 1971, 1990; Mink 1986). More recently, Andrew Gyory has argued that the driving force was opportunistic politicians who falsely claimed that labor unions were calling for exclusion (Gyory 1998). Although anti-Chinese sentiment was indeed strong in California, Gyory argues that workers in the east had little interest in the Chinese in the eastern United States, and that hostility toward the Chinese was minimal in most of the country.

While historians disagree over the reasons for Chinese exclusion, few debate that this policy marked a significant turning point in the history of race in America. The Chinese Exclusion Act limited immigration to small categories such as students or merchants, and the Page Act helped create a tremendous gender imbalance, which meant that relatively few Chinese American men could find wives. Thus the Chinese American population began a long decline. The next four decades saw ever-expanding efforts to ban immigration from Asia.[7] This happened at the same time as the southern United States was entering the era of Jim Crow, when racial segregation and other forms of discrimination were enacted in an effort to mire African Americans in permanent positions of inferiority. The Chinese Exclusion Act helped to mark the beginning of an era where public policy was used aggressively to benefit those seen as white, and to place tremendous disadvantages on those considered to be nonwhite.

Demand for laborers did not end, however, and employers began to turn elsewhere in Asia for workers, particularly Japan. By the early twentieth century, Japanese immigration had grown substantially and was attracting considerable opposition. Calls for restrictions were particularly vociferous from white farmers, who feared losing out to the extremely productive Japanese farms. Once again, Asian immigrants began to be racialized. This time it was the

Japanese who were portrayed as the inferior race, just as the Chinese had been twenty years before.

Hostility toward the Japanese was brought to a head in the spring of 1905, when the San Francisco School Board proposed a plan to segregate Japanese American schoolchildren, as Chinese American schoolchildren had already been segregated. Japanese American schoolchildren, declared the board, were "vicious" and "immoral" (Chuman 1976, 20). In stark contrast, the teachers of the children praised them and considered them to be "well behaved, studious, and remarkably bright" (Chuman 1976, 24).

In the fall of 1906, the segregation plan began, triggering a significant negative reaction in Japan. What happened next illustrates the important role that international relations has played – and continues to play – in shaping immigration policy in the United States. The United States could not afford to ignore Japan's displeasure at what it regarded as a blatant insult toward Japanese immigrants. Japan was considered to be a much more formidable nation than China. In 1895 it had defeated China in war, and only a few years earlier it had shocked much of the world by triumphing over Russia in the Russo-Japanese War of 1904–5. Wishing to avoid unnecessary conflict, President Theodore Roosevelt and his cabinet worked to defuse the situation.

The result was the so-called "Gentlemen's Agreement." Similar to the Chinese Exclusion acts, the Gentlemen's Agreement sought to stop or at least greatly reduce Japanese immigration. However, given the much more formidable status of Japan, the agreement offered some concessions to the Japanese. Perhaps most important for the Japanese American population was a provision that allowed Japanese already in the United States to bring "parents, wives and children" to America. This concession enabled the Japanese American population to grow rapidly in the early twentieth century, even though immigration was reduced. The growing native-born population gave the Japanese American community a small measure of protection against discriminatory measures, as native-born persons were automatically citizens and therefore enjoyed some constitutional protections not extended to aliens.

Efforts to restrict Asian immigration continued. In 1917, the "Barred Zone Act" was passed, which essentially banned immigration from all of Asia, except for Japan, where immigration was still governed by the terms of the Gentlemen's Agreement. Less than a decade later, the Immigration Act of 1924 further limited immigration from all Asian nations except the Philippines, which had become a United States territory in 1898, when it was acquired during the Spanish American War. Although most other Asian immigration had already been banned by 1917, the 1924 act officially extended that ban to Japan, leaving only the Philippines as a source of legal immigration from Asia. In 1934 the Tydings–McDuffie Act closed that last door by granting independence to the Philippines and thereby preventing Filipinos from moving relatively easily to the United States (Hing 1993, ch. 2).

Small numbers of immigrants always managed to enter, despite restrictions, but Asian immigration was relatively low in the years prior to World War II. Restrictions were eased modestly during and after World War II, and immigration increased but did not again hit high levels until after landmark immigration reform in 1965.

Why should we care about immigration laws of the past? Because each of these laws contributed to the perception that Asian groups were inherently different from other people in the United States. The laws racialized one Asian group after another, categorizing each group as part of a separate "Oriental" or "Asian" race that should be excluded. This racialization not only affected immigrants in the first half of the twentieth century, but also affects Asian Americans today. By treating Asians as different and undesirable, these laws helped to reinforce the idea that someone with "Asian" features could not be an American, and so, in the early twenty first-century, even third- and fourth-generation Asian Americans are often assumed to be foreigners. In addition, because Asian populations could not increase for decades, the potential Asian voting population could not grow. In the post-World War II period, Asian Americans lagged behind African Americans and Latinos in getting elected to Congress and state legislatures.

Defining "White" and the Effort to Naturalize

For Asians who did make it to the United States, legal discrimination placed them at a tremendous political disadvantage. Early on, however, it was not clear how extensive that discrimination would be. Perhaps the most important political question centered on the Immigration and Naturalization Act of 1790, which declared that naturalization (the process by which an immigrant becomes a citizen) would be open to "free white persons." The legislation clearly excluded African Americans and American Indians from citizenship, but Asians were not a significant presence in the United States at the time, and the law's applicability to them remained unclear.

The uncertainty stemmed from a question of immense political importance: who is "white"? As noted earlier in this chapter, the meaning of "white" has changed over time, and has no basis in genetics. Rather, "white" – and all racial groupings – are defined through a complex interaction of individual beliefs and political actions. In the mid-nineteenth century, it was not clear whether or not Asians were "white."

What *was* clear was that much was at stake. If Asians were white, then they could become citizens and enjoy substantial benefits. If they were not white, then they would be vulnerable to a wider range of discriminatory policies. Not surprisingly, therefore, Asian fought to be declared "white." The battleground was usually the federal courts. Since naturalization was a national government power, state and local governments played a lesser role.

In the earliest years of Asian immigration, some Chinese were able to naturalize, perhaps because government authorities did not give the matter much

<table>
<tr><th>Chinese</th><th>Japanese</th><th>Koreans</th><th>Asian Indians</th><th>Filipinos</th></tr>
<tr><td>(1848 Gold Rush in California)</td><td></td><td></td><td></td><td></td></tr>
<tr><td colspan="2">1875 Page Law, bans entry of prostitutes</td><td></td><td></td><td></td></tr>
<tr><td>1882 Chinese Exclusion Law, banned entry of laborers for 10 yrs

1892 Geary Act, renewed 1882 law, required registration

1902 Renewed exclusion

1904 Exclusion made permanent</td><td>(1885 Japanese Gov't started sending laborers to Hawai'i)

1907–8 Gentlemen's Agreement, Japanese Gov't stopped issuing passports for laborers</td><td>(1902–5 Koreans immigrated to Hawai'i until the 1904–5 Russo-Japan War)</td><td>(1907–10 Asian Indians immigrated to California in thousands)</td><td>(1898 the Philippines became U.S. territories)

(1907 Filipinos began to be recruited to Hawai'i)</td></tr>
<tr><td colspan="4">1917 "Barred Zone Act," banned entry from a designated wide zone including Arabian Peninsula, India, and Southeast Asia
(did not affect China, which had exclusion acts in effect) (did not affect Japan, which had Gentlemen's Agreement with U.S.)</td><td>(1917 law did not affect the Philippines, U.S. territories)</td></tr>
<tr><td></td><td>1922 Ozawa court case</td><td></td><td>1923 Thind court case</td><td></td></tr>
<tr><td colspan="4">1924 Immigration Act, banning "aliens ineligible to citizenship," thus excluded Japanese (and all Asian) immigration</td><td>(1924 law did not affect either)</td></tr>
<tr><td></td><td></td><td></td><td></td><td>1934 Tydings–McDuffie Act, limiting Filipino entries to 50/year</td></tr>
<tr><td>1943 Chinese Exclusion Act repealed, allowing naturalization and entry of 105/year</td><td></td><td></td><td colspan="2">1946 Lucy–Celler Act, Asian Indians and Filipinos allowed naturalization and given an entry quota of 100/year</td></tr>
<tr><td></td><td colspan="2">1952 McCarran–Walter Act, allowing naturalization and entry quota of 185/year to Japanese (and 100/year to Koreans)</td><td></td><td></td></tr>
<tr><td colspan="5">1965 Immigration Act, abolishing national quotas and enabling mass Asian immigration</td></tr>
</table>

Sources: Complied by the authors from S. Chan (1991), Hing (1993), Avakion (2002), and Reimers (2005)

Figure 1.1 *History of Asian immigration restriction laws, by target ethnic groups.*

thought. In 1873, an error led to the word "white" being omitted from the statute on naturalization, and some Chinese were able to become citizens before the error was corrected in early 1875 (S. Chan 1991, 92). In 1878, however, a federal circuit court ruled that Chinese were ineligible for citizenship (S. Chan 1991, 47).[8] Ah Yup's case (*In re Ah Yup*, 1F.Cas. 223–224 [1878], quoted in Haney López 1996, 5–6) was the first of its kind to reach federal court, and it was followed by many more. Between 1878 and 1945, over four dozen more cases were heard on the question of who qualifies as "white" (Haney López 1996, 203–8).

The inability of the courts to resolve this question and the inconsistent reasoning used in court opinions amply demonstrates the constructed nature of race. A continuing stream of petitioners continued to expand the legal definition of "whiteness," with their efforts testifying to the value of being placed in the "white" race in a country where a color line divided those who enjoyed full access to opportunities from those who faced extensive discrimination.

The underlying problem for the courts was that no objective definition of race can possibly exist, as we noted earlier in this chapter. Racial categorization was simply a tool used by those in power to oppress others. Few judges, however, appeared willing to acknowledge legally the fact that race is a political category even if they understood it. Instead, they continued to struggle to develop an objective test that could clearly distinguish those who were "white" from those who were not.

As Ian Haney López (1996) has shown, the courts' definition changed from case to case, at times relying on "common understanding," while at other times relying on allegedly scientific evidence. In Ah Yup's case, the circuit court claimed to draw on both. The court wrote that "The words 'white person' . . . in this country, at least, have undoubtedly acquired a well settled meaning in common popular speech". Elsewhere in the opinion, however, the judge cited scholarly authority to justify the idea that humanity was divided into different races.

> In speaking of the various classifications of races, Webster in his dictionary says "The common classification is that of Blumenbach, who makes five. 1. The Caucasian, or white race, to which belong the greater part of European nations and those of Western Asia; 2. The Mongolian, or yellow race, occupying Tartary, China, Japan, etc.; 3. The Ethiopian or Negro (black) race, occupying all of Africa except the north; 4. The American, or red race, containing the Indians of North and South America; and 5. The Malay, or Brown race, occupying the islands of the Indian Archipelago," etc. This division was adopted from Buffon . . . and is founded on the combined characteristics of complexion, hair and skull . . . [N]o one includes the white, or Caucasian, with the Mongolian or yellow race. (Haney López 1996, 5–6)

Although racial categories are described in a way that many today would think obvious – except, perhaps, for the definition of the "Malay race" – the writer seemed to find the classification of Chinese much more difficult than we would. Although today most of us would think it obvious that Chinese were of the Asian race, in 1878 the court examined a wide body of evidence before concluding that "a native of China . . . is not a white person." We have so come to accept the court's conclusions that we fail to understand that our racial categories do not have very firm foundations.

This was further highlighted in two cases to reach the United States Supreme Court. The first case of this type to reach the Supreme Court was *Ozawa v. United States* (1922), involving a Japanese immigrant, Takao Ozawa, who had been educated at the University of California (Berkeley) and then settled in Hawai'i. Ozawa challenged the notion that Japanese could not assimilate, noting that he had not maintained ties to Japan, he was not a member of any Japanese organizations in the United States, and his children spoke no Japanese. Ozawa offered convincing evidence that he was fully assimilated, and argued that his skin color qualified him as "white." Ozawa's brief observed that the skin color of Japanese was lighter than that of "the average Italian, Spaniard or Portuguese" – all of whom were by then considered to be white. The Supreme Court accepted Ozawa's description of his life, declaring "That he was well qualified by character and education for citizenship is conceded." However, the court declared, scientific classification required them to rule against Ozawa. "[T]he words 'white person' are synonymous with the words 'a person of the Caucasian race,' " the court asserted, and Ozawa "is clearly of a race which is not Caucasian. . . A large number of the federal and state courts have so decided. . . . These decisions are sustained by numerous scientific authorities, which we do not deem it necessary to review" (quoted in Haney López 1996, 81, 218, 220–1).

Shortly after rejecting Ozawa's claim, the Court heard the case of *United States v. Bhagat Singh Thind* (1923), a case similar to *Ozawa*, but with one important difference. Bhagat Singh Thind, an immigrant from India, had petitioned for naturalization, which a district court approved. Thind's argument seemed to be consistent with the Court's ruling in *Ozawa*, because anthropologists considered Asian Indians to be "Caucasians," not "Mongolians." The federal government appealed, and Thind's case was eventually heard by the Supreme Court only three months after the Court had issued its decision in the *Ozawa* case. In a striking demonstration of the nature of race, the Court abandoned its supposedly scientific position, which equated "Caucasian" with "white," and instead turned to "common understanding" as its basis for deciding racial classification.

> It may be true that the blond Scandinavian and the brown Hindu have a common ancestor in the dim reaches of antiquity, but the average man knows perfectly well that there are unmistakable and profound differences between them to-day. . . . What we now hold is that the words "free white persons" are words of common speech, to be interpreted in accordance with the understanding of the common man, synonymous with the word "Caucasian" only as that word is popularly understood. (Quoted in Haney López 1996, 223–5)

The Court, in essence, was declaring that "white" should be defined by the prejudices of the time.

Viewed collectively, the many court cases dealing with racial classification reveal the lack of any firm basis for defining race. Syrians apparently presented a particular challenge, with some courts ruling on several occasions that Syrians were white, and other courts ruling on several occasions that Syrians were not white. Arabs were likewise ruled both white and nonwhite by different courts. Armenians were found to be white, but Afghanis were not white (Haney López 1996, 204–8). Ian Haney López identified fifty-two court cases on race-related naturalization eligibility in 1878–1944. A glance at the list of the cases (Haney López 1996, 204–8) reveals not only inconsistency across these judicial decisions but the impossibility of classifying peoples into arbitrarily defined categories of race.

Despite numerous setbacks, Asian Americans continued to appeal to the courts for equal treatment under the law. One of the most important victories for Asian Americans – and for many others – occurred in 1898, in the case *U.S. v. Wong Kim Ark*. The case dealt with the question of birthright citizenship, which had been established after the Civil War. The Fourteenth Amendment, one of the three passed in the wake of the Civil War, stated that "All persons born or naturalized in the United States, and subject to the jurisdiction thereof, are citizens of the United States and of the State wherein they reside." Although this seemed to clarify citizenship for those born in the United States, two classes of people remained in question: Native Americans, and those born in the United States to non-citizen parents. In 1884 the U.S. Supreme Court had ruled that Native Americans did not acquire automatic citizenship by virtue of being born in the United States (*Elk v. Wilkins* 112 U.S. 94 [1884]). In 1898, however, in *Wong Kim Ark*, the Court found that U.S.-born children of aliens (people who did not have American citizenship) still had birthright citizenship, even if their parents were not eligible for citizenship. Birthright citizenship became particularly important to Japanese Americans, who had relatively large numbers of children born in the United States in the early twentieth century.

Alien Land Laws

Citizenship, or eligibility for citizenship, was important. Aliens ineligible for citizenship were vulnerable to other discriminatory tactics designed to make life difficult. One important example involved alien land laws, statutes that limited the ability of non-citizens to own land. In most cases, they were aimed specifically at Japanese Americans and specified that they applied to "aliens ineligible for citizenship." As noted earlier in this chapter, Japanese were considered to be nonwhite.

The push for alien land laws was often fueled by fears of the "yellow peril." An image pushed by some writers, politicians, and German propagandists, the idea received wide circulation through the Hearst newspaper chain in the first few decades of the twentieth century. In 1921 the *Sacramento Bee* warned:

> The intent on the part of the Japanese, it is quite evident, now is to secure upon this continent a foothold for their race, not as individual units to be absorbed and assimilated in the great American melting pot, but as a compact body of loyal subjects of the Mikado [Japanese emperor], to serve his interests in every way possible. (Quoted in Melendy 1984, 126)

United States Senator James D. Phelan, one of the most prominent supporters of alien land laws, declared that a "Jap is a Jap," and that "native Japanese are as undesirable as the imported" (Chuman 1976, 77). In this environment, support grew for legislation that would deny Japanese Americans the ability to own land.

Alien land laws provide an excellent illustration of the process of racialization. The groundwork for them was laid over a century earlier, when the 1790 naturalization act declared certain peoples – African Americans and American Indians – unfit for membership in American society. Those who were seen as acceptable would be called "white." By the latter part of the nineteenth century, prejudice against Asian Americans was very effectively strengthened by defining them as "not white," which would help to deny them equal access to legal protections, most notably the opportunity to naturalize. Prevented from obtaining citizenship, Asian immigrants would lose the opportunity to defend their interests through elections and representative governance, thus becoming much more vulnerable to oppressive measures such as alien land laws. By singling out Asian Americans for discriminatory treatment, alien land laws helped to reinforce the image of Asian Americans as unacceptable foreigners and also made it much harder for them to build wealth. If alien land laws worked as supporters hoped, Asian Americans would find it difficult to escape poverty, further reinforcing their image as inferior aliens.

At least sixteen states enacted alien land laws (Chuman 1976, 76–7; S. Chan 1991, 47). California passed its first in 1913, but then enacted another in 1920 in an effort to plug loopholes in the 1913 act. Among the notable provisions of the 1920 were provisions forbidding aliens ineligible to own land from serving as trustees for land held by their children (section 4), provisions forbidding the lease of land to aliens (section 8), and provisions forbidding aliens from giving money to someone else to buy land for them (section 9). The 1920 revisions suggest the often-successful efforts of Japanese Americans to find ways to circumvent the law, such as having a friendly white purchase the land, or buying land in an American-born child's name.

In addition to efforts to circumvent the laws, Japanese Americans challenged them in court. Although the courts usually upheld alien land laws, petitioners won a few cases. In *Estate of Tetsubumi Yano* (1922), the California Supreme Court ruled that section 4 of the 1920 law – the section which prohibited alien parents from serving as trustees for land owned by their children – was unconstitutional. Ultimately, the laws had come too late. Japanese farmers had enough options to prevent them from being all driven off their farms, although the laws undermined their economic security by making it

difficult for them to own the land. But although many managed to stay on –
or even move to – farms, a more devastating blow awaited.

The Imprisonment of Japanese Americans

By the early 1940s, optimists among the Japanese felt that they were coming
close to winning public acceptance from whites, and the younger generation
was building substantial human capital, despite the lack of prospects for
highly educated Japanese Americans. But the surprise attack on Pearl Harbor
on December 7, 1941, set in motion a chain of events that was to thwart their
hopes and inflict losses that could not be overcome in their lifetime. On
February 9, 1942, President Franklin D. Roosevelt issued Executive Order 9066,
giving the military the authority to "designate 'military areas' from which
'any or all persons may be excluded'" (Daniels 1981, 70; Hatamiya 1993, 14).
Although the order did not specifically call for the removal of Japanese
Americans, it provided the legal authority for their mass imprisonment, per-
manently altering the lives of thousands of Japanese Americans.[9]

Careful examination of the government's justification shows again the
power of racial thinking in American society. The legal justification, defended
in court, was military necessity. In fact, however, the best-informed government officials saw no compelling reasons for a mass evacuation of Japanese
Americans.

Racialization made Japanese Americans an easy target. Individual prejudice
and governmental discrimination combined to project an image of this group
as fundamentally alien, unable ever to become good Americans. Their racialization made it easy for other Americans to believe outlandish claims and for
officials to ignore their civil rights.

That racial hostility was the catalyst for this policy is clear when one notes
that German Americans and Italian Americans, considered white, were not
subjected to similar treatment. Although community leaders of all groups
were arrested, there was no mass evacuation of the European American
groups. DeWitt expressed concern over German and Italian aliens (non-
citizens), but he considered Japanese to be the greatest threat. Even native-
born Japanese Americans – that is, American citizens – were seen as a threat
by DeWitt (Daniels 1981, 54). Ultimately, almost 120,000 Japanese Americans
were imprisoned in the ten War Relocation Authority camps.

The beginning of the end of internment came with the Supreme Court case,
Ex Parte Endo (1944). Mitsuye Endo, a native Californian who was employed by
the state and had a brother in the armed forces, had cooperated with the evacuation, but, once arriving at the Tule Lake Relocation Center, had "filed a petition for a writ of *habeas corpus*, requesting that she be discharged from the
center and that she be freed from detention." She argued that "she was a loyal
citizen who was detained against her own will." In 1944, the Supreme Court
unanimously ruled in her favor, although the Court majority opinion had to

Internment: Two Stories

On February 19, 1942, the Portland, Oregon, office of the Federal Bureau of Investigation (FBI) telegraphed the United States Attorney General: "Emergency apprehension reported. Shigeru Aoki, Japan alien at Portland."

Aoki's crime? His membership in the local Buddhist church, the Portland Japanese Chamber of Commerce, and in the Sokoko Kai (meaning "homeland association"). The latter was considered to be particularly serious, as the group was said to be "one of the most aggressive Japanese nationalist organizations, whose members are selected by reason of their intense loyalty and subservience." All evidence, however, suggested that Aoki was a casual member at best, taking no part in the group's activities, and only on the membership list because a friend had paid the fee. Despite the paucity of evidence, the Alien Enemy Hearing Board declared that Aoki was "potentially dangerous to the public peace and safety." Within a week of his arrest, he found himself imprisoned at Fort Missoula, Montana, with his family left scrambling to learn his fate.

The camps where Shigeru was sent were different than the facilities that held most Japanese Americans. The relocation centers that held over 100,000 Japanese Americans were supposedly just to provide living facilities for Japanese Americans who were moved away from the West Coast, but the camps where Shigeru was imprisoned never hid the fact that they were detention centers. Some held German and Italian prisoners of war, in addition to Japanese Americans considered to be high security risks. By mid-1942, Japanese American prisoners were being transferred from Justice Department to Army custody, and Shigeru was moved to camps at Lordsburg, New Mexico, and later to Santa Fe.

Meanwhile, his wife and only child, Toki, had been imprisoned at the Minidoka relocation center, a short distance from Twin Falls, Idaho. Like many immigrants, the parents had long relied on their American-born son for help in understanding English, and so it fell to the eighteen-year-old Toki to learn the fate of his father and appeal for his release.

Fortunately, Shigeru was receiving positive evaluations from camp officials, and authorities eventually agreed that he posed little risk. In early 1944 they granted Shigeru's request to join his family in Minidoka, and he reunited with them in March, over two years after his arrest. Not until August 14, 1945, however, was he finally allowed to leave Minidoka.

In central California, the Yasumura family faced other traumas of relocation. the two oldest girls, Mary and Tomoe, were at the top of their high-school class, with dreams of going to college. But, when the evacuation order came, their lives were changed forever. Their teachers came to their door in tears, grieving over their shattered hopes. Unlike the Aokis, the entire Yasumura family was detained together, at the Amache relocation center in southeastern Colorado. As the war drew to a close and the detainees were allowed to begin to leave, Mary and Tomoe abandoned their earlier dreams of college, opting instead to find work in Denver as quickly as possible, so that they could help their family rebuild their lives.

Only the second youngest child, Grace, made it to college. After graduation, she migrated west to Portland, where she met Toki, who became her husband. Toki and Grace had two sons, one of whom would become a co-author of this book.

Sources: National Archives; Tetsuden Kashima, *Judgment without Trial: Japanese American Imprisonment during World War II* (Seattle: University of Washington Press, 2003).

engage in some intellectual gymnastics to argue that the civilian War Relocation Authority (WRA) had no authority to detain loyal citizens. In reality, the WRA had received authority to do exactly this from Congress, but the Court made the disingenuous claim that Congress had only authorized the detention of other citizens, not loyal ones (H. Kim 1994, 137). Gradually, Japanese Americans left the camps and began to rebuild their lives (we discuss this entire process in more detail in chapter 8).

The Post-war Era

After World War II, conditions did not improve immediately for Asian Americans, but there was gradual change. U.S. troops posted in Asia began to create ties through which small numbers of immigrants flowed, often as spouses of military personnel. The most dramatic change occurred in the 1960s, however.

Post-World War II to 1965

The post-war years saw some improvement for Asian Americans. Those seen as allies of the United States had already seen some small improvements during the war. As a goodwill gesture toward a wartime ally, Congress had lifted the ban on Chinese immigration in 1943 (although it was replaced with a quota allowing only 105 immigrants per year), and Chinese Americans were allowed to become citizens. In 1946 immigration exclusion against Filipinos and people from the Indian subcontinent was ended, and they too were allowed to naturalize. Even Japanese Americans saw some modest gains. Nisei soldiers from Hawai'i had fought in the 100th Battalion, which was later merged with the 442nd Regimental Combat Team, that included soldiers from the internment camps as well as Hawai'i. The two units, which are often referred to as the 442nd, became some of the most highly decorated soldiers of the war, and their efforts helped to win more support for Japanese Americans in general. For the most part, though, Japanese Americans faced intense bigotry in the post-war years. This was amply demonstrated when Daniel Inouye, a decorated veteran who had lost part of his right arm in combat, went to a barbershop shortly after the war, still wearing his army jacket covered with medals, and was told "We don't serve Japs here" (S. Chan 1991, 122).

Conditions for Chinese Americans actually deteriorated again somewhat in the 1950s, with the growing fear of communism, but other Asian Americans made gains. The McCarran–Walter Immigration Act of 1952 made it easier to deport immigrants, but it also ended the ban on immigration and naturalization for Japanese and Korean Americans (who had not benefited from liberalization of laws during or immediately after World War II), at long last allowing those immigrants to become citizens.

The end of World War II and the easing of immigration restrictions in the 1940s and 1950s were important factors in a renewed surge in Asian immigration, but the watershed event in contemporary immigration came in 1965, with the passage of the Immigration Act of 1965 (Hart–Celler Act). The law ended the national origins basis for immigration, an approach based on racist views that held some races to be superior and others inferior. Instead of national origins, immigrants would be selected based on family reunification and needed skills. In other words, priority would be given to applicants who had certain family ties to individuals already living in the United States, and to those who had skills that were in short supply in the U.S.

There is widespread agreement among historians that supporters of the 1965 act did not anticipate its consequences. The expectation seemed to be that the law would produce minor changes in the number of immigrants to the United States. In fact, however, the new quotas created under the law (and the immigration allowed without regard to quota) helped to make possible the massive immigration of the late twentieth and early twenty-first centuries.

The Asian American Movement

Just as the next great wave of immigration was starting to build, the third generation of Asian Americans was coming of age. For the most established immigrant groups – primarily Chinese and Japanese Americans – large numbers of third-generation youth were entering adulthood. As these youth moved into college in large numbers, some helped to create what became known as the Asian American Movement (Wei 1993), which we examine further in chapter 4.

Influenced in part by other civil rights movements of the time – most notably the black civil rights movement – the Asian American movement helped to create the very notion of Asian America. First- and second-generation Asian immigrants tended to identify by national origin rather than seeing themselves as part of a larger grouping of Asian-ancestry peoples. For instance, immigrants from China or Japan tended to identify as Chinese or Japanese, not as "Asian" or "Oriental." Their children also identified primarily by nationality. But many of the grandchildren of the immigrants saw more commonalities than differences with other Asian Americans. Activists noted that Chinese, Japanese, Korean, Filipino, and other Asian Americans faced common challenges. Non-Asian Americans tended not to distinguish between Asian ethnic groups. This was most notable in the ways that bigots used ethnic slurs indiscriminately: for instance, many Japanese or Korean Americans were called "Chinks," while many Chinese Americans had been called "Japs." Bigots almost certainly did not care about the ethnicity of their victims; they just searched their small brains to find the first racist term that applied to Asians. For bigots, any Asian American could be a "Jap," "Chink," "Gook," or "Dink." Realizing this, many third-generation Asian Americans urged the separate Asian American ethnic groups to join together. On campuses, in churches, and anywhere else that Asian Americans gathered, young people encouraged their elders to identify not just by ethnicity (e.g. Japanese), but also panethnicity – as Asian Americans.

Ironically, however, the Asian American Movement was emerging just as the conditions that helped to create it were ending. The Asian American Movement was fueled by young adults who had little or no direct knowledge of their grandparents' native countries, and who were focused on developments in the United States. By the 1980s and 1990s, however, the huge surge of immigration brought new groups of first-generation Asian Americans into the country, with strong national identities. Asian America was again becoming more diverse, and, as it did, the viability of a unified "Asian American" identity was once again in question. The story of Asians in America was beginning a new chapter.

CHAPTER TWO

Asian Americans Today

The latter half of the twentieth century saw a dramatic growth in immigration to the United States, which has transformed the Asian American population. People from overseas have arrived in growing numbers, sometimes sponsored by family members already in the U.S., other times by employers seeking their specialized skills (Park and Park 2005). Just as immigration was beginning to swell in the 1960s, the civil rights movements ushered in new types of racial projects that helped to undermine older racial formations. Newer racial projects have struggled to develop deep roots, however, and racial formation in America has remained in flux. In this chapter, we describe Asian America in the current era, one of changing racial formation. You will learn about:

1 The meaning of the concepts of ethnic, panethnic, and racial identity.
2 The current size and distribution of the Asian American population and of the major Asian subgroups.
3 Sources of diversity in today's Asian American population.
4 The prospects for the development of a panethnic identity among Asian Americans.

Our ideas about race shape the very way we think about Asian Americans. Therefore, before we present some basic data, it is useful to clarify the terms we use to describe Asian Americans and other ethnoracial groups.

Ethnicity, Race, Panethnicity, and Identity

Race is not the only way to conceptualize the kinds of differences normally associated with such categories as "Black," "White," "Latino," and "Asian." *Ethnicity* and *panethnicity* are possible alternatives to the concept of race. While ethnicity may be a familiar term, "panethnicity" probably is not. In the simplest sense, a panethnic group is just a collection of ethnic groups. Panethnicity is more complicated than that, of course, but before we explain some of the complexity, it is useful first to explain more precisely what we mean when we use the word "ethnicity."

Ethnic Identity

Like racial identity, ethnic identity is constructed by social forces. In practice, though, ethnic identity functions very differently than race. By "functions," we mean that it has different effects on the way people think about themselves and the way they are treated by others. To be considered a member of an ethnic group is a very different experience than to be considered a member of a racial group.

Ethnic groups are often considered to be subsets of racial categories. So, for instance, Americans who are considered to be "white" can be subdivided into a variety of ethnic groups, such as Greek, Norwegian, or Scottish. Ethnic groupings are often assumed to be synonymous with national groupings – thus "Korean" and "Mexican" designate both national and ethnic identities – but this is not always the case. For example, Hmong Americans have ancestral roots in a region that overlaps a number of national boundaries, including China, Vietnam, Laos, and Thailand.

Studies of immigrants and their descendants have shown that ethnic traditions brought to the United States by a first generation of newcomers to the United States are largely abandoned by the next few generations.[1] Perhaps the best example of this erosion of ethnic distinctions is language. Although the first generation usually is fluent in a language other than English, the second generation quickly acquires English, and the grandchildren of immigrants often speak only English. Small traces of the immigrant traditions survive, but most have greatly diminished or disappeared by the third generation.

This does not mean that later generations of immigrants just melt into the larger population, becoming the same as everyone else. In the early 1960s, Nathan Glazer and Daniel Patrick Moynihan studied immigrants and their descendants in New York City and found that many maintained some distinctiveness, even though they became increasingly similar to other Americans. Furthermore, Glazer and Moynihan found that many second- and third-generation descendants of immigrants continue to identify themselves in *ethnic* terms, such as Irish American or Italian American (Glazer and Moynihan 1970/1963).

Many people incorrectly believe that this persistence of ethnic identity reflects the persistence of immigrant traditions. But Glazer and Moynihan concluded that "The ethnic group in American society became not a survival from the age of mass immigration, but a new social form" (1970/1963, 16). Glazer and Moynihan's point is this: although most of an immigrant-generation's ethnic traditions are usually lost by the third generation, the ethnic identity does not simply disappear as new generations grow up in the United States. Instead, the original ethnic identity is supplanted by new forms that, though they perhaps share a family resemblance to the old traditions are distinctively American.

Practical benefits encourage the emergence of such new ethnic identities. By organizing into ethnic groups, individuals find that they can have more influence in politics and other spheres of life. Glazer and Moynihan observed that "The ethnic groups in New York are also *interest groups*" (1970/1963, 17; emphasis in original).

New forms of ethnic identity can also be shaped by the perceptions of others. Immigrants from Italy, for instance, did not initially identify themselves by their country of origin (Italy), but rather by their region, such as Sicily.[2] An Italian American identity developed only after people from many regions of Italy arrived in America and found that others tended to lump them together with immigrants from other parts of Italy.

Today, scholars feel that ethnic identity is largely symbolic, voluntary, and cost-free (Gans 1979; Alba 1990; Waters 1990). This too is in sharp contrast to the identity that immigrants brought with them.

For the first generation of immigrants, making a change in one's ethnic identity probably seems about as realistic a thing to do as choosing new parents; any effort to distance oneself from one's ethnic group was likely to carry at least social costs. For most immigrants, ethnic identity shaped where they lived, whom they married, where they worshipped, and more. Marrying outside the group was strongly discouraged, at the very least, and moving far from the ethnic neighborhood could meet with strong disapproval. The American-grown symbolic ethnicity, in contrast, exercises few such constraints on those who adopt it. For many Americans, "being ethnic" is a matter of style, like choosing to wear bright clothes or hats. Someone can choose to be a Greek American, simply by letting this identity shape the movies they see, the books they read, and the restaurants they patronize. And the costs of this choice are few: people who identify as Greek Americans can usually choose to marry non-Greek Americans or to live outside Greek American neighborhoods without fear of condemnation from other members of their chosen ethnic group, unlike their immigrant predecessors. A person who identifies as Italian American is far more likely to live in the suburbs with neighbors of a variety of ethnic identities, rather than live in a "little Italy," which was often where Italian immigrants clustered a century ago.

Mary Waters has written insightfully about the ethnic options available to white Americans (Waters 1990). They can choose to "be ethnic" or to blend in indistinguishably with the majority population. They can also take on a wide range of ethnic identities. Someone might choose to "be" Irish, even if she has no Irish ancestry. For those who are perceived to be white, the options are many. Ethnic identity for most whites has become a lifestyle choice, like choosing to be a vegetarian or a birdwatcher. It is a source of enjoyment, with little cost.

Choice about one's ethnic identity is an important phenomenon in America today, but Asian Americans are not likely to be able to take advantage of it as white Americans can. Visible minorities – those who do not appear to be "white" – do not have these choices, because their appearance makes them vulnerable to definition by others. African Americans are sure to stand out in a crowd with few blacks, and to be defined as "black" no matter what identity they might choose. Asian Americans not only stand out, but also are likely to be perceived as alien – an important phenomenon that we explore in detail later in this chapter.

For those who are seen as nonwhite, race plays a powerful role in shaping how others define them. As we noted above, race functions differently than ethnicity. Those who are perceived to be of a nonwhite race cannot simply drop or switch their racial identity. Asian Americans can "change" their ethnic identity, but they cannot escape their racial identity. For example, a Korean American could consider himself to be Chinese, and few Americans would question it, but it is very unlikely that that same individual could get most Americans to consider him to be white. Some African Americans have told moving stories of how they first became aware that they were perceived differently because of their so-called "racial" characteristics. (Tatum 1997). As young children, they played with other children without regard to color, but, as they grew older, they found themselves increasingly shut out of the world of their white friends.

Asian Americans – particularly ones who have lived in the U.S. for several decades – can often tell similar stories of going into a crowded place where Asians were rare, and seeing heads swivel as they entered.

The imposition of identity on Asian immigrants has a long history in the United States. In the nineteenth and early twentieth centuries, East Asians were defined as "Oriental," inscrutable, untrustworthy, forever foreign. Sikh immigrants from India were labeled "Hindus" (Sikhism and Hinduism are different religions. Calling Sikhs "Hindus" is a little like calling Catholics "Muslims"). When Japanese and Chinese immigrants attempted to define themselves simply as "American," their efforts were rejected.

If intermarriage rates increase, the vulnerability of Asian Americans to definition by others could change as the visible markers of race become less and less easy to perceive. If more and more individuals of different racial groups marry each other and raise families, perceived racial boundaries could weaken, and symbolic ethnicity might become an option for visible minorities. This seems unlikely to happen in the near future, however. Instead, for those whose physical features are defined as nonwhite, the most likely "ethnic option" is panethnicity.

Panethnic Identity

In the late 1960s, the grandchildren of Asian immigrants began to assert control over their identity. Although they did not reject the specific ethnic identities of their ancestors, the young activists declared that what they shared was more important than what was different, and they sought to unite all Americans of Asian ancestry under a new designation: a *panethnic* identity.

"Panethnic" means a collection of ethnic groups ("pan" is the Greek term for "all"). A common example of a panethnic group might be African Americans, who include people from many different parts of Africa. From a pan ethnic perspective, immigrants and their offspring from all Asian countries – whether Japan, China, Vietnam, or elsewhere – might be included in a panethnic category of Asian Americans. Superficially, panethnicity may seem identical to race. Why not simply call such labels racial groups?

The reason is that the two concepts refer to very different racial projects. Indeed, one of the leading scholars of Asian American panethnicity, Yen Le Espiritu, has noted that she used the "racial formation perspective" of Omi and Winant when she developed the notion of a pan-Asian American identity (Espiritu 2004, 217).

Both the imposition of an identity (e.g. labeling Sikhs as "Hindus") and the declaration of one's own identity ("Asian American") are racial projects, but the former kind of project is usually undertaken by others at the expense of the group being labeled, while the latter is undertaken to benefit the group being labeled. Although the assertion of panethnicity seems superficially similar to racialization, the implications of the labels are very different: racial labels are imposed, while a panethnic identity is one that an individual may choose.[3]

This is not to claim that panethnicity is only the product of individual choice. Panethnic identity is similar to "white" ethnic identities, in that it does reflect a personal choice, but the panethnic choice occurs within more constraints. A white American can refer to her ethnic identity as "nothing," but that is not a meaningful option for those viewed as nonwhite. Most whites have not had the experience of strangers approaching them and asking them "what are you?" or "where are you from?" Most Asians have. Asians do not have the option to be "nothing," because they have been racialized as nonwhite. As Espiritu has noted, "panethnic boundaries are shaped and reshaped in the continuing interaction between both external and internal forces" (Espiritu 1992, 7). Americans of Asian ancestry are confronted by racialization that they cannot erase, but they can strive to gain control of that process and use it to serve their interests, and one way to do this is to assert a panethnic identity of their own choosing. We agree with Michael Omi, who argues that panethnicity is "a phenomenon of racialization" (Omi 1993, 203), but we think it is beneficial to maintain some distinction between the development of panethnicity and racialization.

> Adopting the dominant group's categorization of them, Asian Americans have institutionalized pan-Asianism as their political instrument, thereby enlarging their own capacities to challenge and transform the existing structure of power. In other words, Asian Americans did not just adopt the pan-Asian concept but also transformed it to conform to their political, economic, and ideological needs. (Espiritu 2004, 216)

Panethnic identity is an increasingly important issue because immigration has created growing challenges to racialization. One challenge comes from immigrants themselves. Although native-born Americans are unlikely to know other racial structures and therefore often accept the American racial categories as "natural," immigrants know better. Confronted with American racial categories that often seem strange, new Americans often resist accepting the labels placed on them by others. This resistance is unlikely to make established racialization projects disappear, but racial boundaries may become more unstable as millions of newcomers and their children question the racial categories used today.

This has certainly been the case for Asian immigrants. Recall that "Asia" covers a large part of the world, whether or not one includes west Asia. Within that large expanse of territory are countries that have sometimes been bitter enemies. For example, although the tensions have diminished, lingering anger over conflicts from World War II can still dredge up hostilities between Koreans and Japanese. Vietnam and China have occasionally had border skirmishes, and Pakistan and India continue to station large numbers of troops across each other's borders, although tensions may have lessened somewhat in recent years. Asian immigrants who come to the United States and find that they have been lumped together with people they may consider to be their enemies may respond by asserting strong separate ethnic boundaries. This dynamic makes them less likely to embrace a pan-Asian coalition than others, with more "porous" ethnic boundaries (Hein 2006).

More importantly, new immigrants may find that they have little in common with other, more established Asian Americans. A middle-aged Hmong immigrant with little or no formal education, accustomed to a rural agrarian lifestyle, may find it hard to identify with a fourth-generation, college-educated Japanese American living in an upscale suburb. After the devastating civil disturbances in South Central Los Angeles in 1992 (discussed further in chapter 6), questions arose about Asian American panethnic unity, as some Korean Americans felt abandoned by other Asian American groups (Zia 2000, 184).

After a short time, immigrants may become familiar with the basic American racial scheme, but their perceptions may differ greatly from those of native-born Americans. Some dark-skinned African-ancestry Caribbean immigrants (also known as West Indians), for example, are reluctant to call themselves "black," because they see that as a term describing native-born African Americans (Vickerman 1999; Waters 1999).

On the other hand, "racial lumping" can strengthen panethnic unity. If outsiders fail to observe distinctions among subgroups, there may be a greater tendency for those same subgroups to embrace panethnic ties as a defensive measure. This appears to be happening with some Americans of Afro-Caribbean ancestry. Mary Waters found that the children of immigrants were particularly likely to conclude that white Americans would lump all dark-skinned individuals together. Her West Indian American respondents often found themselves subject to the same discriminatory treatment that long-established African Americans had experienced. As a result, many West Indian Americans decided that they might as well embrace an African American identity (Waters 1999).

Asian immigrants and their children sometimes have similar experiences. Anti-Asian prejudices often make no distinctions among subgroups. When those prejudices rise to the level of violence, it can have a powerful unifying effect, as a wide range of Asian American subgroups join together to combat and protest such treatment (see "Vincent Chin and Asian American Politics" text box).

Nevertheless, while immigrants from Cambodia or Korea may all be labeled "Asian American," we should keep in mind that the immigrants themselves are not likely to use that label when they first arrive. The effort to unite these diverse immigrants under a common label is what Omi and Winant call a racial project, whose outcome is uncertain. We cannot be certain how they will identify themselves, but we do know that a child of Vietnamese immigrants can refer to herself as Vietnamese, Vietnamese American, or Asian American. Immigrants and their descendants can embrace or reject a panethnic identity. What is also clear is that there is much at stake over whether several million Americans of Asian ancestry embrace a common identity or choose to go their separate ways.

Who Are the Asian Americans Today?

Do Asian-ancestry Americans perceive a common panethnic identity? To answer that question, it helps to look more closely at who makes up the Asian American subpopulation. Doing so is not a straightforward task, however, as we first need to consider how Asians are defined by those whose job it is to count them.

Defining "Asian American"

In the simplest sense, Asian Americans are Americans with ancestral roots in Asia. However, there is no universally accepted definition of "Asia." Geographers usually consider Asia to extend from a line running through Turkey (west of the Bosporus), along the Black Sea to the Caspian Sea, and up to the Ural Mountains. By this definition, countries such as Turkey, Iraq, and Israel are all "Asian." In East Asian countries, this definition is widely used in high-school geography classes today, together with the notion of "West Asia" (which ranges from Turkey to Afghanistan).

In the United States, however, Americans of "West Asian" ancestry – for example, Syrian or Iranian – are more commonly considered to be "Middle Eastern." Central Asia, which includes Afghanistan, Armenia, Azerbaijan, Kazakhstan, Tajikistan, Turkmenistan, and Uzbekistan, is a gray area in American definitions. Immigrants from those areas have historically been

Vincent Chin and Asian American Politics

Vincent Chin's murder is a watershed in Asian American politics. Never before had a single issue so strongly united Asian American groups, helping to forge a stronger panethnic identity.

On June 9, 1982, Vincent Chin had gone to a bar with some friends. It was a time when prominent leaders had been making blatantly anti-Japanese statements in response to rising sales of Japanese cars. Anti-Japanese sentiments were particularly high in Detroit, where the growing popularity of imports was blamed for lay-offs. At the bar, Chin and his friends got into an altercation with Ronald Ebens, a Chrysler auto plant worker, and Ebens's stepson, Michael Nitz, a laid-off autoworker. Chin's friends heard Ebens use racial slurs such as "chink" and "nip," while one of the bar employees heard him say "It's because of motherfuckers like you that we're out of work." Chin responded, and a fight ensued. Both groups were ejected and left the area. Ebens and Nitz (with the help of a third man) then searched for Chin, and beat him with a baseball bat when they found him. Chin died four days later.

In March 1983 Ebens and Nitz received three years' probation, and were fined $3,780. Chinese Americans were outraged, and the small community began to organize to protest the verdict. They formed American Citizens for Justice, and began to seek allies. As awareness of the Vincent Chin case grew throughout the country, other groups offered their support. There was a wide range of Chinese American groups, but also the Japanese American Citizens League (JACL), the Korean American Association of Illinois, and, in the Detroit area, the Korean Society of Greater Detroit and the Korean American Women's Association. Although there was initially skepticism from some established civil rights groups, support eventually also came from many organizations with roots outside Asian American communities.

For the Chin family, the effort ended unhappily. Ebens and Nitz were tried in a federal court in 1984, charged with violating Chin's civil rights, and Ebens was found guilty while Nitz was acquitted. However, a retrial was ordered on the grounds that there had been excessive pretrial publicity, and also that there were legal errors with some of the evidence. The retrial was held in Cincinnati in 1987, where Ebens was acquitted by a largely male, blue-collar jury. Ebens never apologized.

Although Asian American activists lost the important legal battles of the Vincent Chin murder, they gained a great deal. Out of it came a determination to continue the fight against anti-Asian violence, and the case had a galvanizing effect on many Asian Americans. Perhaps most importantly, it helped to build alliances between different Asian American groups, and between Asian Americans and others, laying the groundwork for a much more effective politics in the years to come. Vincent Chin did not die in vain, and his legacy can be seen in the pan-Asian American coalitions that were inspired by his cause.

Source: This description of the Vincent Chin case draws heavily on chapter 3 of Helen Zia's *Asian American Dreams: The Emergence of an American People* (New York: Farrar, Straus, and Giroux, 2000). Zia was a leading activist in the American Citizens for Justice group.

subject to incoherent naturalization decisions by U.S. courts, sometimes declared white, sometimes nonwhite.

This confusion further illustrates the way that "race" is a historically constructed concept, not a scientific one. The Census Bureau shares this view, noting that racial "categories are socio-political constructs and should not be interpreted as being scientific or anthropological in nature" (U.S. Bureau of Census 2005a, B-12). Further reflecting the fluid, socially constructed nature of racial categories is the fact that the names for racial categories used in the U.S. decennial census have changed with almost every census.

Today, official definitions of "Asian" come from the Office of Management and Budget (OMB), which attempts to create standardized racial categories for U.S. national government agencies. The OMB does not operate in a vacuum, however, and its decisions on racial categories are frequently the target of lobbying efforts of various groups (Espiritu 1992; Rodríguez 2000).

The racial classification scheme for the 2000 census was set by an October 1997 OMB document entitled "Revisions to the Standards for the Classification of Federal Data on Race and Ethnicity." According to this scheme, an Asian is defined as "[a] person having origins in any of the original peoples of the Far East, Southeast Asia, or the Indian subcontinent, including, Cambodia, China, India, Japan, Korea, Malaysia, Pakistan, the Philippine Islands, Thailand, and Vietnam" (Barnes and Bennett 2002, 1; U.S. Bureau of Census 2005a, B-13). This definition is followed by the statement that "Asian groups are not limited to nationalities but include ethnic terms as well, such as Hmong" (Reeves and Bennett 2004, 2). This is important, because, as we have noted above, in many parts of Asia, especially in Southeast Asia, ethnic and national boundaries do not overlap with each other. For example, Hmong in the Laos–Thailand region and Karen in the Burma–Thailand region do not have their own countries.

How Many Asians are There in the United States?

Using Census Bureau definitions, how many Asians are there in the United States, and what percentage of the U.S. population do they comprise? Unfortunately, the question is not so easy to answer. In 2000, for the first time in census history, respondents were allowed to mark "one or more races" (see figure 2.1). About 6.8 million respondents, or 2.4 per cent of the total population, checked multiple racial categories. Although most of them checked just two of the six racial group categories, 823 individuals in the nation marked all the six categories. The "check one or more" provision, widely celebrated as the "Tiger Woods option,"[4] is a result of lobbying efforts of multiracial groups such as the Association for MultiEthnic Americans (AMEA), who do not want to be categorized into one racial group or forced to suppress some of their ethnic roots. The option to check multiple boxes was adopted after lengthy debates on proper ways to recognize the identity of those who fit into multiple racial categories. A major concern of those who opposed a "multiracial" category was that such a category could lead to a reduction in the number of people placing themselves in the already existing racial categories (Williams-León and Nakashima 2001). The "check more than one" approach was a compromise. While not fully satisfying those pushing for a multiracial category, "check more than one" seemed like considerable progress from the days of the

NOTE: Please answer BOTH Questions 5 and 6.

5. Is this person Spanish/Hispanic/Latino? *Mark the "No" box if not Spanish/Hispanic/Latino.*

___**No,** not Spanish / Hispanic / Latino   ___Yes, Puerto Rican

___Yes, Mexican, Mexican Am., Chicano   ___Yes, Cuban

___Yes, other Spanish / Hispanic / Latino — *Print group.*

_____

6. What is this person's race? *Mark one or more races* *to indicate what this person considers himself/herself to be.*

___White

___Black, African Am., or Negro

___American Indian or Alaska Native — *Print name of enrolled or principal tribe.*

_____

___Asian Indian	___Japanese	___Native Hawaiian
___Chinese	___Korean	___Guamanian or Chamorro
___Filipino	___Vietnamese	___Samoan
___Other Asian — *Print race.*		___Other Pacific Islander — *Print race.*

_____

___Some other race — *Print race.*

_____

Source: U.S. Census Bureau, Census 2000 questionnaire.

Figure 2.1 *Census race and ethnicity questions.*

"one-drop rule," when even a very small amount of African ancestry meant that one would be classified only as "black," or when census takers were instructed to classify multiracial individuals by the race of the darker skin (cf. Espiritu 2001, 27). "Check more than one" allowed respondents to identify with their full range of racial identities, if they wished to do so.

How to tabulate the respondents who reported two or more races has proven to be a practical challenge. The Census bureau has solved this problem by releasing two tabulations whenever racial categories are involved.

In one tabulation, only the respondents who reported a single racial group were reported in each racial category. If someone checked only "Asian" for their racial classification, that person would be counted in the "Asian" total. However, respondents who checked multiple racial groups were recorded in a category labeled "two or more races."

In the second tabulation, respondents who checked multiple racial groups were counted toward all racial groups they checked among the six racial group categories. In this version, there is no "two or more races" category. In this second tabulation, the totals exceed 100 per cent (in fact, the total became 102.6 per cent), because some respondents are counted more than once. In

TABLE 2.1 U.S. population by race

	One race		One or more races	
	no.	%	no.	%
White	216,036,244	75.6	220,707,536	77.3
Black or African American	34,772,381	12.2	36,597,015	12.8
American Indian and Alaskan Native (AIAN)	2,151,322	0.8	4,006,160	1.4
Asian	12,097,281	4.2	13,466,479	4.7
Native Hawaiian and Pacific Islander (NHPI)	403,832	0.1	743,314	0.3

Source: 2004 American Community Survey, U.S. Census Bureau.

addition, the population of each racial group is larger than the one reported in the first version, because those who marked several races "in combination with" others are now added toward each group. Because relatively few individuals indicated more than one race, the differences are fairly small, but they do create challenges for measuring the population of racial groups.

Table 2.1 shows the numbers for each racial group, for those who chose only one race, and also for those who chose only one race plus those who chose more than one race. In the first tabulation (for "One race"), Asians comprise 4.2 per cent (12.1 million people) of the U.S. population. In the second version (which counts both those who checked one race only and those who checked more than one race), Asians are 4.7 per cent (13.5 million) of the U.S. population. Either count represents a rapid increase from 1990, which tallied 6.9 million Asians, comprising just below 3 per cent of the U.S. population. Between 1990 and 2000, the Asian population increased 48.3 per cent when measured by those who chose only one race, and 72.2 per cent if those who chose more than one race are included. In fact, Asians' 57.9 per cent growth rate in the second tabulation is even larger than the Hispanic growth rate (U.S. Bureau of Census 2001), which is why Asians are sometimes called the fastest growing group in the nation. It should be noted that the Hispanic growth was much larger than Asians' when measured by the number of individuals. Asian growth exceeded Hispanic growth in *rate* of increase (the percentage increase). Having been smaller in number, in part due to the discriminatory immigration laws, the Asian population increased at a higher rate, because they started from a smaller base.

It should also be noted that table 2.1 includes those who identified as Hispanic. Because the Census Bureau does not consider "Hispanic" to be a racial identity, Hispanics can be of any race. Distinguishing non-Hispanic whites from all whites produces significantly different numbers (the 2004 count for non-Hispanic whites choosing only one race was 192 million, 24 million fewer than the count when Hispanic whites are included). However, including Hispanics does not produce significant changes for the other racial groups, including Asians.

TABLE 2.2 Detailed Asian groups, 2000

	One race no.	%Asian	One or more races no.	%Asian	%Multiple race (%)[a]
Chinese (except Taiwanese)	2,314,537	22.6	2,734,841	23.0	15
Filipino	1,850,314	18.1	2,364,815	19.9	22
Asian Indian	1,678,765	16.4	1,899,599	16.0	12
Vietnamese	1,122,528	11.0	1,223,736	10.3	8
Korean	1,076,872	10.5	1,228,427	10.3	12
Japanese	796,700	7.8	1,148,932	9.7	31
Cambodian	171,937	1.7	206,052	1.7	17
Hmong	169,428	1.7	186,310	1.6	9
Laotian	168,707	1.6	198,203	1.7	15
Pakistani	153,533	1.5	204,309	1.7	25
Taiwanese	118,048	1.2	144,795	1.2	18
Thai	112,989	1.1	150,283	1.3	25
Bangladeshi	41,280	0.4	57,412	0.5	28
Indonesian	39,757	0.4	63,073	0.5	37
Sri Lankan	20,145	0.2	24,587	0.2	18
Malaysian	10,690	0.1	18,566	0.2	42
Other Asian[b]	26,310	0.3	52,602	0.4	50
Other Asian; not specified[c]	146,870	1.4	369,430	3.1	60

[a] Calculated by subtracting the "one race" column from the "one or more races" column, and dividing by the latter.

[b] "Bhutanese," "Burmese," "Indo Chinese," "Iwo Jiman," "Maldivian," "Nepalese," "Okinawan" and "Singaporean".

[c] Those who checked "Other Asian" category and wrote in a "generic term such as 'Asian' or 'Asiatic'."

Source: Census 2000 Summary File 1 (SF 1) 100-per cent data, custom tables QT-P6, PCT5, PCT7.

Table 2.2 lists the population of the major Asian ethnic groups, and the percentage each one comprises of the total Asian American population. In the census question about race, Asian respondents were instructed either to check some of the six already printed group names (Asian Indian, Chinese, Filipino, Japanese, Korean, and Vietnamese), or to check the "other Asians" box and then specify their ethnic group name (for example, Cambodians). They could check both if they were multiethnic Asian (for example, part Chinese and part Cambodian).[5]

The tabulations in table 2.2 show that there is potentially great diversity among Asian Americans. If they identify primarily by ethnicity or nation of origin, Asian Americans become a jumble of groups with even the largest making up less than 1 per cent of the entire U.S. population.

Not surprisingly, the six Asian groups printed on the census form had the largest populations. For both the "One race" and the "One or more races" tabulations, Chinese are the largest Asian ethnic group (exceeding 2 million in both versions of count), Filipinos second (exceeding 2 million in the second version of count), and Asian Indians third. Vietnamese, Koreans, and Japanese follow. Although each of these groups comprises a small share – less than 1 per cent – of the entire U.S. population, each has fairly a large population, exceeding 1 million in the second version of count.

Most of the "other Asian" groups are of Southeast Asian backgrounds (including Cambodians, Hmong, Laotian, Thai, Indonesian, and Malaysian) and South Asian (including Pakistani, Bangladeshi, and Sri Lankan). Not shown in table 2.2 are other Asian groups such as Burmese, Maldivians (from in the islands of Maldives on the Indian Ocean) and Okinawans, (who immigrated, mostly to Hawai'i. from the southern-island region of Japan known as Okinawa, but who have a distinctive identity partly because immigrants from the Japanese main islands used to look down upon them) (Barnes and Bennett 2002, 9). Among the "other Asian" groups, Cambodians, Hmong, Laotian, Pakistani, and Thai number the fewest at no more than 100,000 each. Together with the six larger Asian groups already discussed, there are eleven groups that surpass the 1 per cent threshold (excluding Taiwanese, who will be discussed shortly) (Reeves and Bennett 2004).

When we compare the ranks of the six largest Asian groups in 1990 and 2000, we see some notable changes. Chinese and Filipinos were the first and second largest groups in both censuses, but the third largest in 1990 were the Japanese (table 2.3). Since then, Asian Indians and Vietnamese have experienced remarkable population gains. Comparing the 1990 figures with the smaller, Asian-alone tabulation in 2000, Asian Indians and Vietnamese increased 105 per cent and 83 per cent respectively. The rapid population growth of these two groups, along with that of many other Asian groups, is not surprising, given immigration trends and the large number of immigrants of child-bearing age. The relative decline of Japanese in ranked population size (and their *decrease* in number when looking at the "Asian alone" number in 2000) is noteworthy and an exception among Asians. "The explanations given for the apparent decrease [have] included low birth rates, high rates of outmarriage and assimilation, and low levels of immigration." It is important to note that the 1990 figure included "some of the mixed ancestry people who are part-Japanese" (Lai and Arguelles 2003, 73). The "Asian only" population for Japanese in 1990, therefore, might have been smaller than the 2000 figure of 796,700. Although the image of "declining Japanese" is widespread among Asian activists, some warn that this is not necessarily an accurate picture. There has been steady flow of Japanese immigration (in the order of a few thousand per year) throughout the post-1965

TABLE 2.3 Ten largest Asian American groups, 1990 and 2000

Rank	1990		2000	
1	Chinese	1,645,472	Chinese	2,314,537
2	Filipino	1,406,770	Filipino	1,850,314
3	Japanese	847,562	Asian Indian	1,678,765
4	Asian Indian	815,447	Vietnamese	1,122,528
5	Korean	798,849	Korean	1,076,872
6	Vietnamese	614,547	Japanese	796,700
7	Laotian	149,014	Cambodians	171,937
8	Cambodians	147,411	Hmong	169,428
9	Thai	91,275	Laotian	168,707
10	Hmong	90,082	Pakistan	153,533

Source: Census 1990 Summary File 1 (STF 1) 100-per cent data, table P007; Census 2000 Summary File 1 (SF 1) 100-per cent data, Custom Tables QT-P6, PCT5, PCT7.

period, and the number of Japanese in the part-Asian population is quite large (Lai and Arguelles 2003, 73–8).

Asians are known to marry people of other races (demographers refer to this as "outmarriage") more frequently than other racial groups. The data in table 2.2 support that claim. When we calculate the percentage of the multiracial population in each racial group (called "in combination with one or more races" by the Census Bureau), we find that 14 per cent (1.6 million), or roughly one in seven Asians are multiracial. Asians are much more likely to be multiracial than whites and blacks, 3 per cent and 5 per cent of whom reported that they are multiracial, respectively. Of the 1.6 million multiracial Asians, a majority (868,000) are racially Asian and white. This combination is the second largest in all combinations of two races in the 2000 census, second only to the combination of American Indians and white (1.1 million) (Grieco and Cassidy 2001).

Among the six largest Asian groups, Japanese have the highest multiracial rate (31 per cent), followed by Filipinos (22 per cent). The reasons for outmarriage vary among Asian groups, but include an early history as a bachelor society due to laws banning entry of Asian women (particularly the case for Chinese); U.S. colonialism in the Philippines in the pre-World War II era; U.S. military bases in Japan and Korea in the postwar era (where some women married U.S. men in uniform and came to America as "war brides"); and upward socioeconomic mobility of some Asian groups (such as the Japanese) that made it easier for them to find spouses of other races. The 1990s saw a rapid increase in community and scholarly attention to multiracial and multiethnic Asians. The term *hapa*, originally used in Hawai'i to refer to part-Japanese and part-white people, began to be used by college-age multiracial Asians to describe themselves. Today, some people use "hapa" to include all multiracial Asians (plus multiracial Native Hawaiians and Pacific Islanders), not just multiracial

Japanese Americans (Lai and Arguelles 2003, 113–21). The experience and identity of multiracial Asians raise distinctive social and policy issues, including their recognition not only in U.S. society in general, but among Asian Americans (Lai and Arguelles 2003, 17–21). They also pose challenging questions as to who Asian Americans really are, and challenge the old images of "pureblood" Asians – such as pure Chinese or pure Japanese (Williams-León and Nakashima 2001).

Demographic Data: Where do Asian Americans Live?

Table 2.4 shows the number and percentage of "Asian alone" (those who marked the Asian race alone, which do not include multiracial Asians) in the fifty states and the District of Columbia. People often assume that Asians are numerous in California, Hawai'i, and New York but not elsewhere. The data reveals that the perception is only half right. Although it is true that the three states are indeed population centers for Asians, other areas are seeing rapid growth.

Table 2.5 ranks states by the number and percentage of Asians in the state. As one might expect, California, Hawai'i, and New York are among the top five in both ranks, reflecting the immigration history of Asians since the nineteenth century. Substantial growth has recently occurred in southern states and the "sunbelt" areas, as many professional Asians migrated to those regions, pursuing the expanding job market (Lai and Arguelles 2003).

The suburban Asian American population has grown considerably. Historically, Asians tended to live in "ethnic enclaves" in cities (such as Chinatowns around the country and Little Tokyo in Los Angeles), as they were discriminated against and could not live freely wherever they chose. With the postwar national trend of suburbanization and with federal laws banning racial discrimination in housing, however, Asians began to move into the suburbs, some living in predominantly white neighborhoods and others creating new Asian communities (Min 2006, 39–40). Many of the post-1965 Asian immigrants have settled in the suburbs. While a typical pattern of social mobility for immigrants to the U.S. used to be to settle in urban enclaves first and then move out to the suburbs once they accumulated greater financial resources, many recent immigrants go directly to the suburbs without stopping by urban areas first. This partially explains why some states have relatively large Asian populations. New Jersey serves as a suburb of New York City; it has a large Korean community across the Hudson River on the opposite side of Manhattan, as well as South Asian communities. Maryland and Virginia (which rank eighth and tenth in the percentage of Asians in the state) include the suburbs of Washington, D.C. In each state, more than 100,000 Asians, or approximately half of those in the state, concentrate in one county (Montgomery County and Fairfax County) on the borders of Washington, D.C.

Different Asian ethnic groups cluster in different areas, forming ethnically distinct communities. For example, Monterey Park, located just east of Los

TABLE 2.4 Population by race alone and state

	Asian (no.)	Asian (%)	White (%)	African American (%)	American Indian (%)	Pacific Islander (%)
Alabama	31,346	0.7	71.1	26.0	0.5	0.0
Alaska	25,116	4.0	69.3	3.5	15.6	0.5
Arizona	92,236	1.8	75.5	3.1	5.0	0.1
Arkansas	20,220	0.8	80.0	15.7	0.7	0.1
California	3,697,513	10.9	59.5	6.7	1.0	0.3
Colorado	95,213	2.2	82.8	3.8	1.0	0.1
Connecticut	82,313	2.4	81.6	9.1	0.3	0.0
Delaware	16,259	2.1	74.6	19.2	0.3	0.0
District of Columbia	15,189	2.7	30.8	60.0	0.3	0.1
Florida	266,256	1.7	78.0	14.6	0.3	0.1
Georgia	173,170	2.1	65.1	28.7	0.3	0.1
Hawai'i	503,868	41.6	24.3	1.8	0.3	9.4
Idaho	11,889	0.9	91.0	0.4	1.4	0.1
Illinois	423,603	3.4	73.5	15.1	0.2	0.0
Indiana	59,126	1.0	87.5	8.4	0.3	0.0
Iowa	36,635	1.3	93.9	2.1	0.3	0.0
Kansas	46,806	1.7	86.1	5.7	0.9	0.0
Kentucky	29,744	0.7	90.1	7.3	0.2	0.0
Louisiana	54,758	1.2	63.9	32.5	0.6	0.0
Maine	9,111	0.7	96.9	0.5	0.6	0.0
Maryland	210,929	4.0	64.0	27.9	0.3	0.0
Massachusetts	238,124	3.8	84.5	5.4	0.2	0.0
Michigan	176,510	1.8	80.2	14.2	0.6	0.0
Minnesota	141,968	2.9	89.4	3.5	1.1	0.0
Mississippi	18,626	0.7	61.4	36.3	0.4	0.0
Missouri	61,595	1.1	84.9	11.2	0.4	0.1
Montana	4,691	0.5	90.6	0.3	6.2	0.1
Nebraska	21,931	1.3	89.6	4.0	0.9	0.0
Nevada	90,266	4.5	75.2	6.8	1.3	0.4
New Hampshire	15,931	1.3	96.0	0.7	0.2	0.0
New Jersey	480,276	5.7	72.6	13.6	0.2	0.0
New Mexico	19,255	1.1	66.8	1.9	9.5	0.1
New York	1,044,976	5.5	67.9	15.9	0.4	0.0
North Carolina	113,689	1.4	72.1	21.6	1.2	0.0

TABLE 2.4 *continued*

	Asian (no.)	Asian (%)	White (%)	African American (%)	American Indian (%)	Pacific Islander (%)
North Dakota	3,606	0.6	92.4	0.6	4.9	0.0
Ohio	132,633	1.2	85.0	11.5	0.2	0.0
Oklahoma	46,767	1.4	76.2	7.6	7.9	0.1
Oregon	101,350	3.0	86.6	1.6	1.3	0.2
Pennsylvania	219,813	1.8	85.4	10.0	0.1	0.0
Rhode Island	23,665	2.3	85.0	4.5	0.5	0.1
South Carolina	36,014	0.9	67.2	29.5	0.3	0.0
South Dakota	4,378	0.6	88.7	0.6	8.3	0.0
Tennessee	56,662	1.0	80.2	16.4	0.3	0.0
Texas	562,319	2.7	71.0	11.5	0.6	0.1
Utah	37,108	1.7	89.2	0.8	1.3	0.7
Vermont	5,217	0.9	96.8	0.5	0.4	0.0
Virginia	261,025	3.7	72.3	19.6	0.3	0.1
Washington	322,335	5.5	81.8	3.2	1.6	0.4
West Virginia	9,434	0.5	95.0	3.2	0.2	0.0
Wisconsin	88,763	1.7	88.9	5.7	0.9	0.0
Wyoming	2,771	0.6	92.1	0.8	2.3	0.1
United States	10,242,998	3.6	75.1	12.3	0.9	0.1

Note: Figures are for those selecting one race only.

Source: Census 2000 Summary File 1 (SF 1) 100-per cent data, table P3.

Angeles, became "the first suburban Chinatown" where, by 1990, the majority of the population was Chinese (Horton 1994; T.P. Fong 1994). Many new Asian communities are located in California – for example, Westminster and Garden Grove (Vietnamese) and Long Beach (Cambodians). Asians have also built new communities outside California, however. There is a large Vietnamese community in Houston, and many Asian Indians live in the South, outnumbering Chinese (Lai and Arguelles 2003, 179). Some Asian American communities have been intentionally dispersed across the country by official policy. For example, Southeast Asian refugees were dispersed widely across the country. Other times, the diffusion is the result of individual and family decisions. Whatever the reason, the result is that Asians now live across the nation, not just in the western states.

To be sure, the Asian populations of states like Texas and New Jersey are not as large and concentrated as those of California and New York, the only states with more than one million Asians. Only Hawai'i and California have a total population that is more than 10 per cent Asian. Yet 5 or 10 per cent is large

TABLE 2.5 Largest Asian American populations, by state, 2000 Census

Ranked by number of Asians		Ranked by % of Asians	
California	3,697,513	Hawai'i	41.6
New York	1,044,976	California	10.9
Texas	562,319	New Jersey	5.7
Hawai'i	503,868	New York	5.5
New Jersey	480,276	Washington	5.5
Illinois	423,603	Nevada	4.5
Washington	322,335	Alaska	4.0
Florida	266,256	Maryland	4.0
Virginia	261,025	Massachusetts	3.8
Massachusetts	238,124	Virginia	3.7

Note: Figures do not include those who chose more than one race.

Source: Census 2000 Summary File 1 (SF 1) 100 per cent data, table P3.

enough to be visible and significant when we consider issues of public policy and political representation. Although their numbers may not give them a great deal of political power, Asians may be numerous enough to become targets of hate crimes or to be blamed for suburban overdevelopment (Horton 1994, ch. 4). We will return to these issues in chapter 4.

Asian American Diversity

We know that ethnic and national distinctions are often of great importance to the first generation of immigrants, and, with the exception of Japanese Americans, the majority of every Asian American subgroup today is foreign-born. This has important implications for policies such as health care. Because life experiences can be so different in different countries, Asian Americans who have immigrated from different countries may have very different health patterns.[6] Health care professionals can serve immigrants more effectively if they are aware of these ethnic variations.

Another source of diversity among Asian Americans of different ethnicities is socioeconomic status (SES). Socioeconomic levels are most often measured by income and education. As figures 2.2–2.6 and table 2.6 demonstrate, SES differences among Asian subgroups are very large (education is addressed in chapter 8; those figures show a pattern of differences similar to those reported in this chapter).

We should be careful about interpreting income statistics for Asian Americans. Figure 2.2 reports the median family incomes of all Asian Americans in the 2000 census. Comparing these panethnic income statistics

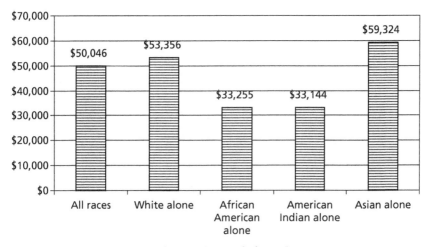

Source: Census summary file 4 (SF4) – sample data, PCT113

Figure 2.2 *Median family income, by racial group, 1999. Data from Census 2000, but income figures are for 1999.*

with those of other groups can give the impression that Asians are all high earners – even higher than whites. This view occasionally appears in intro-ductory American government textbooks, creating an impression that Asian Americans are "the superachievers of the minority majority" whose "median family income has already surpassed that of non-Hispanic Whites" (Edwards et al. 2006, 182).[7] However, this perception is misleading, because – among other problems – the statistics do not take into account differences among families and number of workers per family.

How this distortion happens can be seen by looking at per capita income. Family income does not take family size into account. We know from census data that Asian American families actually have more individuals (3.57 persons) than the overall population (3.14 persons), because many Asian immigrants (including those who came to the country as refugees) have more than two chil-dren, and because many Asian couples also have to support their elderly parents as a condition of obtaining an immigrant visa for them. Statistics show that more Asians live in multigenerational families than the overall population (Sakamoto and Xie 2006, 54). When we compare racial groups' per capita income, the income advantage of Asian Americans disappears (figure 2.3). A median white individual ($23,918) earns more than a median Asian American individual ($21,823).[8]

Another ground for caution in interpreting panethnic statistics is the tremendous variation among subgroups. While Asians of Japanese and Indian descent do tend to have high median family incomes, others, such as Koreans and Vietnamese, not only earn less than whites but also less than the median for all races (figure 2.5). Some Asian subgroups, such as Cambodians and

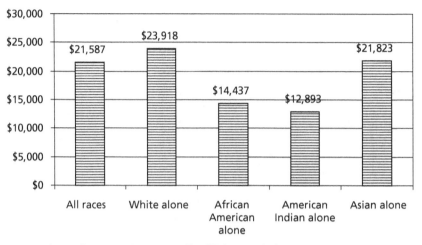

Source: Census 2000 summary file 4(SF4) – sample data, PCT130.

Figure 2.3 Per capita income by racial group, 1999.

Hmong, have median family incomes about the same as African Americans and American Indians. Figure 2.4 gives median family income by Asian American subgroups, showing the considerable difference that exists between the highest and lowest-earning groups.

The differences among Asian American ethnic groups become even more apparent when comparing per capita income (table 2.6). Japanese ($30,075) and Asian Indians ($27,514) still earn more than whites, but the number of Asian American groups who earn less than the overall population is even larger by this measure. For example, Filipinos, who earn more *family* income ($65,189) than the overall population, are found to earn *less per capita* income ($21,267) than the overall population. This is partially because Filipinos tend to have relatively large family sizes (3.77 persons) among Asian Americans. Likewise, Pakistanis, who have 4.14 family members on average, earn slightly larger family income ($50,189) but less per capita income ($18,096) than the overall population. All Asian American ethnic groups with refugee history have four or more family members on average. It is no coincidence that Laotians, Cambodians, and Hmong appear near the bottom of the table for per capita income. Their median per capita income is about half or less than half of the overall population ($21,587). In particular, Hmong median per capita income ($6,600) is less than one-third of that of the overall population and approximately half of the median for African Americans ($14,437) and American Indians ($12,893).

Poverty rates reveal similar diversity among Asian American subgroups. The U.S. government sets a poverty threshold for various types of families according to family size and the number of family members under 18 years old. For example, in 1999, if a family of three had one child below 18, the threshold was set at $13,410; it was set at $16,895 for a family of four with two children

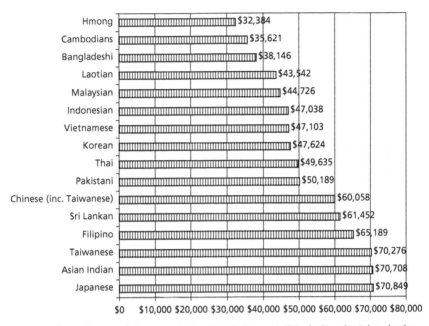

Source: Terrance J. Reeves and Claudette E. Bennett, "We the People: Asians in the United States," Census 2000 Special Reports (Dec. 2004), Census 2000 special tabulation.

Figure 2.4 *Median family income by detailed Asian American group, 1999. Data for those who identified with one group only (e.g. only Japanese).*

below 18. All members of a family whose income is lower than this threshold are defined as poor by the federal government (Bishaw and Iceland 2003, 2). Poverty rates are slightly greater for Asian Americans than for the overall population (figure 2.5). Although the poverty rate for Asian Americans is lower than that for African Americans, American Indians, Pacific Islanders, and Hispanics, it is higher than that for non-Hispanic whites.

Once again, we can see large differences in poverty rates among Asian American ethnic groups (figure 2.6). Not surprisingly, some Southeastern Asian American groups have high poverty rates, while Filipinos, Japanese, and Asian Indians have relatively low rates. Although it is certainly not true that all Southeast Asian Americans are poor, substantial numbers are in poverty, in sharp contrast to some other Asian American groups.

Asian Americans and Panethnic Identity

Influences on Panethnicity

Although Asian Americans are a very diverse subpopulation, a few interests are widely shared by all. The most powerful is probably opposition to anti-Asian violence. Few people, Asian American or otherwise, enjoy being beaten

TABLE 2.6 Per capita income by detailed Asian American group, 1999[a] ($)

Japanese	30,075
Asian Indian	27,514
Sri Lankan	27,478
Taiwanese	25,890
Chinese[b]	23,756
[PER CAPITA INCOME FOR ENTIRE U.S.]	21, 587
Filipino	21,267
Malaysian	19,895
Thai	19,066
Indonesian	18,932
Korean	18,805
Pakistani	18,096
Vietnamese	15,655
Bangladeshi	13,971
Laotian	11,830
Cambodians	10,366
Hmong	6,600

[a.] Data for those who identified with one group only (e.g. only Japanese).
[b.] Includes Taiwanese.
Source: Terrance J. Reeves and Claudette E. Bennett, "We the People: Asians in the United States," *Census 2000 Special Reports* (Dec. 2004), Census 2000 special tabulation.

senseless. While many Asian American organizations do not make anti-Asian violence their primary concern, it has played a critical role in forging a pan-Asian American political coalition.

Anti-Asian bigotry helped to forge a panethnic identity among Asian Americans in the 1960s. As we noted in chapter 1, bigoted whites care little for ethnic distinctions, sometimes calling Japanese Americans "chinks," and sometimes referring to Chinese Americans as "japs". By the late 1960s, many racists had updated their slurs, adding "gook" to their limited vocabulary, again applying it to Asian Americans of a wide variety of ancestries.[9] The fact that bigots made no distinctions helped to encourage panethnic thinking, particularly in the third generation, many of whom were just reaching adulthood. Although they recognized ethnic differences, many came to believe that their shared experiences – particularly their experiences with bigotry – were far greater than their differences.

On the other hand, the tremendous disparities among Asian Americans have created diverging economic interests that have inhibited the formation of panethnic identity. Some South Asian American entrepreneurs may be

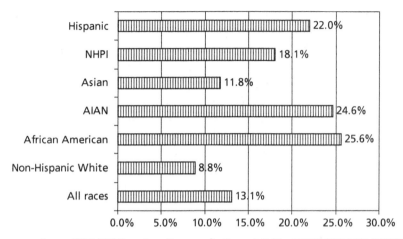

Source: 2004 ACS (American Community Survey), Tables B1700B-B17001E, B17001H, B17001I.

Figure 2.5 *Poverty by ethnoracial group, 2004. Each group includes Hispanic and non-Hispanic, unless noted.*

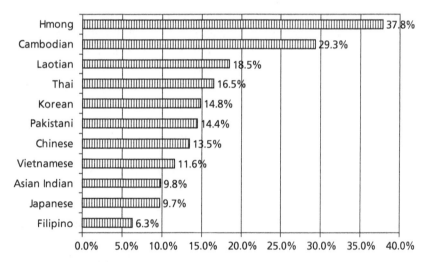

Source: Terrace J. Reeves and Claudette E. Bennett, "We the People: Asians in the United States," Census 2000 Special Reports (Dec. 2004), Census 2000 special tabulation.

Figure 2.6 *Poverty by detailed Asian American group, 1999. Data for Asian Americans reporting one race only.*

concerned about investments and the capital gains tax, while some Hmong American families might be concerned about a potential end to their government assistance. Although common ground might be found, language barriers can also make it more difficult to bridge the gap among ethnic groups. For Asian immigrants, there is no single language that most will speak fluently.

Social structures and institutions can play an important role in forging identities; they can help people to recognize and act on the kinds of shared interests we discussed above. Society can be structured in ways that reward or
penalize panethnic alliances. In the past, Asian American subgroups had
strong disincentives to ally with each other. For example, the legal structure –
while it discriminated against Chinese – encouraged Japanese Americans to
stress their differences in the first few decades of the twentieth century, and
bitter anti-Japanese sentiments during World War II led many Chinese to
return the favor. By the late twentieth century, however, government and non-
governmental routines were working in the opposite direction. Public and
private agencies organized their clientele into ethnoracial groups, usually
following OMB Directive 15, which recognized four (later five) racial groups,
plus a "Hispanic" category. As a result, Asian American subgroups found it necessary and in their interests to work together when dealing with government
officials or large private organizations. In chapter 4, we look in more detail at
examples of pan-Asian American political coalitions.

The geographical distribution of a subpopulation can also be important.
One of the most striking cases of the development of a panethnic identity has
occurred among the aboriginal peoples of the United States who cluster in
urban areas. "Urban Indians," who in the 2000 census made up almost 60 per
cent of American Indians, are more likely to interact with Indians from other
tribes than their rural counterparts, and so have played an important role in
the creation of a panethnic Native American identity.[10] Although many still
emphasize a tribal affiliation, they have also been willing to embrace a panethnic identity ("American Indian"). Ceremonies have been designed to incorporate multiple tribal rituals, serving a broader population and creating a
panethnic culture. The high concentration of Asian Americans in urban areas
may facilitate similar inter-ethnic contact and cooperation.

The structure of colleges and universities can also promote panethnic thinking. Not surprisingly, pan-Asian organizations exist on many college campuses. With pan-Asian groups drawing them together, new Asian American
students often conclude that their common panethnic perspective trumps
their ethnic differences. Asian American studies programs can play a similar
role. For some Asian American students, the university might offer the first
chance to interact with large numbers of Asians of other ancestries.
Interacting with professors and fellow students, they are likely to learn of the
experiences and challenges that Asian Americans share.

Another potentially important site for forging a panethnic identity is the
church. In the past, churches have served as important foci for Asian American
ethnic groups such as Japanese Americans (Fugita and O'Brien 1991). Today,
argues Russell Jeung, new Asian American churches are drawing together Asians
of different nationalities, building panethnic identity in the process (Jeung 2005).

The institution of marriage is another important force promoting panethnic formation. Discussions of intermarriage usually focus on interracial

couplings (e.g., black and white), but research has shown that intra-Asian inter-marriage is growing considerably. Asian American studies programs, pan-Asian American churches, and other similar venues can facilitate socializing, courtship, and marriage. Nazli Kibria's interviews with young adults also found evidence for at least some acceptance of panethnic marriage. Although her respondents reported that some of their parents insisted on intra-ethnic marriage (e.g. Korean Americans marrying other Korean Americans), many saw their parents as at least willing to tolerate marriage to other Asian Americans, although the parents sometimes found some Asian groups much more desirable than others (Kibria 2002, 171–4).

Politics can play an important role in the formation of a panethnic identity as well. Nagel describes how the "Red Power" movement played a major role in the creation of an American Indian panethnic identity, organizing on a pan-tribal basis (sometimes drawing bitter opposition from tribal leaders) and helping unite Native Americans around common concerns and panethnic pride (Nagel 1996, ch. 6). In Chicago, Puerto Ricans and Mexican Americans formed a coalition over specific goals, such as affirmative action (Padilla 1985). One of the leading students of Asian American politics, Pei-te Lien, has argued that a pan-Asian American identity has been forged through political partici-pation (Lien 2001).

Other common causes help to create panethnic unity. One example of this could be seen in the Asian American movement, which was spearheaded by activists concerned with pursuing changes at San Francisco State and the University of California, Berkeley (Wei 1993, ch. 1). In chapters 4 and 8, we describe in more detail how intra-Asian alliances have been formed over spe-cific issues.

Panethnicity among Immigrants and Native-born

In the early twenty-first century, the majority of Asian Americans are foreign-born, so we would hypothesize that most would not embrace a panethnic identity as their primary one. Over time, however, their children and grand-children are likely to move through institutions and have experiences that encourage panethnic thinking, but the immigrant generation is more likely to identify in narrower terms. This pattern was confirmed in the landmark Pilot National Asian American Political Survey (PNAAPS). About two-thirds of PNAAPS respondents chose either ethnic (e.g. "Korean") or "ethnic American" (e.g. "Korean American") when asked how they thought of themselves.

Further confirmation was found when respondents were distinguished by nativity. Approximately 70 per cent of Asian immigrants identify primarily in ethnic or ethnic American terms. On the other hand, 50 per cent of native-born Asian Americans said that they think of themselves in panethnic terms ("Asian American"), or simply as "American." Another third of the U.S.-born used an ethnic American label.

However, while only 15 per cent of Asian immigrants chose "Asian American" as their primary identity, the number jumped to 55 per cent when respondents were asked if they *ever* thought of themselves as "Asian American" (Lien et al. 2004, 38–44). It would appear that many Americans of Asian ancestry are most likely to embrace their ancestral identity (e.g. Vietnamese) but also see themselves as Asian American, although the latter identity is less prominent.

Such attitudes illustrate the flexible and variable nature of identity (Lowe 1991). Individuals may identify in different ways at different times, with their identity shifting with the context. For instance, a student at the Northeastern, visiting a friend at Boston College might identify herself to new acquaintances as "from Northeastern." However, if that same student were to visit a relative in another part of the country, she might instead respond that she was "from Massachusetts." If that same student studied abroad, she might tell new friends that she was "from the U.S."

Asian American Uncertainty: The Case of South Asian Americans

While all immigrant groups are likely to be uncertain about panethnic labels, South Asian Americans are a particularly significant case. With their sizable numbers (primarily Asian Indian Americans), they represent an important segment of any potential Asian American coalition. In addition, however, because of their distinct history and geography, South Asians have perhaps the most tenuous ties to a pan-Asian identity of all Asian American groups.

Although geographers usually define Asia as extending westward to Turkey, other definitions place India and Pakistan as the western boundary. Culturally and geographically distinct, South Asians also have historically had limited interaction with East Asians.

Physical appearances differ as well. Reflecting the different migration patterns from centuries past, South Asians tend to be physically distinct from East and Southeast Asians. This has led to continuing uncertainties as to how South Asians should be classified in the American racial scheme. From 1920 to 1940, they had been classified as "Asians" (under the inappropriate label of "Hindu"), but they had disappeared from the Asian category in the 1950 census, not to return until 1980 (Lott 1998, 82).

Although South Asian Americans have formed alliances with other Asian Americans, doubts remain. South Asian activists sometimes feel that they are underrepresented in leadership positions in pan-Asian coalitions, and some wonder if the interests of South Asians are too different from those of other Asian Americans. We discuss South Asian Americans further in chapter 4.

Panethnicity and Politics

While panethnic identity can be of great interest, how is it politically important? It might seem as if it is largely a matter of personal choice, but, in fact, it is extremely important for the study of Asian American politics. The most obvious significance involves numbers. Asian Americans still make up a fairly small portion of the population – even when combined together. But the separate Asian subgroups make up even smaller percentages, of course. In politics, numbers can equal power. Although other factors – such as organization – affect political power, having more supporters is always a valuable resource. The more people who identify as "Asian American," the more potential clout Asian American political groups are likely to have. In local, state, and national government, elected officials are likely to pay more attention to issues that are a concern to large numbers of people.

Interestingly, panethnicity and politics may be related in the opposite way as well. While stronger panethnic identity might produce more political success, more political success might produce a stronger panethnic identity. Pei-te Lien has argued that a pan-Asian American identity has been built through political activity. Lien (2001, Ch. 2) describes cases of Asian American elected officials and activists working across ethnic lines. One notable example was the response to media depictions of the so-called Asian fund-raising scandal, where a wide range of Asian American groups joined together to protest at what they saw as biased and inflammatory reporting.

In the 1996 election campaign, there had been charges that three Asian Americans (John Huang, Charles Trie, and Johnny Chung) had solicited campaign contributions from sources not eligible to make donations. As news of the charges spread, the recipients – who included the Democratic National Committee – began to react with alarm. The controversy snowballed to the point where all Asian Americans seemed to be considered guilty until proven innocent. In striking and ugly fashion, the "forever foreigner" image seemed to pop up again, generating suspicions against many Asian Americans donors, who were asked about their citizenship and investigated in ways done to no other donors. Had an American of European ancestry been implicated in fundraising illegalities, it is unlikely that officials would have questioned all white donors. Asian American donors increasingly felt singled out and profiled as suspicious based on their racial identity.

The precipitating event for many Asian Americans was a mocking *National Review* cover that featured a caricature where President Clinton and his wife Hillary had been drawn with stereotypical East Asian features. Although there were differences over strategy and tactics, many activists agreed that this represented an attack on Asian Americans, and some response was essential.

While elite-level coalition-building has blossomed on many occasions, grassroots effects are less certain. A *Los Angeles Times* poll (*Los Angeles Times* 1997b) of Southern California Chinese Americans' response to the fundraising scandal found that approximately 37 per cent were offended by the focus on contributors with Asian surnames, but 27 per cent were not, and while 39 per cent felt that the investigation was discriminatory, 36 per cent did not. The panethnic consciousness that grows so readily in the welcoming environ-ments of such places as university Asian American studies programs seems not to have taken root in the minds of large numbers of Asian Americans, who, most likely, will never find themselves in such settings.

What is clear, though, is that the willingness of Asian Americans to join together can have an important impact on their political prospects. We take this up this issue in detail in the next chapter.

Transnational Asian Americans?

Another important question about Asian American identity regards ances-tral roots. How important are Asian Americans' ties to Asia? Today there is much discussion of the ways that immigrants can continue to be influenced by connections to their countries of origin. The connections that immigrants feel to their home countries is part of what is called transnationalism (Basch et al. 1993). Although transnationalism appears to be an important factor in Asian American politics, we need to be careful not to exaggerate the importance.

Transnationalism and Return Migration over Time

Immigrants have always retained interest in their homelands, but it is easier today to maintain contact. International communication is much easier than it was fifty, or even twenty, years ago. Although overseas travel is prohibitively expensive for many, and political conditions make it even more difficult in some cases, today's immigrants usually find it far easier to journey back to their native lands than did those of previous generations.

However, it is incorrect to assume that Asians – or other immigrants – are now less willing to become part of American society. As we will discuss in chapter 7, this assumption feeds the "forever foreigner" stereotype, an image of Asian Americans that is both harmful and inaccurate. For instance, contrary to what some people believe, the evidence indicates that English is learned fairly quickly. Adults – immigrant or otherwise – may have diffi-culty learning a new language, but their children usually become fluent, prefer to speak English rather than their parents' native language, and con-sider the U.S. to be their homeland (Portes and Shauffler 1996; Rumbaut 2002).

There is also a misconception that immigrants of an earlier era came with a stronger commitment to stay, while immigrants of today are less committed to their new country. In fact, however, immigrants have long felt the pull of their native lands, and large numbers of nineteenth- and early twentieth-century immigrants were return migrants, leaving the America to live the rest of their lives in the lands where they were born (Piore 1979, ch. 6). Just as is the case today, many never came with the intention of staying.

Like return migration, transnationalism is nothing new. However, the specific effects of transnationalism change over time as conditions change. For example, the greatly enhanced communications options make it much easier for immigrants to be active in the politics of their former country (Foner 2001). Candidates can travel to America to campaign for support from emigrants, who may retain the right to vote in their native land.

Globalization, Transnationalism, and Immigration

"Globalization" refers to worldwide shifts in power, particularly changes with political, economic, and cultural consequences (Smith, et al. 2001, 18). Globalization and transnationalism have a powerful combined effect on some immigration flows.

To understand this, it is necessary to understand a little about the economic restructuring that has led to much low-skill production moving "offshore," to countries where wages are very low by U.S. standards (Sassen 1990). Advances in transportation have allowed many goods to be manufactured thousands of miles away and sold in the U.S. for much lower prices than if they were made in America. The key, of course, is that workers making these products are receiving wages that are much lower than U.S. workers usually receive. You may have noticed, for instance, that it is difficult to find clothes still made in the U.S. When American manufacturing of goods such as clothing does survive, it requires that labor costs be kept extremely low.

Frequently, only immigrants are willing to work for such low wages. In some cases, newcomers have an additional incentive because they are here without proper authorization, making it more difficult for them to find other jobs. In addition, some unauthorized migrants owe large sums to the smugglers who got them to the U.S., and the smugglers place heavy pressure on those immigrants to pay off their debts (Kwong 1996/1987, 179–88).

Many immigrants are attracted to ethnic enclaves – communities with large numbers of people with the same ethnicity. The traditional Chinatowns found in many U.S. cities are classic examples of ethnic enclaves. Such enclaves are valued by many immigrants, but they are especially attractive to unauthorized immigrants because they allow individuals to blend into the neighborhood, making them less conspicuous to authorities. Unauthorized immigrants often settle in these enclaves where they find work in restaurants, in clothing and other manufacturing, and other very low-paying jobs. The low pay and isolation of these workers can make it very difficult for them to escape poverty. Often, they have little or no knowledge of English, a much greater burden for them than for legal immigrants who do not need to fear accidentally drawing attention to themselves. As a result, many unauthorized immigrants stay on, heavily dependent on employers who speak their language, and who claim they need to pay very low wages to stay in business. These low-paid workers contrast sharply with the image of highly successful Asian Americans (we discuss this "model minority" image in chapter 7).

Transnationalism and Asian American Diversity

Understanding transnationalism is important for a full understanding of Asian American politics. Transnationalism is likely to be high among Asian Americans, because of the high percentage of Asian Americans who are first-generation immigrants. In later chapters, we explore the political implications of transnationalism further. Here, we note how transnational ties vary from group to group among Asian Americans, contributing to Asian American diversity.

The effects of transnationalism can vary by country of origin. The way that Hmong refugees relate to the land of their birth is likely to be very different from South Asian immigrants, who can maintain much stronger connections to their native land. Some Chinese immigrants may be accustomed to migrating widely across Asia, while others may have come to the U.S. directly from China. Not surprisingly, research has found variation in transnational ties among Chinese Americans who grew up in different countries (Lien 2006).

In addition to national differences, transnationalism can vary by generation, gender, and social class. Immigrants are most likely to retain ties to another country, but those connections usually become increasingly thin with each additional generation (Jones-Correa 2002; Levitt and Waters 2002). The third generation often do not speak the native language of their grandparents, making transnational ties much more difficult.

Gender can be another important source of difference. Although there are certainly similarities, there can be important differences in the ways that men and women build and maintain connections with their countries of birth. For example, the transnational connections of women may be shaped more by concerns over childrearing or giving support to aging parents than those of men (Viruell-Fuentes 2006).

Social class can matter as well. For poor immigrants, transnational connections are much harder to maintain. Only middle- and upper-class immigrants are likely to have the resources for frequent travel back and forth between countries.

While transnationalism helps to increase Asian American diversity, other factors may have opposite effects. In the next chapter, we turn to political participation, which sometimes helps Asian Americans overcome their differences and build larger coalitions.

CHAPTER THREE

Political Participation and Public Opinion

Studying Asian Americans' political participation can tell us much about their political incorporation – the degree to which they are allowed to participate on equal terms with other Americans. Our focus in this chapter will be on individual participation, although we continue to be interested in the larger patterns created by the participation of large numbers of individuals. These patterns of participation can give us a better idea of the nature of Asian American politics.

A quick glance at the data shows that Asian Americans do not participate in voting very much. But this does not necessarily mean that Asian Americans are apolitical. In this chapter, we look at the data more closely, and identify institutional barriers to Asian American political incorporation and participation. As we saw when looking at socioeconomic profiles, some broad perceptions about Asian Americans do not hold up upon more careful analysis. Perhaps equally importantly, there is evidence that Asian American political participation is playing a major role in creating a meaningful Asian American identity (Lien 2001). In this chapter, you will learn about:

1 Asian American voting patterns, and the steps needed for immigrants to get to the voting booth.
2 Asian American political participation in activities other than voting.
3 The major influences on Asian American participation.
4 Asian American political preferences and attitudes.
5 Gender-based differences in political participation of Asian Americans.
6 How political participation may be shaping an Asian American identity.

In this chapter, we focus primarily on individual participation. The activities of interest groups – a very important type of political participation – are examined in depth in the next chapter. Elite-level participation in political decision making (by elected and other government officials) is discussed extensively in chapter 5.

Political science studies of political participation tend to focus on voting. Voting studies have much to tell us, but there is much more to the story, particularly for subpopulations such as Asian Americans. Indeed, before the 1990s, when fewer Asian Americans voted and ran for offices than do now, Asian American politics was "characterized as 'politics by other means,' for example, indirect influence through interest group lobbying,

TABLE 3.1 Voting rates in the 2004 election (% of all individuals 18 and older)

	% voted
Total	58.3
White alone	60.3
White non-Hispanic alone	65.8
Black alone	56.3
Asian alone	29.8
Hispanic (of any race)	28.0

Note: Hispanics can be of any race, so the "Black alone" and the "Asian alone" categories may include small numbers of respondents who are also identified as Hispanic. We give a separate tabulation for Hispanics, because it can be useful to compare them to Asian Americans. See the appendix at the end of this book for additional information

Source: U.S. Census Bureau, Current Population Survey, November 2004, table 4a.

targeted campaign contributions, litigation, and protest" (Brackman and Erie 1995, 282). As Nakanishi (1986) cautions, an exclusive focus on voting and elections would overlook a very substantial portion of Asian American politics. With these caveats, we turn to a discussion of participation through voting.

Political Participation: Voting

There is a widely held view that Asian Americans are not politically active. Table 3.1 shows one of the sources for that view. The table draws on Census Bureau data to tabulate voting rates by ethnoracial group, for the 2004 elections. Clearly, Asian and Hispanic voting rates are dramatically lower than those for whites and blacks. We show only results for the 2004 election, but the same pattern holds for other national elections (Lien 2001, 115, table 3.3). Why is turnout so low?

The similarities between Asian and Hispanic voting rates on one hand, and between white and black voting rates on the other, suggest one part of the explanation. We know that the Latino and Asian subpopulations include high percentages of immigrants, while there are relatively few immigrants among whites and blacks. Individuals born in the U.S. are automatically citizens, but immigrants must apply and pass a test for citizenship, usually after a five-year waiting period. As a consequence, substantial percentages of Latinos and Asians are not citizens. Non-citizens cannot legally vote, so groups that include large numbers of non-citizens will have lower turnout rates than groups that have few non-citizens, when turnout is measured as a percentage of all voting-age individuals. Because the census data is based on all individuals 18 or older (citizen and non-citizen), it includes many immigrants who are not yet eligible to vote.

Can You Pass the Test?

If you were born in the United States, you are automatically a citizen. However, immigrants must successfully complete an interview and test before they can naturalize (become a citizen), demonstrating basic English skills and knowledge of U.S. history and government. The USCIS is currently preparing a new test which is scheduled to be in full use by 2008, but applicants will still be asked ten questions, many of which require specific knowledge. See if you can answer these ten questions from the new test:

1 What is the supreme law of the land?
2 What do we call the first ten amendments to the Constitution?
3 What are the two parts of the United States Congress?
4 We elect a U.S. Senator for how many years?
5 The House of Representatives has how many voting members?
6 Who vetoes bills?
7 Who confirms Supreme Court justices?
8 When was the Constitution drafted?
9 What group of essays supported passage of the U.S. Constitution?
10 Who was President during World War I?

Answers are on the next page. How did you do? Citizenship applicants must answer at least six out of ten. Would you have passed the test?

Sources: U.S. Citizenship and Immigration Services. "Fact Sheet." November 30, 2006. http://www.uscis.gov/files/pressrelease/FactSheetNatzTest113006.pdf.

Voting as a Three-Step Process

Getting to a polling place requires more than one step. For the immigrants who make up a large percentage of Asian American populations, voting is a "three-step process:" naturalization, registration, and voting (Lien et al. 2001, 625).

For immigrants, the first step toward voting is the process of naturalization, that is, of becoming a citizen (Step 1). Most immigrants become eligible to file naturalization papers five years after becoming permanent residents; those who are spouses of U.S. citizens become eligible in three years.[1] Filing an application does not automatically lead to citizenship, however. Applicants must go through an interview where they must demonstrate basic skills in English and also pass a civics test on U.S. history and government.

After becoming citizens, immigrants can take the second step on the road to the polling place: registration. Native-born and naturalized citizens are subject to the same registration rules, but research has shown that naturalized citizens do not register as frequently as the native-born. Naturalized citizens may not be aware of need to register. Many native-born Americans learn about registration in school, from teachers and classmates, and some high schools place voter registration forms in prominent places in the school building. Immigrants who arrive as adults would not have this assistance, of course, and

Answers to citizenship test
1 The Constitution.
2 The Bill of Rights.
3 The House of Representatives and the Senate.
4 Six years.
5 435.
6 The President.
7 The Senate.
8 1787.
9 *The Federalist Papers.*
10 Woodrow Wilson.

those who are able to learn about the registration requirements may not have sufficient English skills to fill out the forms.

Still, many naturalized citizens register, becoming eligible to move to the third stage of the voting process: actually casting a ballot. Language and other barriers can still block their way, however. In jurisdictions where a language minority is 5 per cent or more of the population, the Voting Rights Act stipulates that bilingual election materials must be prepared, but problems remain. For example, the Asian American Legal Defense and Education Fund (AALDEF) found that in New York City candidate names were mistranslated in Chinese and Korean languages; interpreters were not doing their jobs and their availability was not advertised; poll workers were not aware of bilingual ballots; and some workers demanded identification from Asian American voters even though voters were not required to show identification (Magpantay 2004). In the 2004 general election, AALDEF monitored far more polling places with high Asian American voter concentration, covering 167 sites in eight states on the East Coast and in the Midwest. It found widespread violations of the voting rights of Asian Americans, especially those with limited English proficiency (AALDEF 2005a).

Table 3.2 compares voting rates by ethnoracial group, breaking them down by stages in the three-step voting process. For meaningful comparisons, it is necessary to compare individuals at comparable stages in the voting process. Therefore, the first column shows overall turnout rates for everyone in the given category (e.g. for all whites or for all Asian Americans), but the second column only shows voting rates for citizens. The third column shows voting rates only for those who are registered. The variation is dramatic. When only those eligible to vote are included (i.e. only those who are citizens), both Latino and Asian American voting rates increase by 50 per cent or more. And, in both groups, most of those who register go on to vote. Research on previous years produces similar results, with Asian American voting rates for those registered very similar to the rates for whites (Ong and Nakanishi 1996; Lien 2001, 115).

The data, however, still leaves us with the question of why Asian Americans register at such low rates. In 2004 only a little over half of Asian Americans

TABLE 3.2 Voting rates by race and Hispanic origin, individuals 18 and older, 2004 (%)

	Total who voted	Citizens who voted	Registered who voted
All races	58.3	63.8	88.5
White alone	60.3	65.4	88.9
White non-Hispanic alone	65.8	67.2	89.4
Black alone	56.3	60.0	87.4
Asian alone	29.8	44.1	85.2
Hispanic (of any race)	28.0	47.2	81.5

Source: U.S. Census Bureau, Current Population Survey, November 2004, table 4a.

TABLE 3.3 Voting turnout for native-born and naturalized citizens (%)

	U.S.-born citizens	Naturalized citizens
All races	64.5	53.7
White alone	65.8	57.4
White non-Hispanic alone	67.3	61.8
Black alone	60.4	54.4
Asian alone	40.5	46.4
Hispanic (of any race)	45.5	52.1

Source: U.S. Census Bureau, Current Population Survey, November 2004, table 13.

were registered to vote, compared to 72 per cent of the entire population, and 75 per cent of non-Hispanic whites.

One possibility might be that naturalized citizens are less interested in voting than U.S.-born citizens. Those uninterested in voting might see no reason to register. Naturalized citizens might continue to be more interested in the politics of their native country, or they might anticipate more difficulty voting, given language barriers and other aspects of the process which might be more unfamiliar for them than for a native-born citizen. However, as table 3.3 demonstrates, this is not the case. The table compares turnout of native-born citizens to that of naturalized citizens. Although white and black naturalized citizens voted at lower rates than white and black native-born citizens, Asian and Hispanic naturalized citizens actually voted at higher rates than Asian and Hispanic native-born citizens in 2004. A similar analysis of the 2000 election found voting rates essentially the same for native-born and naturalized Asian American citizens (Lien et al. 2004, 150). Also, although the gap with other groups has become smaller, Asian Americans still vote at lower rates than other groups, even when comparing only naturalized citizens. The lower Asian American voting rates do not appear to be simply a statistical artifact created because of the higher percentage of immigrants. Rather, the reason for the low turnout rate of Asian Americans seems likely to lie in their low registration rate.

Why don't Asian Americans register as frequently as other racial groups? One of the most extensive studies of Asian American political participation and opinions, the Pilot National Asian American Political Survey (PNAAPS), looked at factors that differentiated registered Asian Americans from non-registered Asian Americans (Lien et al. 2004, 155–7). Interestingly, education level, income, and English language use were not found to have significant effects. Rather, registered Asian Americans are different from non-registered ones only in two aspects: they have more political interests, and they are more likely to be contacted by political parties and organizations.

Political Participation: A Broader View

Before we examine voting further, it is useful to consider political partici-pation more broadly. Although voting is the most common type of political participation, other kinds of participation may be better measures of overall participation for subpopulations such as Asian Americans who have a large percentage of non-citizens (and therefore a large percentage not eligible to vote). Many of the kinds of participation other than voting are open to every-one, although some forms of participation, such as contributing money to political candidates, are limited to citizens and permanent resident aliens. We look briefly at other types of political participation, and then examine expla-nations for this broader range of political participation.

Participation Other than Voting

Figure 3.1 shows participation levels for some of the most commonly mea-sured activities other than voting. Past research on political participation (Verba et al. 1995, ch. 3) has found that Americans are most likely to engage in voting and much less likely to do any of the other activities. Asian Americans follow the same general pattern.

We can see that most Asian Americans do not engage in any political activity other than voting. Of the other forms of activity, only "worked with others to solve a community problem" even approaches a fifth of the total subpopulation, and all others (except voting) have attracted little more than a tenth, at most.

Important to note, however, is the pattern in the graph. For every activity, foreign-born citizens participate at higher levels than non-citizens but at lower levels than U.S.-born respondents.[2] This trend suggests that Asian Americans tend to participate more as they become more knowledgeable about the U.S.

Figure 3.2 gives comparable political participation rates for the entire U.S. population from the 2004 National Election Study. As you can see, although native-born Asian Americans vote at somewhat lower rates than the general population, participation levels for other activities are fairly similar. These two

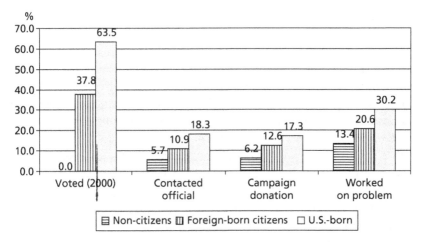

Sources: Pilot National Asian American Political Survey (PNAAPS), 2000–1.
Question was: "During the past four years, have you ever participated in any of the following types of political activity in your community?"
"Worked on problem" was phrased "worked with others in your community to solve a problem"; "Govt, board or commission" was "served on any government board or commission." The question has some other choices, such as "signed a petition for a political cause" and "worked for a political campaign" (Lien et al. 2004, 150).

Figure 3.1 *Asian American political participation (%).*

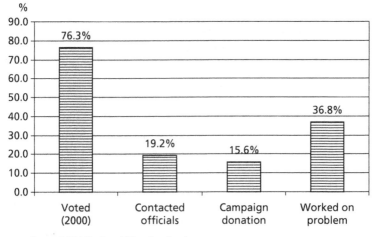

Source: 2004 National Election Study.

Figure 3.2 *Political participation (%) – general population.*

figures suggest that low levels of participation are in large part a reflection of a fact that a high percentage of Asian Americans are still fairly new to the U.S., and that participation rates will be higher for their children and grandchildren.

Campaign Contributions

Campaign contributions have loomed large in discussions of Asian American political participation. Some observers have suggested that Asian Americans are becoming major players as campaign donors (e.g. Espiritu 1992, 61), but further evidence has raised questions about that. Nevertheless, many Asian Americans do contribute to campaigns, and, because of campaign finance laws that disclose contributors and recipients of campaign donations, we have more detailed data on this form of participation than on most others besides voting.

The PNAAPS found that only about 12 per cent of respondents had contributed money in the past four years, although the percentage rises to 17 per cent when only native-born Asian Americans are considered. Significantly, the PNAAPS data suggests that Asian Americans are less likely to contribute than the general population, and even native-born Asian Americans are only slightly more likely to contribute. Although "it is now widely believed that Asian Americans are unique political animals because they combine general political apathy with generous campaign giving" (Cho 2002, 349), the evidence does not support that description.

In addition to the survey data, we also have information gathered by the Federal Elections Commission (FEC). The FEC requires federal campaigns (campaigns for congressional office or the presidency) to file reports on contributions and expenditures. Contributions over $200 must include the contributor's name, occupation, and employer (Federal Election Commission 2003).

Wendy Tam Cho's analysis of FEC data shows that Asian Americans in the FEC database are most likely to contribute to Asian American candidates, suggesting symbolic support for co-ethnics rather than strategic maximization of influence. If Asian Americans were more strategic donors, larger percentages of their money would go to the candidates who have the best chance of winning, and highly strategic givers would give most to candidates in close races. The FEC data, however, suggests that Asian Americans are most often motivated to show support to co-ethnics, rather than direct their money to those who have the best chance of success (Cho 2002, 367–70). Asian Americans' contributions to Asian American candidates do not seem to be affected by the strength of the candidacy. Another sign of strategic giving could be heavy early donations, since early money delivers the greatest leverage for building a successful campaign, but Cho found that Asian American donors did not particularly tend to make early contributions either (Cho 2002, 372–6).

Identity seems to be an important influence on Asian American contributions. Most of the donors studied by Cho gave to members of their ethnic group: for example, Chinese Americans contributed mostly to Chinese American candidates. In a more narrowly focused study, Cho and Lad (2004) found that virtually all of Asian American contributors to South Asian candidates for congressional races were South Asians. However, Cho also found some evidence that panethnic giving might increase for candidates who are in office for a long time. The evidence is very limited, however, since there are only two long-term Asian American members of Congress: Norman Mineta and Robert Matsui, both House Democrats from California (Matsui died in office in January 2005). Cho found some evidence that Mineta and Matsui, both Japanese Americans, picked up more contributions from non-Japanese Asian Americans as they built their careers in Congress (Cho 2002, 372).

A few cautions are in order for Cho's analysis. First, her analysis inevitably misses some Asian Americans (Cho 2002, 353; Cho and Lad 2004, 261 n.9). Although she has probably the best existing name dictionary not in corporate hands, it is almost impossible to detect Asian Americans with non-Asian names. Asian women who have married non-Asian men and taken their husbands' names will be undetectable, unless they have Asian first names – which is unlikely for third or later generation Asian Americans. In addition, children of Asian–non-Asian parents may have non-Asian names (first and last). As we explained in chapter 2, it is these second- and third-generation Asian Americans who are most likely more likely to have a panethnic orientation. Limiting the analysis to Asian names is unavoidable, but it probably creates a small bias toward individuals who are less likely to have a panethnic orientation.

Two other cautions should also be noted. As explained earlier, the FEC database only provides information for individuals who gave over $200. For analyses focused on campaign finance, this limitation in the data is a minor concern, since most campaign funds come from larger donors. However, the lack of information about small donors is a concern for our study, since we are interested not in the amount of money donors give, but in their ethnicity. A final caution is that this is a database of contributors to *federal* elections (candidates for members of Congress and the president). For state and local elections, candidates may be able to have more personal contact with potential contributors, so different dynamics may develop. Unfortunately, no national database of contributors to state and local campaigns exists, so it would be extremely difficult to replicate Cho's study for state and local races nationwide.

James Lai has analyzed patterns of contributions to Asian American candidates for a 1991 California House race (Lai et al. 2001). His findings are similar to Cho's. Most Asian American donors give to co-ethnics, but some panethnic support is evident as well. Paralleling our discussion in chapter 2, it would appear that most Asian American contributors are currently focused on ethnic rather than panethnic participation in the political process, but the latter could grow in the future.

Explaining Political Participation

Political scientists have developed some models to help us understand the factors that affect participation levels, but these models have mixed success in explaining Asian American participation.

The "SES Model"

Perhaps the best-known explanation for voting draws on social class, otherwise known as socioeconomic status (SES). The SES model grew out of repeated observations that people with higher levels of education and income had much higher voting rates than people with low levels of education and income. Further analysis showed that education was the most powerful factor, although income levels had a modest impact on participation (Wolfinger and Rosenstone 1980).

The SES model seems clearly inadequate to explain Asian American voting rates. Although there is tremendous diversity among Asian Americans, we have seen that a large percentage have fairly high levels of education. The SES model would predict that Asian Americans vote at *higher* levels than the nation as a whole, not lower. Obviously, other factors need to be considered.

The Civic Voluntarism Model

A more powerful model is known as the "Civic Voluntarism Model" (Verba et al. 1995). It divides influences on political participation into three broad categories: resources, political engagement, and recruitment and mobilization.

Resources include obvious things such as time and money, but also less obvious things such as skills. Some types of participation require considerable individual effort. Certain skills – such as the ability to organize people – can greatly aid participation.

Political engagement, in its simplest sense, refers to interest in politics. However, interest can be measured in more refined ways such as whether someone supports a political party, and, if they do, how strongly.

Recruitment and mobilization refers to efforts of others to encourage involvement in politics. In an earlier era, Asian Americans were discouraged from participating, through a combination of rules and informal efforts. For example, as we noted in chapter 1, immigrants from Asia were not allowed to naturalize throughout the first half of the twentieth century. No one would try to mobilize them to vote, since laws prevented them from becoming eligible. Today, however, legal barriers to participation have been removed.

These three sets of influences are very useful in explaining political participation in the general population, but they appear to be less effective in explaining Asian American participation.[3] With the large percentage of immigrants, there are some additional influences – such as length of time in the country – that do not fit easily within this model. In addition, there may be "home country" effects, sometimes labeled "transnational" influences. We discuss these further in chapters 4 and 8. Nevertheless, the civic voluntarism model can help us develop a better understanding, even though it has some shortcomings. In the next section, we show an analysis of Asian American participation using the Civic Voluntarism Model.

Resources

There is widespread agreement that education is one of the most important resources for political participation. Education does not directly increase participation, but instead allows you to participate more effectively. The American political system is very complex. Those with higher levels of education have acquired greater information-gathering skills, so educated people know how to learn what they need to know to become involved in politics, if they want to. Higher income and education levels also make it likely that they have worked and interacted with others who are knowledgeable about the political system, so they may have easier access to information than less educated people. Education provides resources that make it easier to become politically engaged, *if* people choose to do so (Verba et al. 1995, 360). Lien et al. (2004, 157–8) found that Asian Americans with a higher level of education were somewhat more likely to vote in the 1998 and 2000 elections, and they were more likely to say they are interested in politics, even after controlling for other factors (Lien et al. 2004, 86–9). However, as we have noted, Asian Americans generally have high levels of education but low voting rates. Therefore it is important to take into account other factors that might mitigate the effects of education and income on Asian Americans' participation.

Socialization in the U.S. can be considered to be another political resource. By *socialization*, we mean learning about and orientation to politics. Even immigrants from participatory nations that do foster high levels of participation probably are not oriented to the American political system. Although socialization can take place throughout life, many individuals become oriented to the political system early in life, learning from parents and other adults. If you and your parents were born in this country, by the time you reach 18, you will probably know much about the voting process. Basic information, such as where to vote, can often be learned from your parents. Immigrants have to learn this for themselves, however, and many face the additional challenge of trying to get the information in a language that is unfamiliar to them. Although these challenges may decrease over time, they are likely to inhibit turnout among groups that have large numbers of immigrants.

Groups can also provide resources. Although activities such as praying, playing baseball, or maintaining old friendships are not inherently grounded in ethnicity, minority individuals often engage in these activities with people of their own ethnic groups. They do so because they find it more comfortable or effective, or because they feel excluded from "mainstream," largely white groups of the same kind, or because they can better satisfy their particular needs within ethnically defined groups. For Asian Americans, such "needs" might include associating with those of similar cultural backgrounds or being in a social space where they can freely use their native tongue.

Even when groups have non-political purposes, group involvement can have political effects (Putnam 2000, ch. 21). Active participation in civic organizations can help members develop skills valuable in politics (Verba et al. 1995, ch. 11). Consider, for example, the skills needed to conduct a successful bake sale or other fundraiser. Before the event even happens, you need to recruit volunteers, reserve a location, publicize the event, and then remind your volunteers to show up. During the actual event, considerable managerial skills are often necessary to coordinate volunteers, track and safeguard the money, and generally ensure that things run smoothly. Running a fundraiser requires many of the same skills needed to conduct a political rally. Someone who has helped with numerous church fundraisers may also be effective at mobilizing volunteers for political functions.[4] If you have been a leader in a social or cultural club – perhaps a theater club at school – you may have found yourself chairing meetings, or giving speeches to the membership. Once again, these skills can just as easily be used in politics – say, chairing a meeting of campaign volunteers, or speaking at a political rally. In addition, social networks linking non-political groups can also be used for political purposes. Friends and acquaintances from these social networks are potential political allies.

Often, leadership skills are developed or enhanced in college. Minnesota state Senator Mee Moua (the first Hmong American elected to a state legislature), "found for the first time in her life an environment where people spoke without fear of retribution, and as if they really had power" when she was in college and graduate school in public policy (Yoshikawa 2006, 9).

The PNAAPS data found that membership in groups affects participation for Asian Americans, just as other studies have found for the general population. For example, religious attendance is strongly associated with voting (although not with other forms of participation): Asian Americans who say they attend religious services more often are more likely to vote.[5] Membership in an ethnic organization, while it does not appear to have an effect on voting, is a strong predictor of participation other than voting. Asian Americans who "belong to any organization or take part in any activities that represents the interests and viewpoints" of their ethnic or other Asian groups are likely to participate in a greater number of political activities beyond voting (Lien et al. 2004, 157–60). Although survey data such as this does not yield enough information for us to be certain that skills are being learned in these organizations, the results do have implications for those who want to promote Asian American political activities. Even when other factors are taken into account, Asian Americans who regularly go to church or temple are more likely to go to a voting booth, and Asian Americans who belong to ethnic organizations are more likely to engage in political activities.

Engagement

To say that political engagement influences political participation seems painfully obvious, a little like saying that love of baseball makes you more likely to attend baseball games. However, a close examination of political engagement is useful, because it can tell us valuable things about political participation and help us understand how political participation might be increased.

An analysis of PNAAPS data reveals that Asian Americans who have an interest in politics were indeed more likely to vote in the 2000 election (Lien et al. 2004, 157–8). This was the case even when other relevant factors, such as education, income, and political knowledge (self-reported familiarity with election process) were taken into account. Political interest is not just a function of education or income, but is a distinct trait that leads people to participate more. Even people with low levels of income and education and little knowledge about the political system may be active in politics, if they have the interest.

Does immigrant status reduce engagement in American politics? For native-born Americans, political engagement usually means engagement in U.S. politics, but immigrants may see the political events of their native country as more important than those in their new homes. Could immigrants' interest in the politics of their countries of birth lead them to be less interested in politics in the U.S.?

Data from the Pilot National Asian American Political Survey (PNAAPS) refutes this hypothesis. An analysis of participation among PNAAPS respondents finds that interest in homeland politics did not decrease the likelihood that they would vote in the U.S., and those interested in homeland politics were even more likely (than those not interested in homeland politics) to participate in political activities other than voting (Lien et al. 2004, 159–68).[6]

For immigrants, another important variable influencing political engagement may be length of time in the country. The original civic voluntarism model did not focus on immigrants, and so did not consider length of time in the country (Verba et al. 1995, 343–8). But research has suggested that individuals do participate more as they move from young adulthood to middle age, as familiarity, attachment, and investment in a place grows. For example, new college students often have no interest in local elections. In many cases, they have only recently moved (often to dorm rooms), so the local politics of that area is brand new to them.

Census data and the PNAAPS confirm that political engagement increases with length of residence. When we look at simple relationship between length of residence and participation without taking other factors into account, we learn, for example, that 66 per cent of Asians who have been in the U.S. for six to ten years are registered to vote; that the percentage increases to 78 for Asians in the U.S. for eleven to seventeen years and to 84 for eighteen years (Lien et al. 2004, 166–7).

Recruitment and Mobilization

This brings us to the issue of recruitment and mobilization (see Figure 3.3). Other impediments to participation can be overcome when groups exist that

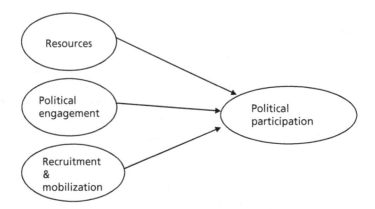

Figure 3.3 *A simple model of political participation.*

are committed to helping newcomers become politically involved. Groups can not only recruit and mobilize, but can also help to increase political engagement by providing information about politics.

In the past, political parties have been the leaders in providing these services. Unlike some European political parties, the major American parties did not have membership fees, and they did not limit recruitment to a narrow segment of people with very similar ideas. Rather, American parties focused on winning elections, which compelled them to attract a wide base of support. By the 1830s, two-party competition had developed, and each major party had a strong interest in issuing broad appeals, since they did not want to lose supporters to their competitor. In the two-party system, one or both parties could be expected to strive to win the support of newcomers, at least in settings where the two parties were of equal strength. In the language of political scientists, the parties were motivated to incorporate immigrants into the political system.

This is what happened during the huge wave of immigration between roughly 1880 and 1920. Although there is considerable debate over the extent and nature of the party efforts (see, for example, Dahl 1961 and Erie 1988), there is strong evidence that the Democratic Party at times found it in its interest to mobilize European immigrant groups (Gamm 1989). While we should not exaggerate the welcoming nature of local party leaders – many appear to have been reluctant to appeal to potential new voters – the party eventually found it beneficial to recruit newcomers, who then helped to build the New Deal coalition that dominated national elections for three decades. Legal and other discrimination limited these recruitment efforts to white immigrants, however.

Political parties today are considerably different. The old party "machines" mobilized supporters in person, sending party workers out to meet and recruit potential new voters where they lived and worked. As communication and media technology advanced, however, parties found themselves relying less on personal contact. Also, reformers succeeded in making it much harder for government officials to hire their supporters, greatly weakening an important link between top party leaders and party workers.

A groundbreaking study by Janelle Wong (2006) examined recruitment of Chinese and Mexican Americans in New York City and Los Angeles. Although many other groups did work with these immigrant populations, Wong found that political parties devoted relatively little effort to drawing them into the political process. In fact, many of Wong's respondents complained about the lack of effort from the major parties to incorporate these groups. The absence of party recruitment can have a considerable effect on participation. As Sidney Verba, Kay Schlozman, and Henry Brady observed in their landmark study of political participation, "those who are recruited often say yes when asked" (Verba et al. 1995, 390).

From a short-term perspective, it may seem to be a rational choice for the parties to limit their recruitment efforts among Asian Americans. Given limited resources, they focus on mobilizing individuals who are most likely to vote. Asian Americans are less likely to vote. Other things being equal, attempting to mobilize more likely voters will produce more votes. But this rational decision may trigger a vicious cycle. The PNAAPS data shows that contact by party and other political elite organizations had a positive influence on Asian Americans' registration and on their voting turnout in 1998 and 2000 (Lien et al. 2004, 156–8). In other words, when political parties did work to mobilize Asian Americans to vote, they often had a powerful effect.[7]

Further undermining the attractiveness of mobilization of Asian American immigrants are size and language. Although the Asian American population has grown rapidly, it is still only about 4 per cent of the population. While most non-English-speaking Latinos communicate in Spanish, Asian immigrants speak many different languages. Recruitment in a multilingual population can be difficult and costly. And, even if the parties are willing to devote the resources necessary to mobilize different Asian American subgroups, the total number of potential votes to be gained is modest compared to Latinos or whites.

Over the long run, however, democracy can suffer, because fewer people participate. If parties were to devote resources to mobilizing less likely voters, more of those immigrants would be likely to vote over the years, and become loyal party supporters. The payoff comes in the longer term, however, and, as we noted above, parties contest elections in the short term.

Recruitment and mobilization can also be driven by individual political elites and other organizations. By "political elites" we mean people in government office, political party leaders, or others in leadership positions in political organizations. Asian American political elites might be successful in getting Asian Americans to participate, but, of course, Asian American political elites are still rare. In Hawai'i, however, and in a few areas of California, where more Asian Americans occupy public offices, rates of participation seem

to be higher. Pei-te Lien studied the states with the five largest Asian popula-
tions, and found that voting rates were by far the highest in Hawai'i, and
second-highest in California, suggesting that the greater number of Asian
American political elites in those two states may make a difference in Asian
American participation rates (Lien 2001, 117–21). Census data for 2004 supports
Lien's findings.

The lower Asian American rates of political participation we have reported
in this chapter appear to be affected by contextual factors; they are not simply
a product of Asian Americans having less inclination to participate. By
"contextual factors" we mean external conditions that can influence behavior.
Rules governing registration are an example of contextual factors, as are the
weak recruitment efforts by political parties. The key point is that lower Asian
American participation does not appear to be due solely to a lesser desire to
participation.

Explaining Participation Other than Voting

Not surprisingly, then, influences on non-voting participation are different
than influences on voting, because voting is different from other forms of participation in important ways (Verba et al. 1995, 360). For instance, although no
activity is costless, voting is one of the less costly types of participation (for
social scientists, *costs* include non-monetary resources such as time and information). To cast a meaningful vote, you need to gather some information, but
that can be done with minimal effort. Furthermore, access to the voting booth
is relatively easy: polling places are usually open for twelve or more hours on
election day; in addition, people are increasingly able to vote by absentee or
mail ballot. All this makes it far less likely that people will be prevented from
voting because of schedule conflicts. On the other hand, research indicates
that most voters get few material or social benefits from voting, and that most
are motivated by a sense of civic duty, and, to a lesser extent, a desire to influence public policy (Verba et al. 1995, 113–18).

The PNAAPS found that Asian Americans with higher incomes are not necessarily more likely to vote, but they are indeed more likely to participate in a
greater number of political activities such as contacting government officials,
attending a political meeting, signing a petition, or taking part in a demonstration (Lien et al. 2004, 159–60). Moreover, Asian Americans who believe that
"what happens generally to other groups of Asians in this country will affect
their own life" and those who have experienced personal discrimination are
more likely to participate in a greater number of political activities. These two
factors, "panethnic linked fate" and experience of discrimination, are not
found to make a difference in whether Asian Americans are more likely to vote.
These results suggest that the panethnic Asian American identity, coupled with
the perception of being a target of racial discrimination, is a driving force for
participation in political activities other than voting.

Assessing the Civic Voluntarism Model

The civic voluntarism model's three sets of factors – resources, engagement, and mobilization – can help us explain Asian American registration and voting patterns, but the explanation is incomplete. The civic voluntarism model is somewhat useful to account for Asian Americans' participation in voting: education level, political interest, and contact by political parties and elites do have a positive relationship with voting by Asian Americans. However, like any model, this one cannot account for every relevant variable. Some excluded ones that are important to Asian American participation are number of years spent in the U.S.; "the correspondence between public officials and constituency in terms of race and ethnicity; the role of legal institutions and requirements such as registration and voting laws; and the strategic calculations of political elites" (Verba et al. 1995, 20–1). The civic voluntarism model gives us a framework for thinking about political participation, but it cannot give us a full picture of the factors which may have an important impact on Asian American participation.

Political Orientations: Voting, Partisanship Preferences, and Political Attitudes

Having considered *why* Asian Americans participate, we turn our attention now to the preferences they express *when* they participate. We look at their political ideology, party identification, and voting patterns. Research has found that party identification – defined as an individual's long-term, "lasting" attachment or "psychological identification" with one political party (Campbell et al. 1960, 121) – is one of the most important predictors of voters' choices, but there are many other influences as well.

Ideology

Social scientists have defined "ideology" in various ways. One noted scholar of African American political opinion defines ideology as "a worldview readily found in the population, including sets of ideas and values that cohere, that are used publicly to justify political stances, and that shape and are shaped by society" (Dawson 2001, 4). Dawson goes on to say "[i]deologies provide the member of a polity with a worldview, with constellations of ideas with which to organize their understanding of the political world" (Dawson 2001, 54). Ideologies give people a way of understanding politics.

   It is common to summarize the ideological position as ranging along a spectrum from very conservative to very liberal. Some claim that Asian Americans are more conservative than other minority groups. For example, one American Government textbook declares "Asian Americans tend to have high incomes and so are economically more conservative and more Republican than Hispanics" (Kernell and Jacobson 2006, 412).

TABLE 3.4 Ideology by ethnoracial group

	All respondents	Asian American[a]	White	African American	Latino[b]
Liberal	23	36	24	13	28
Moderate	26	32	25	29	28
Conservative	32	22	36	15	32

[a.] Pilot National Asian American Political Survey, 2000–1;
[b.] 2006 Pew Religion Survey ("Changing Faiths" 2007).

Sources: American National Election Study (2004).

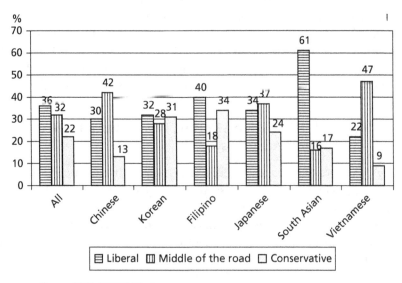

Source: PNAAPS 2000–1.

Figure 3.4 *Ideology, Asian American subgroups (% of group).*

The PNAAPS does not support this claim (Lien et al. 2004, 73–8). In fact, as table 3.4 illustrates, the PNAAPS provides some evidence for the opposite: Asian Americans may be more likely than other groups to identify themselves as *liberal*. More research is needed, though, before we can make confident assertions about Asian American ideology.

The PNAAPS did not find huge variations between Asian subgroups, but there were a few notable differences. It is interesting to note that, although South Asians rank relatively high in socioeconomic terms among Asian subgroups, in this case higher income does not translate into conservatism. Instead, South Asians reported a strikingly high degree of liberalism, with over 60 per cent identifying as either very liberal (18 per cent) or somewhat liberal (43 per cent). Most of the other subgroups had only about a third in the two liberal categories. The next highest totals were for Filipinos – who came in 20 points lower, with 8 per cent identifying as very liberal and 32 per cent as

Measuring Asian American public opinion

Almost every week the media reports results of public opinion polls on political issues such as presidential approval rates or immigration reform. Some of these polls are far more reliable than others. Polls that ask viewers to cast their "votes" on the web and through mobile phones are very unreliable. It is highly unlikely that people who participate in such votes are representative of the opinion of the nation.

Reliable polls use scientific (sometimes called "random") sampling. In a scientific sample, every member of the population has an equal chance of being sampled. However, some degree of "margin of error" (technically, sampling error) is inevitable. Sampling error does not refer to mistakes that people make, but the inevitable variations that come in sample selection. Once you get a sample size of a few hundred or more, though, the sampling error is usually relatively small.

Sampling error is a big problem for small subpopulations, however. Groups such as Asian Americans (and Native Americans) are so small that there will usually be only 20–40 respondents in a sample of 1,000, generating very large sampling error and making it impossible to make reliable generalizations.

There are ways, however, to obtain reliable data on a small group like Asian Americans, but they are very expensive. Extensive surveys have been done for blacks (e.g. Tate 1994; Dawson 2001) and Latinos (e.g. de la Garza et al. 1992; and the Latino National Survey in 2005–6).

Lien et al. (2004) conducted the first nationwide public opinion poll of Asian Americans from November 2000 through January 2001. Titled the Pilot National Asian American Political Survey (PNAAPS), it located Asian Americans living in these areas, by making calls to a sample of households with Asian surnames. Since this method alone would still miss many Asians, the researchers also used random-digit dialing (RDD) in zip code areas in Los Angeles, San Francisco, and Honolulu where it was known that the density of the Asian American population was relatively high. The data is now archived in ICPSR (Inter-University Consortium for Political and Social Research) at the University of Michigan.

Like any public opinion survey, PNAAPS has its own limitations. For example, it misses various segments of Asian Americans in the nation. As it was a phone survey, households without a telephone were not included. Moreover, some individuals who were reached refused to participate. Furthermore, because the survey targeted five metropolitan areas with a large number of Asians, it did not represent Asians living in other cities such as Seattle, Atlanta, or Minneapolis, and Asians in states like Iowa and Tennessee where Asians were only about 1 per cent of the state population.

Constructing a sample that includes all areas would be extremely expensive – only possible for the Census Bureau. In fact, the Census Bureau's Current Population Survey is a good source for data on voting turnout for Asian Americans, but the PNAAPS is the only dataset available on many aspects of Asian American political attitudes and participation, although new multiracial data sets including Asian Americans are being produced by political scientists (Hutchings and Wong 2006).

somewhat liberal. Interestingly, Filipinos also had the largest percentage of conservatives, with 5 per cent identifying as "very conservative" and 29 per cent as "somewhat conservative." Koreans had the second highest percentage of conservatives, with 4 per cent "very conservative" and 27 per cent "somewhat conservative."

Partisanship

Pei-te Lien gathered data from twelve surveys conducted in the 1990s in which Asian Americans were included in sizable numbers, and that asked about party identification. She found that party identification[8] varied from poll to poll, with some polls showing greater identification among Asian Americans with Republicans, and others showing greater identification with Democrats (Lien 2001, 153–5, 162). While Asian Americans were, overall, more supportive of Republicans than were African Americans or Latinos, the surveys suggest that Asian Americans became more likely to identity with Democrats in the late 1990s (Lien 2001, 153–5, 162). The PNAAPS also found much stronger identification with Democrats (Lien et al. 2004, 105–10): with 36 per cent identifying themselves as Democrat and only 14 per cent as Republican; of the others 13 per cent identified as "Independent," while the remainder said they did not identify in partisan terms, were uncertain, or refused to give a response (Lien et al. 2004, 16). We need to be cautious about these figures, however, since the PNAAPS surveyed Asian Americans in five metropolitan areas where Democrats had strong support.

Lien (2001, 188–93) also examined eight surveys that reported responses for Asian American subgroups. All of these surveys were conducted in metropolitan areas with large Asian populations (Southern California, San Francisco Bay Area, and New York City). In these surveys, Japanese, Filipinos, and South Asians were the most consistently Democratic in their leanings. In the PNAAPS, these subgroups favor Democrats over Republicans by a margin of greater than two-to-one (table 3.5). In contrast, Vietnamese often favored Republicans.

Some surveys have found Vietnamese Americans to be among the more conservative Asian Americans (Lien 2001, table 5.7), but the PNAAPS data suggest that their political views may have moderated. It is possible that conservatism among Vietnamese Americans is on the decline as the Vietnam War fades in importance. The first waves of refugees from that war were often intensely anticommunist (Collet 2005, 911), but other issues are likely to capture the attention of the second and third generations (Tran and Berthelsen 2008). In "Little Saigon" in Orange County, for example, more Vietnamese Americans are registering as independents than as Republicans (Collet 2005, 911–12). Vietnamese Americans and Chinese Americans surveyed in the PNAAPS had a high percentage of respondents who replied that they were not sure of their party identification or declined to give any.

Korean Americans have also often been viewed as one of the more conservative Asian American subgroups. Their frequent church attendance (Min 1995, 214–15) fits a more Republican profile, and many pastors and priests in Korean American churches preach conservative social values, such as opposition to gay marriage (see e.g. J. Ma 2000) – a position also more attuned to Republican policy agenda. However, data from the 1990s and the PNNAPS

TABLE 3.5 Asian American partisan identification (% of each group)

	Democrat	Independent	Republican	None given/not sure
Chinese	32	3	9	56
Korean	43	12	22	23
Vietnamese	12	15	16	58
Japanese	40	20	12	28
Filipino	40	14	23	23
South Asian	44	23	16	16

Source: PNAAPS 2000–1.

suggests that Korean Americans' identification with Republicans is not as great as one might suppose.

How do Asian Americans Vote?

We know that voting patterns often follow party identification. People who identify with the Republican Party tend to vote for Republican candidates, and people who identify as Democrats tend to vote for Democratic candidates. However, voters sometimes find reasons to vote against their normal party preferences. Asian American voters, for instance, may cross party lines to vote for an Asian American candidate.

Survey results support the view that Asian Americans have become more supportive of Democratic candidates, although not as much as blacks and Latinos. For the 2000 presidential election, a *Los Angeles Times* national exit poll found Gore, the Democratic candidate, favored by a large margin of Asian Americans, 62 per cent to 37 per cent (*Los Angeles Times Poll* 2000), while Asian American respondents in the PNAAPS gave Gore a 55 to 26 per cent edge (Lien et al. 2004, 16). Table 3.6 summarizes exit poll data from the 2004 presidential election. In 2004, the National Election Pool survey reported that John Kerry (the Democratic candidate) was favored by Asian Americans 56 to 44 per cent over Bush, while the *Los Angeles Times* national survey reported a 64 to 34 per cent advantage for Kerry. Exit polls conducted by advocacy organizations targeting Asian American voters also showed that Kerry was favored over Bush on the East Coast and in the Midwest (AALDEF 2005b) and in Los Angeles County (Asian Pacific American Legal Center 2006). In Orange County, where the general population tends to be very conservative, Asian Americans voters were almost equally split between Kerry and Bush (Asian Pacific American Legal Center 2006).

Why have the Democratic candidates had such a large advantage? Although we cannot provide full answers here, we can see two factors that might have contributed to this trend in the data reported in table 3.7. One is the vote choice of independents and those who refused to name their party affiliation.

TABLE 3.6 Selected exit and other post-election polls, 2004 presidential election (% votes cast)

	Bush	Kerry
Los Angeles Times poll (2004)	34	64
Asian American Legal Defense and Education Fund (2004)	24	74
National Election Pool Poll #2004 (2004)	44	56
Los Angeles County (Asian Pacific American Legal Center 2006)	40	59
Orange County (Asian Pacific American Legal Center 2006)	40	50

TABLE 3.7 Vote choice of Asian Americans 2000 and 2004, according to surveys that focused on Asian American voters (% for each candidate)

PNAAPS (537 voters among 1,218 respondents in Los Angeles, San Francisco, New York City, Honolulu, Chicago)	Gore 55% Bush 26%
AALDEF (11,000 voters in New York State, New Jersey, Massachusetts, Rhode Island, Michigan, Illinois, Pennsylvania, Virginia)	Kerry 74% Bush 24%
APALC (Los Angeles County)	Kerry 59% Bush 40%
APALC (Orange County)	Kerry 40% Bush 50%

Sources: Pilot National Asian American Political Survey (2000–2001); Asian American Legal Defense and Educational Fund (2005b); Asian Pacific American Legal Center (2006).

"Independents" and voters who did "not think in partisan terms" (PNAAPS), voters who did not identify with any party in AALDEF's survey, and voters who declined to state a party affiliation (APALC) all preferred Democratic to Republican candidates. Another possible contributing factor is that partisan voters crossed party lines. Except for Orange County, a larger percentage of Republicans voted for a candidate of the opposite party than did Democrats. For example, in the sample of voters collected by AALDEF (2005b, 1, 9), 7 per cent of Democrats voted for Bush, while 18 per cent of Republicans voted for Kerry.

We have to be cautious in generalizing these results to the entire Asian American population. Asian Americans constitute only a small percentage of those questioned in most national surveys. Moreover, we have to note the general political tendencies of the regions from which the data listed in table 3.7 were collected. The five cities where PNNAPS data were collected, most of the areas in the eight states where AALDEF conducted its exit poll, and Los Angeles County are all heavily Democratic areas. It is possible that Asian Americans elsewhere might be less Democratic. Furthermore, although statistical sampling was used in PNAAPS, this was not done in some of the exit polls conducted by advocacy organizations (Lien 2001, 244). Although APALC selected precincts by random sampling (2006, 20), AALDEF did not (AALDEF 2005b, 3).

Gender-Based Differences

Does gender matter for Asian American political ideology and participation? Examining the influence of gender without regard to ethnicity, the Citizen Participation Study found that men are considerably more likely than women to ask others to participate in a political activity (Verba et al. 1995, 152–4). Often, however, gender differences are small.

This is also the case for Asian American men and women. There are only small differences in political ideology, as roughly equal percentages of men and women identify as conservative or liberal. Also, men and women hold strikingly similar views on a number of public policy questions (Lien et al. 2004, 189, 194).

However, the PNAAPS data found some gender differences similar to those in the larger population. Asian American men appear to be mobilized somewhat more often than women (men are 5 percentage points more likely to be contacted by parties and political organizations, and 7 percentage points more likely to be contacted by individuals for voting). Similarly, a higher percentage of men reported being very interested in politics – 29 per cent to 20 per cent (Lien et al. 2004, 187–8). These differences, however, are less than 10 percentage points.

Without question, there are a number of important ways that women and men differ politically. Specific life circumstances often vary by gender, which can lead to different priorities and political concerns. Women, for instance, are more likely to take time off work for childbirth, and so they may be more concerned about family leave policies than men.[9] Gender can also serve as a powerful unifying force supporting political mobilization (Wong 2006, 129–33). However, racial disadvantages – which, of course, are shared by men and women – might often be a more powerful influence than gender, and so the "gender gap" might vary by ethnoracial group (Lien 1998).

Political Participation and the Shaping of Asian America

As we explained in chapter 2, the study of Asian American politics begins with two basic questions: where do Asian Americans fit in the larger society, and *how* do they fit? What does Asian American political participation tell us about those questions?

Our examination of individual participation suggests that Asian Americans are still on the margins of society. This marginalization is not necessarily only the consequence of bigotry and racial prejudice, as was the case several decades ago. Today, the political marginalization of Asian Americans is a consequence of a more complex set of factors, including the presence of a large number of immigrants and the short-term focus of the major political parties.

At this point, Asian Americans are caught in a bit of a vicious cycle. Political influence belongs to those who participate. The low participation rates of Asian Americans reduce their influence and make political parties less interested in devoting resources to recruiting them. Were participation to increase substantially, they would likely be the targets of much more aggressive mobilization efforts. However, without more aggressive recruitment and mobilization, participation will probably continue to lag.

At the same time, it is important to remember that Asian Americans are very unevenly distributed throughout the country, and their numbers are growing. In some places, especially Hawai'i but also several areas in California, they are important political players.

If Asian Americans begin to receive greater attention from political parties and political elites, it is possible that they could wield disproportionate influence. As we have seen, their partisan patterns do not yet appear to be well established. Although there may be a trend to greater support of Democrats, Asian Americans in the past have not appeared to be highly committed to either party, making them a potentially valuable "swing vote" (Nakanishi 1991). However, Lien and her colleagues have found that the greater their sense of "linked fate" – their sense of having interests and issues in common – the more likely PNAAPS respondents were to identify with Democrats (Lien et al. 2004, 122–3). This suggests that a growing panethnic identity could reduce the potential for Asian Americans to be a swing vote.

Some question whether divided partisanship is a good thing. According to this view, African Americans and Latinos command attention not only because they outnumber Asian Americans but also because they vote heavily for Democratic candidates. Similarly, although Jewish voters make up a bloc smaller than Asian Americans, they exert considerable influence in electoral politics. A group named 80-20 (which we describe in chapter 4) has advocated that Asian Americans should also try to strive for a bloc vote which can be defined as at least 80 per cent voting for the same candidates.

It is important to recall that the apparent divided partisanship may be due to inter-ethnic differences. As we have seen, some Asian American subgroups may lean more toward Republicans, some toward Democrats. If these differences turn out to be substantial and persistent, we might have to concede that the apparent partisan balance among Asian Americans is only a product of racial lumping: the mistaken presumption that very different groups should be treated as one simply because they all are presumed to belong to the same "race." If ethnic political differences continue to be substantial, the dream of a panethnic Asian American bloc vote is unlikely to be realized.

This raises the final important question for this chapter: how similar are the Asian American subgroups? We have presented data suggesting that majorities of Asian Americans do not approach politics from a panethnic perspective. For example, we have seen differences in party identification and in campaign contribution patterns. It seems clear, as others have observed (e.g. Tam 1995), that Asian Americans are not a monolithic political bloc.

On the other hand, there may be the potential for panethnic alliances to grow. For instance, although campaign contributions appear to follow ethnic lines, there is some evidence for panethnic support, especially at the state and local levels. Limited data on voting suggests a similar pattern. Likewise, although there is considerable variation in partisanship, there may be growing similarities across Asian subgroups. In the next chapter, we take a closer look at Asian American organized groups. Some are organized along ethnic lines, but others emphasize a panethnic appeal, attempting to bring together a broad range of Asian Americans.

CHAPTER FOUR

Interest Groups and Social Movements

Organized groups are a fundamental part of any democratic politics. Although individuals play some role, especially in elections, most political influence occurs through groups. Politics, in a sense, is a team sport, and effective participation requires membership on a team. Individuals acting alone will struggle to have a significant impact.

In this book, we are interested in groups and movements tied together by ethnoracial identity. Our concern is primarily with organized groups, rather than informal groupings, but we also look at social movements, which often include formal and informal groups. As we will see, organized interests and social movements have been central to the politics of identity, helping to create an Asian America. In this chapter, you will learn about.

1 Examples of Asian American organized interests.
2 How organized interests are affected and respond to the federal political structure.
3 How organized interests try to exert political influence.
4 How Asian American organized interests and social movements have played a central role in the development of an Asian American identity.
5 Some of the public policy efforts of Asian American groups, including the movement for redress for the internment of Japanese Americans and other World War II-related proposals (we discuss public policy further in chapter 8).

Organized Interests and Social Movements

Our primary focus in this chapter will be on *organized interests*. These are often known as interest groups, but are sometimes called "organized interests" to distinguish them from informal collections of people. Organized interests usually have some administrative structure – someone is officially in charge, or at least designated as the president or chairperson of the group – and there are often rules regarding who is and who is not a member. In addition, organized groups often have mission statements which describe their purpose for existing.

Organized interests are central actors in most democratic politics. Although single individuals can participate through elections and some other avenues, most people will find it difficult to wield meaningful political influence acting alone.

Organized groups can be far more influential than lone individuals. By definition, an organized group brings together multiple individuals and, other things being equal, multiple people can have more political influence than a single person. In addition, organized interests can divide the political labor, making them far more likely to sustain a meaningful effort. Even the most dedicated individual is likely to find it difficult to maintain a lone political crusade. Most people can only spare a limited amount of time away from their job, travel to meet with government officials can get expensive, and countless other things in life compete for an individual's time. Groups, on the other hand, can divide up the work, easing the burden on any one individual. Finally, groups can often raise substantially more resources than a lone individual. The more successful groups are able to hire staff to work full-time on the group's goals, making the group more likely to learn important information and giving more opportunities to try to influence government officials.

Sociologists see social movements as entities that "exist outside the institutional framework of everyday life," and that are "only *partly* organized phenomena" (Harper 1998, 114). A social movement is larger than any single organized interest, but organized groups usually are major players. Social movements differ from organized interests in that social movements draw on the support of many individuals who never formally join the organized groups that are part of the movement. Although social movements have not been a common feature in the Asian American political landscape, one has been of tremendous importance.

Asian American Organized Interests

Thousands of groups serve the interests of Asian Americans, Native Hawaiians, and other Pacific Islander Americans. We are concerned primarily with those that focus on political activity, but it is impossible to draw a sharp distinction between the political and the non-political. Because governments can affect any aspect of life, groups that see themselves as unpolitical can occasionally become involved in politics. Other groups may focus on non-political concerns, but find it necessary to interact with government officials. Groups focusing on health concerns are an excellent example. Even limiting our focus to groups who are primarily or substantially concerned with politics still leaves us with dozens of formal groups operating at the national, state, and local levels. Table 4.1 gives a very partial listing of national politically active Asian American and Pacific Islander groups with websites.

Table 4.1 focuses on groups with explicit political goals, but many other groups also engage in politically important activity. Tax laws require most non-profit groups to avoid involvement in partisan politics, but these non-profits can still engage in voter mobilization and other political activities that

TABLE 4.1 Examples of national Asian Pacific American groups

Group name	Website (as of 2007)	Selected political goals[a]
Asian American Justice Center (AAJC, formerly NAPALC)	www.advancingequality.org	Human and civil rights of Asian Americans.
80–20 Initiative	www.80-20initiative.net	Rally Asian Americans behind single presidential candidate.
APIA Vote	www.apiavote.org	Promote APIA political participation.
Asian American Government Executives Network (AAGEN)	www.aagen.org	Promote APA leadership in all levels of government.
Asian Pacific American for Institute Congressional Studies (APAICS)	www.apaics.org	Increase APA participation in all aspects of the political process.
Hmong National Develoment (HND)	www.hndlink.org	Develop Hmong American leadership, empower Hmong Americans.
Indian American Center for Political Awareness (IACPA)	www.iacfpa.org	Encourage political participation of Indian Americans.
Japanese American Citizens League (JACL)	www.jacl.org	Protect rights of all segments of APA community.
Korean American Coalition (KAC)	www.kacla.org (Los Angeles chapter)	Advocate for Korean Americans, encourage political participation.
Leadership Education for Asian Pacifics (LEAP)	www.leap.org	Develop AAPI leaders, publish policy analyses.
National Asian Pacific American Women's Forum (NAPAWF)	www.napawf.org	Advance social justice and human rights for APA women and girls.
National Association of Korean Americans (NAKA)	www.naka.org	Korean American civil rights, understanding between Korean Americans and other ethnic and racial groups.
National Congress of Vietnamese Americans (NCVA)	www.ncvaonline.org	Promote civic participation of Vietnamese and Asian Pacific Americans.
National Council of Asian Pacific Americans (NCAPA)	www.ncapaonline.org	Coalition of APA groups.

TABLE 4.1 *continued*

Group name	Website (as of 2007)	Selected political goals[a]
National Federation of Filipino American Associations (NaFFAA)	www.naffaa.org	Promote Filipino American participation, advocate for their interests.
National Pacific Islander Educator Network (NPIEN)	www.geocities.com/ npienwebsite/index.html	Increase government representation of and funding for Pacific Islanders.
Organization of Chinese Americans (OCA)	www.ocanatl.org	Promote participation, advocate for APAs.
Sikh American Legal Defense & Educational Fund (SALDEF)	www.saldef.org	Protect civil rights of Sikh Americans.
Southeast Asia Resource Action Center (SERAC)	www.searac.org	Foster civic engagement of Southeast Asian Americans, represent Southeast Asian American interests.
South Asian American Leaders of Tomorrow (SAALT)	www.saalt.org	Build coalitions, provide South Asian American voice on issues of equality and civil rights.

[a] Authors' summary of selected goals, taken from organization website.

does not involve endorsement of political parties or candidates. In addition, many activities that are not explicitly political may provide individuals with resources which make it easier for them to participate in politics. Organizations have an incentive to "provide services that will attract and solidify its potential constituency" (Wong 2006, 91), and some of these services provide resources that make it easier to participate in politics. One of the most obvious examples is assistance with naturalization. Since only citizens are allowed to vote in most elections, naturalization – the process of becoming a citizen – is a necessary step before immigrants can wield influence at the polls. Some small groups provide help learning English, American history and civics, and other things needed to pass the citizenship exam. In addition, organized groups can provide immigrants with a range of information and help them feel connected to others who share their interests, which makes it more likely that newcomers will participate in politics. Later in this chapter, we look in more detail at the things that organized interests do for their members.

Transnationalism and Asian American Groups

Transnational ties shape Asian American groups and the challenges they face. Perspectives that immigrants bring with them from native lands influence the way that immigrants identify themselves, which in turn influences the type of groups they form and the goals they pursue.

Larger global conditions can also be influential. Social scientists sometimes distinguish these from transnationalism, using the term "globalization" when the focus is on the broader worldwide context. The term "transnationalism" is then reserved for somewhat narrower phenomena. So an example of globalization would be the growing worldwide economic connections, while an example of transnationalism would be the ways that cultural practices in China influence the adaptation of Chinese immigrants to the U.S. Transnational studies tend to focus more on connections of individuals, not ignoring the important role played by the political systems we call "states," but looking at much more than that. We look at globalization further in chapter 8,

Transnationalism and Group Formation

Some South Asian Americans experienced transnational ties as something pointing them back toward their native land. In the early twentieth century, many supported independence from British rule (Geron et al. 2001, 620; Khagram et al. 2001, 259), and, many decades later, interest in India was seen by many as an essential part of an Indian American identity (Shukla 2003, 186). In the 1970s, the Indian government promoted the message that Asian Indian immigrants to America could help India not by returning to South Asia but by staying in America. In the U.S., they could promote trade and other links with India, as well as make direct investments in Indian businesses. This message was "distinct from the homeland nostalgia of earlier immigrant groups," focused instead on concrete ways to aid their country of origin (Shukla 1999/2000, 186). Emerging ethnic organizations and newspapers that catered to Indian immigrants also promoted the idea of an Indian community in America (Shukla 1999/2000). The focus of these organizations was on concerns overseas (Geron et al. 2001). "Though living in the United States, both the elite pan-Indian and the cultural association leaders looked to India as the source of their primary purpose and activities" (Khandelwal 2002, 161).

> The pan-Indian organizations formed in the 1960s and 1970s represented principally the Indian professional immigrants and their nationalist Indian culture and elite politics. They perceived themselves as informal ambassadors of India in the United States, with the task of bestowing prestige on its national image in their new country. (Khandelwal 2002, 160)

Substantial time and other resources were devoted to transplanting Indian cultural elements to the U.S., although those elements were often modified in their interaction with American society (Khandelwal 2002).[1]

Other South Asian American groups have been more concerned with adaptation to life in America, but they too are often shaped by life in India. For example, the founders of the SNEHA wanted to offer South Asian American women a supportive group that understood both the importance of extended family and the difficulty of drawing on those resources when most extended family members were thousands of miles away.[2] Most American social service agencies often struggled to understand the specific cultural context of South Asian women. However, SNEHA is not just a provider of more culturally appropriate services, but also helps to empower and mobilize South Asian American women to address their needs more effectively (Purkayastha, Raman, and Bhide 1997).

In other cases, groups formed around structures that immigrants had known in their native country. Chinese migrants, for example, brought with them "the clan and family association from the Old World" (Daniels 1988, 81). A larger organizational form, the district association, was also transferred from China. In America, this evolved into the Chinese Consolidated Benevolent Association – more commonly known as the Chinese Six Companies – and came to be a major political force in Chinese America (Daniels 1988, 24–6). Peter Kwong has argued that "when Cantonese immigrants found their relationship to U.S. authorities similar to what it had been under the Ch'ing government, they transplanted the traditional political institutions to Chinatown . . . Their initial conception may have been nonpolitical, but inevitably the groups became very political indeed" (Kwong 1996/1987, 85).

More recently, many Hmong immigrants have organized around clan groupings that originated before they came to America (Hein 2006, ch. 4). For Hmong Americans, the past casts a particularly long shadow, as the wars of Southeast Asia have not fully ended for them. The Hmong had been recruited by the U.S. during the Vietnam War. Led by their skilled military leader Vang Pao, Hmong forces rescued downed U.S. airmen and attacked North Vietnamese and Pathet Lao forces.[3] Hmong military leaders believed that the U.S. had promised to rescue the Hmong if the communist forces captured Laos, but little assistance emerged when the U.S. left South Vietnam in 1975 (Hein 2006, ch. 4). For years after, Vang Pao and others promised to work to overthrow the communist government in Laos, drawing the support and contributions of Hmong immigrants (Kennedy and McEnroe 2005). For many Hmong Americans, the cause was not only returning to Laos, but also helping thousands left behind, some of whom were living in the bush and doing their best to evade Lao government troops.[4]

In a development seen many times before, however, the pull of Laos appears to be much weaker with the second generation. While Laos-related issues continue to have great power in Hmong America, many younger Hmong see America as their homeland. Hmong Americans appear to be in a transitional stage, where some still feel very strong ties to Laos, others feel the tug of both countries, and yet others feel deeply rooted in America.

Transnationalism can also help span boundaries. Monisha Das Gupta describes how feminist, queer, and labor activists struggled to develop new approaches to political mobilization, cutting across lines that often divided groups in America. For example, those working to create women's shelters found themselves struggling against the model minority stereotype, which led others to believe that South Asian American women were better off than many women facing domestic abuse. In response, the South Asian Women for Action (SAWA) worked to help educate donors and others on the challenges facing South Asian women, both in America and in Asia (Das Gupta 2006, 143). But, rather than simply referring back to perspectives from their country of birth, these South Asian American activists began to envision different ways of thinking about solutions to their challenges, considering, for example, "rights that are *not* contingent on citizenship" (Das Gupta 2006, 26; emphasis in original). Here, transnational experiences contribute to an awareness of limitations of past approaches to political organizing and activism, helping activists to build connections across lines that had divided them.

Transnational Sources of Immigrant Concerns

Transnationalism not only exerts influence on organizing, it also helps explain that diversity of concerns facing many Asian Americans. In some cases, transnational ties can even mute important concerns.

Transnationalism that generates a strong emphasis on the country of origin can lessen involvement in public policy in the U.S. In a seminal article, Ling-chi Wang argued that many Asian immigrants had suffered from "dual domination," manifested through an "assimilation paradigm," which justified racial discrimination in the U.S., and a "loyalty paradigm," which overseas governments could use to pressure their émigrés to focus their political efforts on supporting their native country (Wang 1995). The "loyalty paradigm" could lead to less involvement in domestic policies that can have a big impact on immigrants and their children, with Asian Americans instead focusing on policies that affect their former countries.

In many cases, however, transnationalism simply shapes but does not reduce interest in U.S. politics. One important example of this is tied to the mode of entry, which is influenced by conditions in migrants' country of birth. Although we usually referred to those not born here as "immigrants," the U.S. Citizenship and Immigration Services (USCIS) makes more distinctions between mode of entry. The USCIS reserves "immigrant" for those who come with visas designating them as permanent residents. Most of those in the larger groups – Chinese, Filipino, Asian Indian, and Korean – come through this mode. However, for most of the smaller, Southeast Asian groups – Vietnamese, Cambodian, Hmong, and Laotian – large percentages come as refugees, a different mode of entry than that of "immigrants," under USCIS definitions, and subject to different rules (K. Chan 2001).[5]

The mode of entry can make a big difference. Immigrants usually go through a long application process. The wait can be trying, but it gives some time for preparation – economically, psychologically, and culturally. Potential immigrants can try to save some money, learn English, and gather some information about their new home. Refugees, in contrast, may have no time to prepare. Some Southeast Asian refugees had to flee into the jungle with no more than the clothes on their backs. Many were poor, but even those who lived comfortable lives usually were unable to bring much money with them.

Not surprisingly, refugee subgroups have many of the greatest challenges, as we have noted in data earlier in this chapter and in chapter 2 (K. Chan 2001). Many Southeast Asian groups include high percentages of refugees who arrived here struggling with psychological trauma, culture shock, and poverty. Add to that the relatively low educational levels of groups such as the Hmong, and it is easy to understand why it can be inappropriate to lump them with other Asian American subgroups. Prosperous immigrants may be more concerned about their children being always perceived as foreign, or about the lack of Asian Americans in top management levels, but poor refugees are more likely to focus on their need for affordable and safe housing, or finding a job of any type.

Understanding the importance of transnationalism and modes of entry also helps explain some important differences between Asian Americans on the one hand and native Hawaiians and other Pacific Islanders (NHOPIs) on the other. As we noted earlier, we have consciously not focused on NHOPIs, because of the substantial differences between their experiences and that of Asian Americans – although they are often lumped with Asian Americans in the same racial group (the 2000 census placed them in separate racial groups, however). Native Hawaiians in particular are indigenous people, not refugees or immigrants, and many of their concerns are similar to those of other indigenous peoples: for example, regaining control over their ancestral lands, especially those lands sacred to their society.

Perceptions of Transnationalism and Hostility toward Asian Americans

For Asian Americans, being perceived as transnational has long had negative consequences. Asian Americans' connections to other places – imagined or real – has helped to fuel the belief that they are fundamentally foreign: the "forever foreigner" stereotype which we will discuss further in chapter 7. Even in the mid-twentieth century, when most young Asian Americans were born in the U.S., virtually every Asian American had encountered this perception by their teenage years.

This perception contributed to the repression of Japanese Americans in World War II (we return to this in chapter 8). In the 1950s and 1960s, as Japan and China switched places as ally and enemy of the U.S., Chinese

Americans became more likely to suffer the consequences of this image, during a time that is sometimes known as the Cold War. The Wen Ho Lee case we discuss in chapter 7 is a good example of how this continues to this day, although tensions with China are somewhat less than they were in the 1960s.

We emphasize that these are *perceptions*, and usually inaccurate ones.[6] In the case of many Japanese Americans, they had few if any meaningful transnational ties. In other cases, the transnational ties that did exist were very unlikely to lead to treasonous behavior toward the U.S. but instead affected the way that Asian Americans related to others, identified themselves, or went about their daily lives.

However, inaccurate perceptions can be important when people believe them. For Asian Americans, they have sometimes led to public policies hostile toward them. Non-Asian Americans have also suffered from similar negative perceptions, – for example, German Americans during the two world wars – but, for Americans considered to be white, this has been the exception rather than the rule.[7]

Organized Interests and the Federal Political Structure

To comprehend the universe of organized interests, it is important to understand the federal political structure. In a federal system, power is divided between national and subnational governments. In the United States, the state governments are the most powerful subnational units, and substantial power is given to both the state and the national governments. In addition, local governments perform important functions and often have some significant authority. Because of that, interest groups find it beneficial to form at all levels, national, state, and local.

Some groups, such as the Organization of Chinese Americans (OCA) and the Japanese Americans Citizens League (JACL), have both a national organization and local chapters. The national offices, located in Washington, D.C., allow easier interaction with federal government officials, while the local chapters are able to monitor local developments and engage in more extensive outreach than is possible from a single national office. Other groups may be largely independent, although loosely affiliated with state or national organizations.

States with larger Asian American populations often have Asian American Republican and Democratic groups. The American political party system, which also reflects the federal system, is highly decentralized, although that has declined in the past few decades. The national party organizations often have only modest ties with state and local parties, and the state and local units take the lead in many activities, such as recruiting candidates for office.

What Organized Interests Do

As with all interest groups, Asian American organized interests vary in the approaches they take. While most engage in at least some grassroots activism, some focus most of their efforts there, while others engage in substantial lobbying. Most see education as part of their mission as well. In addition, some organizations focus on enhancing Asian American political influence by bringing together multiple groups in a coalition.

Public Education

For Asian American organized interests, public education is often an important challenge. While most groups engage in some educational efforts, Asian American groups often find it particularly important because of the lack of information – or misinformation – about Asian Americans. For instance, as we noted in chapter 1, there is now a widespread perception of Asian Americans as affluent and well-educated. While there certainly are a number of Asian Americans who fit that description, there are also large numbers with low levels of education and in poverty. Many of these are also immigrants struggling with other challenges, such as limited knowledge of English. The "model minority" image of Asian Americans – depicting them as highly prosperous – can leave policymakers unaware of the many Asian Americans in need of services to help them improve their education and move out of poverty. In response to this potential pitfall, the Asian American Justice Center, the Asian Pacific American Legal Center of Southern California, the Asian Law Caucus, and the Asian American Institute collaborated to tabulate and distribute census data which showed the high level of need in some Asian American communities (*A Community of Contrasts*). Because the groups with the greatest needs are relatively small (e.g. Hmong Americans and Cambodian Americans) the Census Bureau rarely releases separate information on them, so these tabulations are an important and often unique source of information about the level of need in those communities. In addition to tabulating this data, the sponsoring groups also traveled around the country distributing free copies and drawing attention to it, helping to raise awareness of the range of needs within the diverse population of Asian Americans.

Asian American organizations engage in public education in a wide variety of ways. In addition to collecting and disseminating information to the general public, many groups devote considerable resources to distributing information through the media, using press releases, news conferences, letters to the editor, and other means. Groups have also put together materials for public displays in schools or other public places. For example, the Japanese American Citizens League (JACL) has assembled a curriculum and resource guide for schools that want to teach about the Japanese American internment during World War II. With the spread of the internet, organizations are finding it easier to make educational materials widely available.

In addition to educating non-Asian Americans, many groups also devote significant resources to informing their members. All interest groups provide information to members, but the need is more acute for many Asian American organizations, because many of the people they serve are not fluent in English. Government information can be difficult for native English speakers to locate, but the challenge increases exponentially for those whose first language does not even use the same alphabet. In addition, Asian Americans with lower levels of education – like other Americans of similar educational levels – can find it particularly difficult to navigate the maze of government agencies and offices. Also, coming from a different political system, immigrant Asians are often uncertain about their rights, or what they can expect from government. Even immigrants already fluent in English can struggle to understand the large and complex American political system. Helping with these challenges is a major goal of many Asian American groups.

For example, the Southeast Asian Resource Action Center (SEARAC) "monitors and disseminates information on programs, policies, and legislation of interest to Southeast Asian Americans in areas such as health care, safety, economic development, and civil rights" (www.searac.org). The Indian American Center for Political Awareness (IACPA) monitors public policies and publishes an Indian American political issues newsletter. Many smaller groups focus on providing social services, but also help educate Asian Americans about government and public policies.

Lobbying

Another common emphasis of groups is lobbying. Organized interests of all types do this, as it is one of the most effective ways to influence government officials. Lobbying often has an unsavory image in the United States, with some equating it with bribery or other underhanded efforts at wielding influence. In fact, however, lobbying in its simplest sense is merely communicating with government officials, trying to get them to understand your point of view.

Lobbying can also be seen as an educational activity. It is impossible for elected officials to be highly knowledgeable about the circumstances of the thousands of people they represent. A lobbyist can help inform government officials about the unique challenges facing the individuals who the lobbyist represents. The Asian Pacific Environmental Network (APEN), for instance, has helped to inform the California Environmental Protection Agency about the range of environment hazards faced by low-income Asian Americans and others. The Asian & Pacific Islander American Health Forum (APIAHF) works to influence state and national government policies affecting the health of Asian Americans and Pacific Islander Americans. APIAHF staff work extensively with members of Congress and other government officials, educating them about the health challenges facing Asian Pacific Americans.

Organizing and Mobilization

A third major effort of many organizations is political mobilization. Many Asian American groups seek to increase Asian American political participation. This is done in many ways. APIA Vote focuses on voter registration and get-out-the-vote drives, seeking to increase Asian American voting. Others, such as Leadership Education for Asian Pacifics (LEAP), emphasize leadership training, conducting seminars and other events designed to help Asian Americans move into positions of political leadership. Helping individuals organize into groups that can wield more influence is yet another form of political mobilization. This is a common goal of groups working with lower income workers. For example, the Koreatown Immigrant Workers Alliance has helped low-wage workers organize and press employers for better compensation and working conditions.

Coalitions and Asian Americans

Coalition-building is important in any democratic politics, and particularly important for Asian American groups. Although the subpopulation has grown rapidly, Asian Americans still make up a relatively small percentage of the American population (approximately 4 per cent). If their numbers are divided even further, as a consequence of interest groups competing for support, their political influence could dwindle to almost nothing. Because of this, it is beneficial for Asian American groups to join with others.

One of the most prominent examples of this is the National Council of Asian Pacific Americans (NCAPA). Founded in 1996, the NCAPA brings together over twenty APA organizations. In recent years, some of the NCAPA's efforts have included endorsing a set of national policy priorities, enunciating principles for comprehensive immigration reform, and formulating legislative priorities for their dealings with Congress.

Another notable example is the organization known as 80–20. Officially a non-partisan political action committee (PAC), 80–20 was formed to try to build Asian American support for a single presidential candidate, in the belief that unified support would magnify Asian American influence. The name comes from the goal of having 80 per cent of Asian American voters choose the same presidential candidate. Given the diversity of views that we noted in chapter 3, that goal seems like a very ambitious one. As table 3.6 showed, most polls found that 80–20 fell considerably short of their goal.

In addition to pan-Asian coalitions, Asian American activists have also sought to build broader alliances with other communities of color. A good example of this is the Rights Working Group (RWG). Composed of national, state, and local organizations, the RWG brings together a diverse collection of

Daphne Kwok and Asian American Organized Interests

The career of Daphne Kwok provides a mini-tour of important Asian American groups. Kwok has been executive director of the Asian Pacific American Institute for Congressional Studies (APAICS), one of the leading institutions working to increase the Asian Pacific American presence in positions of political leadership. Before that, Kwok was executive director of the Organization of Chinese Americans (OCA), a long-established leader in the fight for civil rights for Asian Pacific Americans. After heading APAICS, Kwok was executive director of the Angel Island Immigration Station Foundation, a nonprofit group promoting education about immigration to the west coast, which has been the primary entryway for Asian immigrants to the U.S.

Kwok is widely recognized as one of the most important Asian American political activists. Kwok's work has taken her to the White House, to Capitol Hill, and throughout the country in her efforts to advance the interests of Asian Americans.

One of her most important roles has been working to link Americans with their government. This is done in part by informing government officials of the concerns of Asian Americans, but it also includes mobilizing Asian Americans to participate directly in the political process. In 1996 Kwok coordinated the first national Asian Pacific American voter registration drive.

Kwok has also served on the boards of numerous important Asian American groups, including the National Council of Asian Pacific Americans (she was the first elected chair), APIA Vote, and the Southeast Asian Resource Action Center. Among the many other positions she has held are spots on the U.S. Secretary of Energy Advisory Board, the Wesleyan University Board of Trustees, and the D.C. Mayor's Office for Asian and Pacific Islander Affairs.

Kwok's career exemplifies another important aspect of the politics of racial and ethnic minorities: the cooperation that takes place between academics and political activists. Kwok has served as co-chair of the Asian Pacific American Caucus (APAC), which was formed by members of the American Political Science Association. One of the goals of APAC was to facilitate more cooperation between scholars in the universities and Asian American political groups, and Kwok has been instrumental in helping to strengthen that cooperation.

organized interests that share concerns about individual rights. The Asian American Justice Center, American-Arab Anti-Discrimination Committee, American Civil Liberties Union, Mexican American Legal Defense and Education Fund, Muslim Public Affairs Council, and numerous other groups comprise the RWG membership. Collectively, they can rally a much wider range of people in support of civil and human rights, and their tremendous diversity also guarantees that supporters will be found throughout the country, increasing their influence with members of Congress. We consider these broader coalitions further in chapter 6.

Interest Groups, Social Movements, and the Development of Asian America

Asian American organized interests reflect and shape Asian America. A leading scholar of Asian American politics, Pei-te Lien, has argued that the very development of an Asian American identity has been greatly fueled by political activity. In part, this is a consequence of the way that politics works in the United States.

To put it simply, numbers matter. If people are not denied basic political rights, they can gain political influence if they join together in large numbers and push for common goals. Asian Americans *were* denied basic political rights for many years, but, even when legal discrimination finally ended, they found that their relatively small numbers meant they needed to build coalitions. As we explained in chapter 2, one starting point has been for the different Asian American groups to join in a panethnic coalition.[8]

The Emergence of Asian American Organized Interests and Coalitions

While the need for coalition-building might seem self-evident, it did not happen overnight. For many years, identification with individual Asian ethnic groups was very strong, and not until the latter half of the twentieth century did strong movement toward panethnic coalitions emerge.

The Japanese American Citizens League (JACL) is a good example of this. The JACL started out focusing heavily on the concerns of Japanese Americans. Although its role in the internment of Japanese Americans was highly controversial (see text box, p. 175), there is little question that it was trying to defend the interests of Japanese Americans. Founded in 1929, primarily by second-generation Japanese Americans, known as *Nisei*, the JACL for much of its history was an organized focused on the concerns of Japanese Americans.

In the last few decades of the twentieth century, however, the JACL began to broaden its mission. In part this was driven by the demographics of Japanese Americans, who went from being the largest Asian American group in 1970 to the being only the sixth-largest in 2000. In addition, however, it reflected an increasing acknowledgement of the ways that the fate of Japanese Americans are tied to those of other Asian Americans. The JACL website is quite explicit about this, noting that its founding mission was to protect the civil rights of Japanese Americans, but that it has expanded its concerns to those of all in the Asian Pacific American community. Like many others, the JACL cites the case of Vincent Chin, after which "It became apparent that those who would do harm to Japanese Americans did not discriminate in their hatred and bigotry against Asians or other people of color" (http://www.jacl.org).

The Organization of Chinese Americans (OCA) is another example of this evolution. Officially started in 1973, the OCA grew out of the Chinese American Leadership Council, and saw itself as "a voice for Chinese Americans as the National Association for the Advancement of Colored People (NAACP) and the Japanese American Citizens League (JACL) were for their respective ethnic groups" (www.ocanatl.org). Today, however, the OCA, like the JACL, explicitly states that it "aims to embrace the hopes and aspirations of nearly 12 million Asian Pacific Americans in the United States" (www.ocanatl.org).

At the same time, organizations representing more recent immigrant subpopulations often still continue to focus on a single ethnic group. The Sikh American Legal Defense and Educational Fund (SALDEF) mission statement illustrates this: "SALDEF's mission is to protect the civil rights of Sikh Americans and ensure a fostering environment in the United States for our future generations" (www.saldef.org). The more difficult environment for Sikh Americans in the post-9/11 environment has probably helped keep SALDEF focused on the rights of Sikhs, as they continue to encounter cases of discrimination based on issues such as physical appearance (especially over the wearing of turbans and beards). Similarly, the National Association of Korean Americans (NAKA) continues to focus on the interest of Korean Americans. The NAKA emerged in the wake of devastating civil disturbances in Los Angeles in 1992 (see chapter 6), which saw Korean American businesses suffer extensive and extremely costly damage. Although the NAKA seeks to promote understanding between Korean Americans and other racial and ethnic groups, it continues to see its role as representing the interests of Korean Americans.

Organizing and Identity

Working together can shape one's sense of identity as well as increase the chance of accomplishing concrete goals. Humans tend to identify with those around them, and that sense of identification is often strengthened when a group is united by common goals. Team sports are a good example. On the first day of practice, team members are often strangers, but by the time the season is well underway, a strong group identity has usually developed. Even if an individual already identified with a group, that identity can be strengthened, and new ties may develop.

An Asian American identity can be strengthened by organized interests. Groups that seek to serve panethnic interests are likely to bring together Asians of different ancestries. A Hmong American, for instance, might find herself working with Japanese or Chinese Americans for the first time. South Asian Americans might interact with Filipino Americans. Over time, a sense of a shared pan-Asian identity develops alongside the ethnic one, so, for example, one might identify both as Asian American *and* as Korean American.

Panethnic identification can grow even in organizations focusing on a single ethnic group. Although members of that group may interact primarily with individuals of their ethnicity, they will sometimes find it beneficial to join in coalitions with other groups, many of which may be composed of Asians of different ancestries. Once again, interaction is likely to lead to some shared panethnic identity, not displacing, but existing along with the ethnic one.

The Asian American Movement and the Establishment of a Panethnic Identity

The greatest impetus for a panethnic identity probably grew out of the social movement sometimes known as the Asian American Movement. Known by other names as well – most notably "Yellow Power" – this effort encompassed organized groups as well as many informal collections of activists. The movement was a watershed in Asian American history, helping to fuel a panethnic consciousness that continues to this day. Dominated by young adults, the movement was the first widespread effort to declare that all Asian Americans were more united by their similarities than separated by their differences.

The Asian American Movement – also referred to as the Asian Pacific American Movement – was a vast array of activists. While they shared a commitment to advancing the interests of Asian Americans, such a large body of people was bound to have a wide range of political perspectives. To this day, fierce arguments continue over how the movement should be defined. Even dating the movement can be contested, although most would agree that it emerged and was most prominent from the late 1960s into the 1970s.

Although most activists were arrayed on the left of the political spectrum, there were still considerable ideological differences. Some were avowedly radical, while others pushed for more moderate approaches. One sign of the depths of the differences is that there continues to be strong disagreement over the interpretation of the movement. Those who see its political goals as more moderate have been strongly criticized by those who prefer to emphasize the radical elements.

There is considerable agreement, however, that the Asian American Movement drew together Asian Americans of different ethnicities. For many, this was a striking development, breaking down distinctions that immigrant parents or grandparents had brought with them to the United States. While there may have been some casual acknowledgement that Americans of Asian ancestry shared some similarities, they perceived themselves as distinct groups. Although there was some interaction, including intermarriage, there was rarely a sense of common identity. For example, many older Japanese Americans reacted with surprise to hear young adults proclaim that Japanese, Chinese, Koreans, Filipinos, and others should identify themselves under the common label "Asian American." It is likely that this sense of identity never took strong hold among many adults socialized into the notion that each group was distinct, but a younger generation found it easier to embrace. For third-generation Asian Americans, the differences that their grandparents took for granted seemed minor compared to the similarities they saw between themselves and Asians of other ethnic backgrounds. The coming wave of immigration would present new challenges to a pan-Asian identity, but the Asian American Movement played an important role in helping to diffuse that identity among a generation of youth and young adults.

Challenges to Panethnicity

As we observed in chapter 3, there appear to be many challenges to a stronger Asian American panethnic identity. We have stressed ethnic divisions, but our discussion of interest groups helps to point out other factors which have the potential to divide Asian Americans.

One of the most notable cross-cutting factors is social class, also known as socioeconomic status (SES). Although we do not have good data about how Asian American political participation varies by SES, we know that there is tremendous variation in educational and income levels. There are many Indian Americans who have prospered in the high technology sector, and there are many others who are struggling to survive as cab drivers or in other modestly paid positions. Some Chinese immigrants came to this country with substantial wealth, while others toil away in sweatshops at very low wages. While individuals with dramatically different SES levels can become political allies, they often have very different concerns

The development of a panethnic identity can be strongly influenced by others. Racial prejudice and racial lumping often provide a strong incentive to overcome ethnic differences to confront a common foe. In many cases, there may be enough shared interest to bring groups together in a temporary coalition. Creating alliances is essential for Asian Americans seeking more extensive political influence, and coalition-building is a fundamental requirement for electing candidates. In the next chapter, we look at how successful Asian Americans have been in making their way into public office.

CHAPTER FIVE

Elected Officials and Representation

Representation is a critical part of politics. Although many people can represent the interests of others, the most influential political representatives are usually elected officials. However, not everyone is able to have representatives of their choosing. In contested elections, the candidate you support may lose. More troubling is that entire groups of people may have great difficulty electing representatives of their choosing. This has been the case for Asian Americans. In this chapter, you will learn:

1 What concepts of representation are applied to Asian American politics and how.
2 To what extent Asian Americans have been represented in the U.S. Congress and the California State Legislature.
3 Why Asian Americans have been underrepresented in these legislatures.
4 The representation of Asian Americans in the executive and judicial branches.

Two Concepts of Representation

A large-scale democracy must use representatives. As civics classes often note, only small groups such as the ancient Athenians, high-school classes, or small-town residents in New England, can make political decisions directly; the rest of us need to elect people to represent us in government.

But what is "representation"? Hanna Fenichel Pitkin's seminal work *The Concept of Representation* (1967) discusses two different forms of representation that are indispensable to discussion of representation of women and minorities.[1] One is called descriptive representation. In this form, "a representative body is distinguished by an accurate correspondence or resemblance to what it represents, by reflecting without distortion." The quality of representation "depends on the representative's characteristics, on what *he* is or is *like*, on being something rather than doing something" (Pitkin 1967, 60, 61; emphases in original). Following this definition, descriptive representation for Asian Americans means having Asian American faces in the government (most importantly in legislatures, but in the executive and judiciary branches as well) in proportion to the percentage of Asian Americans living in the nation or the relevant geographical area.

The second form of representation is called substantive representation. While a descriptive representative "represents by what he is or how he is regarded," a substantive representative is "acting for others, an activity on behalf of, in the interest of, as the agent of, someone else." In this notion of representation the key factor is not who the representative is but what he or she does for the people who should be represented: "the substance of representing is activity" (Pitkin 1967, 113, 116). In the context of Asian American politics, substantive representation means having someone in the government who works for the causes and issues important to Asian Americans. A representative does not have to be an Asian American to do a good job in this regard.

Scholars have debated which of these forms of representation is most important for the political representation of women and racial minorities. Our choice can have a direct impact on the forms of government and elections we employ – for example, proportional representation and majority-minority districts (for the wide array of opinions, see Grofman and Davidson 1992). Some argue against descriptive representation, saying that it takes our thinking away from what representatives do (Pitkin 1967). Moreover, one empirical study of white–black relations in the context of representative–constituency communication suggests that white House members can represent black interests effectively in districts with high percentages of black residents (Swain 1993).

Despite these and other criticisms, many people involved in women's and minority politics believe descriptive representation should be promoted rather than dismissed. Mansbridge (1999) makes this argument in an article entitled "Should Blacks Represent Blacks and Women Represent Women? A Contingent 'Yes.'" Mansbridge, herself an activist who campaigned for the Equal Rights Amendment (ERA), presents two scenarios in which descriptive representation advances substantive representation.

The first is a case in which the presence of women and minority representatives enhances communication between a deliberative body and constituents. Mansbridge (1999, 642) points out that women and minority members in legislatures often have to work as "surrogate" representatives of the entire country, region, or state for the group they belong to, even though they are elected from smaller districts and are primarily supposed to work for the constituents there. This is a well-known story for Asian Americans, who are most likely to be represented by non-Asians and must rely on whichever Asian American members they find in Congress or other legislatures. For women and minority members, having to work for their own group in the entire nation creates additional tasks but also makes them proud to serve. Many Asian American representatives express their sense of responsibilities in serving the entire group to which they belong.[2] This is not just lip service: in chapter 8 we see that a handful of Japanese American members of Congress worked tirelessly for Japanese Americans in the entire country in pushing the bill to redress the wartime Japanese internment.

   The second case Mansbridge (1999, 643–8) makes in favor of descriptive representation is better representation of future concerns. During a campaign, there will be important issues that have not yet been the focus of attention, and so candidate views will be unknown and possibly unformed. When these issues do become more prominent, representatives who share many of their constituents' experiences and characteristics are more likely to be able to anticipate their constituents' views on those issues. What this means in the context of Asian American politics is that Asian American representatives can be expected to work for the interests of Asian Americans better than non-Asian representatives, if an issue which will have a great impact on Asian Americans unexpectedly arises. Asian Americans have lived this story many times; Asian Americans seldom see what they think of "their" issues – which may be immigrant rights, racial discrimination, hate crime, or health policies – fully discussed in election campaigns. Rather, history tells that Asian Americans have often been thrust on the political agenda unexpectedly and unwillingly, as negative examples or political targets. Due to the "forever foreigner" images, for example, Asian Americans suddenly found themselves to be conspirators in the Democratic campaign finance scandal or in the alleged "espionage" of Chinese American scientist Wen Ho Lee (see chapter 7). When unexpected issues like these occur, it is most likely to be Asian American representatives who will take actions to protect the safety and interests of Asian Americans. When Wen Ho Lee's case was revealed in the media in the spring of 1999, it was David Wu (D-OR), a Chinese American member of the House of Representatives, who introduced a resolution "expressing the sense of Congress relating to recent allegations of espionage and illegal campaign financing that have brought into question the loyalty and probity of Americans of Asian ancestry" (House Concurrent Resolution no. 124). Although the resolution was co sponsored with many non-Asian members from districts with a large proportion of Asian Americans (and was adopted in the House but not in the Senate) (Takeda 2001), it might not have been introduced or considered at all had there been no Asian American members in Congress.
   As we can see from these two scenarios, descriptive and substantive representation are not mutually exclusive. If, as Mansbridge argues, descriptive representation can lead to enhancement of substantive representation, why do we have to keep comparing these two forms of representation? It is because many Asian Americans are not sure about substantive representation – that is, they are not fully convinced that they can entrust non-Asian representatives to defend their interests in the long term. When the PNNAPS survey (examined in chapter 3) asked "If you have an opportunity to decide on two candidates for political office, one of whom is Asian American, would you be more likely to vote for the Asian American candidate if the two are equally qualified?", 60 per cent of the Asian American respondents answered "Yes" (Lien et al. 2004, 17, 235).
   Some additional benefits can stem from descriptive representation. Asian American faces in governing bodies can be role models, leading Asian

Americans (and the general public as well) to think that Asian Americans can legislate and govern, and creating a sense that Asian Americans are indeed part of the representative process (Mansbridge 1999, 648–52).

However, the issues surrounding representation are not so simple, even if we set aside, for the moment, a frequently made criticism that a descriptive representative may not be the one with the best talent (Pitkin 1967, 89). Several complications arise if we naively press for descriptive representation. First, does a descriptive representative always work for the interests of the group which he or she is supposed to represent? Many African Americans do not see Clarence Thomas as "their own" Justice on the Supreme Court, as Thomas repeatedly writes or joins opinions against affirmative action. Similarly, S. I. (Samuel Ichiye) Hayakawa, a Japanese Canadian who immigrated to the U.S. and served one term as a U.S. Senator (R-CA), was generally not seen as the champion of Japanese or Asian American interests. In 1978, when the Japanese American Citizens League (JACL) had just begun its full-scale drive for redress for the wartime internment, Hayakawa gave a speech at the JACL national convention to condemn, rather than support, the idea of redress (Hatamiya 1993, 140–41, 232). Of course, Hayakawa did *not* share some important characteristics of those who had been imprisoned, because he was born in Canada and had been living in Chicago (outside of the evacuated areas), not on the West Coast, when people of Japanese descent were removed and interned (Maki et al. 1999, 76–7).

Second, even if an Asian American representative promises to work for the interests of Asian Americans, what are "Asian American interests"? Are there such things at all? The same question applies to other minorities and women, and certainly to Asian Americans, because of their great degree of diversity in ethnicity, socioeconomic backgrounds, religion, and historical experience. Once again, the question of identity is critical. In chapter 2, we noted that it is not clear how strongly Asian Americans will feel a common panethnic identity. Can Chinese Americans and South Asian Americans find enough mutual interests that they agree to want to be represented? Can a fourth-generation Japanese American legislator effectively represent the interests of Southeast Asian refugees? Is it possible that a non-Asian representative who has many good friends of Southeast Asian origin from high school can serve as their better substantive representative? As these questions remind us, descriptive representation always raises the question of which group at which level should be represented (Mansbridge 1999, 634). This question is important for Asian Americans, because some Asian ethnic groups have been more severely excluded than others. In general, a representative can be judged a better descriptive representative if she or he has strong mutual relationships with disadvantaged subgroups within the group represented (Dovi 2002). When we talk about "[g]eneralized notions" such as Asian American interests, we have to remember that such "[i]nclusive language also has its pitfalls" (Dovi 2002, 737). Important differences can be obscured if we lump many groups together under the "Asian American" label.

Descriptive representation, as we have seen, has both benefits and problems. In this chapter, however, we focus on descriptive representation, because it has historically been so low for Asian Americans. Also, studies suggest that increasing Asian Americans in the government triggers other benefits. For example, Lai and Geron's (2006, 70–71) study of Cupertino, a city in Silicon Valley, California, shows that having two Asian Americans on a five-member city council has led to the appointment of more Asian Americans to city commissions, hiring of more Asian Americans as city employees, and institutionalization of Asian cultural events.

Descriptive Representation of Asian Americans in U.S. Congress and State and Local Governments

For the remainder of this chapter, then, we focus on descriptive forms of representation of Asian Americans, leaving the discussion of substantive representation (or the lack thereof) to other studies (Takeda 2001; T.P. Kim 2007). We first examine the U.S. Congress and then move on to legislatures in California and other states.

Descriptive Representation of Women and Minorities

Table 5.1 shows the number and percentage of women and ethnoracial minority representatives and Senators in the U.S. Congress at the beginning of 2007 (broken down by party affiliation). For comparison, the table also shows the percentage of women and ethnoracial minority individuals in the general population. Comparing the percentages for Congress and the general population, we learn that women and all ethnoracial minority groups are underrepresented in Congress. While women constitute slightly more than half of the general population, only around 16 per cent of members are women in both the House and the Senate. Likewise, African Americans and Latinos both account for approximately 13 per cent of the general population, but their shares in the House are only 9 and 5 per cent respectively. The scores are even worse in the Senate, where there are only one African American (Barack Obama (D-IL)) and three Latino members (Mel Martinez (R-FL), Ken Salazar (D-CO), and Bob Menendez (D-NJ)). Asian Americans also suffer from under representation in Congress; their percentages, 1.4 per cent in the House and 2.0 per cent in the Senate, are well below 4 per cent, the proportion of Asian Americans in the general population. Underrepresentation is the most severe for Pacific Islanders and Native Americans. Except for Daniel Akaka (D-HI, part Hawaiian) and Tom Cole (R-OK), there are no members of native origin in Congress, although there have been well-known Native American Senators, such as Ben Nighthorse Campbell (originally a Democrat from Colorado but switched to be a Republican in 1995; served the House in 1987–92 and the Senate in 1993–2004) and Charles Curtis (R-KS, served the House in 1893–1907

TABLE 5.1   Women and racial minority members of U.S. Congress during the 110th Congress (2007–8)

	% in U.S. (2000 census)	House (2007) 435-member Dem. 233 – Rep. 202 – Ind. 0	Senate (2007) 100-member Dem. 49 – Rep. 49 – Ind. 2
Women	50.9	71 (D50 – R21) 16.3%	16 (D9 – R5) 16.0%
African Ams.	12.3	40 (D40 – R0) 9.2%	1 (D1 – R0) 1.0%
Hispanic (any race)	12.5	23 (D20 – R3) 5.3%	3 (D2 – R1) 3.0%
Asian Ams.	3.6	6 (D5 – R1) 1.4% (including Bobby Scott)	2 (D2 – R0) 2.0%
Pacific Islanders	0.1	0 (D0 – R 0) 0.0%	1 (D1 – R0) 1.0%
Native Ams.	0.9	1 (D0 – R1) 0.2%	0 (D0 – R0) 0.0%

Note: Members with two racial backgrounds (such as Senator Akaka) are counted twice. Non-voting members ("delegates") in the House are not counted. Data taken at the beginning of the 110th Congress (before the death of a black woman Representative Juanita Millender-McDonald (D-CA) on April 22, 2007).

Sources: Lois Romano, "Hill Demographic Goes Slightly More Female," *Washington Post* (Nov. 9, 2007), A39; "Women and Minorities in the 110th Congress". *CQ Weekly* (Feb. 26, 2007), 607.

and the Senate in 1907–13 and 1915–29, and then became the vice president in the Hoover Administration) (Edmunds 2001; *Biographical Directory of the United States Congress*).

Why women and racial minorities are all under-represented in the national legislature, more than forty years after the passage of the Civil Rights Act of 1964, is an important question, but too big a question to be addressed fully in this book. Scholars have debated whether the cause is voters' sexism (and racism), tendency of the electoral process to give advantages to incumbents (who are most likely to be white males), or social forces that discourage women (and racial minorities) from becoming candidates for political offices (Lawless and Fox 2005). It is possible that some or all of these factors simultaneously undermine descriptive representation for women and minorities. While minority groups share common causes for under-representation, each of them has its own historical and other reasons for this problem.

Descriptive Representation of Asian Americans in the U.S. Congress

Categorizing the Asian American members of Congress can be complicated. In Table 5.1 we report that the 110th Congress included six Representatives and two Senators who are Asian American. Three of the Representatives – Mike Honda (D-CA), Dorris Matsui (D-CA), Mazie Hirono (D-HI), and one Senator (Daniel Inouye (D-HI) – are Japanese Americans. Former Representative Bobby Jindal (R-LA) is South Asian American (and, while in office, the only Asian American Republican member). One Representative (David Wu, D-OR) and one Senator (Daniel Akaka, D-HI) are of Chinese ancestry, and Akaka is also of

Native Hawaiian ancestry. What complicates matters is the difficulty of categorizing and counting multiracial individuals. In table 5.1, for example, we counted Akaka as both Asian American and Pacific Islander. A more delicate issue is whether to count Robert Cortez Scott (D-VA) as an Asian American member. Scott can be categorized as an African American, but he has one-quarter Filipino heritage. Scott began serving the House in 1993, and his partial Filipino background was not known to Asian American communities until several years later. Although some reports do not count Scott as Asian American (*Congressional Quarterly* 2007), we do so, partly because it helps demonstrate that Asian Americans are under-represented even when including a "borderline" case like Scott.[3]

There have not yet been more than six Asian Americans in the House at the same time. Table 5.2 lists all Asian American voting members who have served in the House and the Senate. The table shows that there have been fewer than twenty Asian American individuals who have served in Congress. The table also indicates several features of Asian American representation in Congress. First, most Asian American members have been elected from Hawai'i or California. This is not surprising given the geographic concentration of Asian American population in the two states. Second, most Asian American members have been Democrats. Again, this is not surprising. Historically, racial and ethnic minorities have championed their causes through the Democratic Party, and Asian Americans are not exceptions. Five Asian American members have been Republican, including S. I. Hayakawa (mentioned above), Jay Kim (the only Korean American member of Congress so far), and Bobby Jindal.

Japanese Americans have been "over-represented" in this small pool of Asian American members of Congress. This is partially a result of the fact that many of the Japanese American members were elected from Hawai'i, where Japanese Americans have risen to the key position within the political structure. From 1977 to 1990 the two Senators from Hawai'i were both Japanese Americans (Daniel Inouye and Spark Matsunaga). There have been three Chinese members, the first of whom was Hiram Fong (R-HI), who was also the first Asian American Senator. No Filipino and Southeast Asian American members have been elected to be voting members of Congress, except for the ambiguous case of Bobby Scott. The absence of Filipinos in Congress is particularly noteworthy, given their population size, which nearly matches that of the Chinese; their long history in the United States; and their fluency in English. Their under-representation may in part stem from lack of success at the local level, where they are struggling to elect Filipino city council members (Lai forthcoming).

Although Japanese American Democrats from Hawai'i predominate, the first Asian American elected to Congress was a naturalized citizen who immigrated from India: Dalip Singh Saund (D-CA). In his autobiography Saund (1960, 99–100) notes that his opponent in the Democratic primary went to the court to disqualify him from running in the 1956 election as he had spent insufficient time since becoming a citizen (the case was dismissed).[4] Saund

TABLE 5.2 Asian Americans who have served in the United States Congress

Years served	Member name	Ethnicity	Party	District
House				
1957–63	Dalip Singh Saund	South Asian Am.	Democrat	California 29th
1959–63	Daniel K. Inouye	Japanese Am.	Democrat	Hawai'i at-large
1963–77	Spark M. Matsunaga	Japanese Am.	Democrat	Hawai'i at-large, then 1st
1965–77	Patsy T. Mink	Japanese Am.	Democrat	Hawai'i at-large, then 2nd
1975–95 (Oct. 10)	Norman Y. Mineta	Japanese Am.	Democrat	California 13th, then 15th
1977–90	Daniel K. Akaka	Chinese & Native Hawaiian	Democrat	Hawai'i 2nd
1979–2005 (Jan. 1)	Robert T. Matsui	Japanese Am.	Democrat	California 3rd, then 5th
1987–91	Patricia F. Saiki	Japanese Am.	Republican	Hawai'i 1st
1990–2002 (Sep. 28)	Patsy T. Mink	Japanese Am.	Democrat	D-Hawai'i 2nd
1993–99	Jay C. Kim	Korean Am.	Republican	California 41st
1993–present	Robert Scott	African & Filipino Am.	Democrat	Virginia 3rd
1999–present	David Wu	Chinese Am.	Democrat	Oregon 1st
2001–present	Mike Honda	Japanese Am.	Democrat	California 15th
2005–2008 (Jan. 14)	Bobby Jindal	South Asian Am.	Republican	Louisiana 1st
2005 (Mar. 8)–present	Doris Matsui	Japanese Am.	Democrat	California 5th
2007–present	Mazie Hirono	Japanese Am.	Democrat	Hawai'i 2nd
Senate				
1959–77	Hiram L. Fong	Chinese Am.	Republican	Hawai'i
1963–present	Daniel K. Inouye	Japanese Am.	Democrat	Hawai'i
1977–83	S. I. Hayakawa	Japanese Am.	Republican	California
1977–90	Spark M. Matsunaga	Japanese Am.	Democrat	Hawai'i
1990–present	Daniel K. Akaka	Chinese & Native Hawaiian	Democrat	Hawai'i

Note: Only voting members are shown (non-voting delegates are not included).

Source: Compiled by authors from *Biographical Directory of the United States Congress* and Nakanishi and Lai (various editions).

prevailed, becoming, in his words, "the first native of Asia elected to the United States Congress" (1960, 111).

Descriptive Representation of Asian Americans in the California State Legislature

In addition to Congress, a natural place to examine descriptive representation is in state legislatures. An important state to examine is California, where more than one-third of the U.S. Asian American population resides (3.7 million in the 2000 census), and where Asian Americans comprise slightly more than 10 per cent of the state population. To have representation that matches the share of their population, Asian Americans would need to have eight members in the 80-member State Assembly and four in the 40-member State Senate.

Table 5.3 lists all Asian Americans who have served in the California State Legislature, both past and present. In the 2007–8 legislative term, there are eight Asian American Assembly members and two Senators. Looking at these numbers, one might say that descriptive representation for Asian Americans has been achieved, at least for the Assembly. However, having more than two Asian American members in the California State Assembly only dates to the dawn of the 21st century. Before 2001, when three Chinese American women – Wilma Chan, Carol Lee, and after a special election Judy Chu – started their terms, the number of Asian American legislators was two at most. That was the case even in the 1990s, when Asian Americans made up at least 9.6 per cent of the state population (2.8 million in the 1990 census). In fact, there were no Asian American state legislators during the period 1981–92. The rapid rise of Asian American state legislators beginning in the late 1990s was due to a growing number of Asian Americans who had been elected to local offices such as mayors, city council members, and school board members (Lai and Geron 2006), and the efforts of grassroots ethnic and panethnic Asian organizations which have promoted voter registration and training of potential candidates for elected offices (see chapter 4).

A careful look at table 5.3 reveals a similar but slightly different pattern of Asian American representation in the California legislature than in the U.S. Congress. First, as in Congress, most Asian American legislators have been Democrats, and many of them have also been Japanese Americans. Chinese Americans have done better in California than in Congress: there have been nine Chinese American state legislators so far, as opposed to eight Japanese Americans. The first of them, March Fong Eu, subsequently served as Secretary of State in 1975–94 (her adopted son, Republican Matt Fong, served as State Treasurer in 1995–8, and was an unsuccessful challenger to Barbara Boxer in a race for the U.S. Senate in 1998). In 2006 another Chinese American, John Chiang, was elected State Controller, a position that oversees and audits state funds.

The first Asian American elected to the California legislature, however, was a Korean American, Alfred Song. Born in Hawai'i, Song started out on the

TABLE 5.3 Asian Americans who have served in the California state legislature

Years served	Member	Ethnicity	Party	District[a]
House				
1963–66	Alfred H. Song	Korean Am.	Democrat	45th (Los Angeles County)
1967–74	March Fong Eu	Chinese Am.	Democrat	15th (Alameda County)
1969–70	Tom Hom	Chinese Am.	Republican	79th (San Diego County)
1973–80 [b]	Paul T. Bannai	Japanese Am.	Republican	53rd (Los Angeles County)
1975–80 [c]	S. Floyd Mori	Japanese Am.	Democrat	15th (Alameda County)
1993–98	Nao Takasugi	Japanese Am.	Republican	37th (Ventura County)
1997–2000	Mike Honda	Japanese Am.	Democrat	23rd (Santa Clara County)
1999–2004 [d]	George Nakano	Japanese Am.	Democrat	53rd (Los Angeles County)
2001–6 [d]	Wilma Chan	Chinese Am.	Democrat	16th (Alameda County)
2001–6 [d]	Carol Liu	Chinese Am.	Democrat	44th (Los Angeles County)
2001[e]–6 [d]	Judy Chu	Chinese Am.	Democrat	49th (Los Angeles County)
2003–present	Alan Nakanishi	Japanese Am.	Republican	10th (San Joaquin County)
2003–present	Shirley Horton	Japanese & White Am.	Republican	78th (San Diego County)
2003–6	Leland Yee	Chinese Am.	Democrat	12th (San Francisco County and City)
2005–present	Alberto Torrico	Japanese Am. & Latino	Democrat	20th (Alameda & Santa Clara Counties)
2005–present	Van Tran	Vietnamese Am.	Republican	68th (Orange County)
2005–present	Ted Lieu	Chinese Am.	Democrat	53rd (Los Angeles County)
2007–present	Mike Eng	Chinese Am.	Democrat	49th (Los Angeles County)
2007–present	Mary Hayashi	Korean Am.	Democrat	18th (Alameda County)
2007–present	Fiona Ma	Chinese Am.	Democrat	12th (San Francisco County)
Senate				
1967–78	Alfred H. Song	Korean Am.	Democrat	26th (Los Angeles County)
2007–present	Leland Yee	Chinese Am.	Democrat	8th (San Francisco County and City)

[a] Some districts include multiple counties but only one county name is shown.
[b] Elected by special election on June 26, 1973 to a seat vacated by a deceased member.

TABLE 5.3 *continued*

(c) Elected by special election on March 4, 1975 to a seat vacated by a deceased member.

(d) Did not run for re-election due to term limits.

(e) Elected by special election on May 15, 2001.

Sources: Complied by the authors from Saito (1998, 217); State of California (1975); Secretary of the State of California (1971– 4,1975– 80,1981–2,1985,1988– 91); Nakanishi and Lai (1995, 1996, 1998–9, 2000–1, 2001, 2003); Nakanishi, Lai, and Kwok (2005); and California State Assembly (2007).

Monterey Park city council and was elected to the State assembly two years later, in 1962. Song was also the first Asian American state Senator, and remained the only one until 2006, when Leland Yee successfully moved to the Senate from the Assembly. Although the "Koreatown" in downtown Los Angeles has not produced a Korean American state legislator yet, in 2006 Mary Chung Hayashi became the second Korean American elected to the Assembly. Known as Mary Chung when she emigrated from South Korea at the age of twelve, she later took the last name of her husband, Dennis Hayashi, a Japanese American who served as Director of the Office of Civil Rights of the Department of Health and Human Services under the Clinton Administration (Hayashi 2003).

As in Congress, Filipino and South Asian Americans are severely under-represented in the California state legislature. The absence of Filipino state legislators in California is striking, since Filipinos have had large settlements in places such as Los Angeles and Stockton at least since the 1920s (Chan 1991, 74–8), and in the post-war period, in places such as San Diego and Daly City. Moreover, the Filipino population in the state (approximately 919,000 in the 2000 census) nearly matches that of Chinese Americans (981,000 in 2000). Their absence is not because few Filipinos run for the state legislature. Several Filipinos did (such as Henry Manayan in the 20th Assembly district in 2004), but they have not been successful. The South Asian population is smaller (315,000 Indians and 20,000 Pakistanis), but it also has a long history in the state. Sihks and Hindus have settled in Stockton and in the Imperial Valley respectively at least since the 1910s (S. Chan 1991, 74–5). Dalip Singh Saund, a Hindu, immigrated to the Imperial Valley (Saund 1960).

At this writing, one Southeast Asian American serves in the California legislature: Van Tran. Tran, who had evacuated from Vietnam in 1975 just before the fall of Saigon, became the first Vietnamese American elected to a state-level office in the country, along with Hubert Vo of the Texas state legislature.[5] Prior to becoming an Assembly member, Tran was a city council member of Garden Grove, a city in Orange County that is home to many Vietnamese refugees and their families and relatives. An adjacent city, Westminister, is popularly known as "Little Saigon." Vietnamese Americans, many of whom are

Republicans, have consistently elected their co-ethnics in the city council and the school board of these two cities since the late 1980s (the roster of which is found in Collet 2005). The election of Van Tran illustrates how some geographically concentrated groups of Asian Americans have successfully elected co-ethnics to the state legislature, first building a pool of potential candidates in city-level and local-level positions (such as Vietnamese Americans in Orange County, Chinese Americans in San Francisco, and Hmong in Minnesota). This ascendance does not automatically take place, however, as shown by the lack of Korean state legislators from Koreatown (in Los Angeles) or Filipino state legislators from San Diego or Daly City.

Asian American women are slightly better represented in the California State Assembly than in the U.S. House of Representatives. There have been seven Asian American women in the State Assembly. While three Chinese American women were "termed out" in 2006, two were newly elected in the same year, so three out of the eight Asian Americans in 2007–8 were women. By contrast, Patsy Takemoto Mink (D-HI) had virtually been the lone Asian American woman in the U.S. House for many years except for the short period of Patricia Saiki's (R-HI) service. The situation became somewhat better with the recent arrival of Doris Matsui and Mazie Hirono, giving Asian American women one-third of the six seats held by Asian Americans. The tendency that women's descriptive representation is better in state legislatures than in Congress is not unique to Asian Americans; the tendency is seen in the general population, too (Lawless and Fox 2005, 18–20, 48–50). The higher the level of office, the more difficulty women and minorities find it to be elected. There have been no Asian American women in the Senate, either in Congress or in the California state legislature.

Descriptive Representation of Asian Americans outside of California and Hawai'i

Asian Americans are under-represented in elective office in most states other than California and Hawai'i. However, a number of Asian Americans have been elected to state and local offices in places where the Asian American population is not very large. A Vietnamese American (Gordon Quan) was elected to the Houston City Council in 2000, and another Vietnamese American (Hubert Vo) was elected to the Texas House of Representatives in 2004 (Nakanishi and Lai 1995, 1996, 1998–9, 2000–1, 2001, 2003; Nakanishi, Lai, and Kwok 2005).

Despite a large number of Chinese and Koreans, Asian Americans have struggled to elect their own candidates in New York City, partly due to the way in which district lines are drawn (Saito 2006). In 2001, however, John Liu became the first Asian American member of the city's council, representing a district that included Flushing, Queens. In recent years, Flushing has attracted a large number of Asians, who made up about half of the population of the area (Hum

2004). In 2004 Jimmy Meng was elected from Flushing, becoming the first Asian American in the New York state assembly. Meng, however, decided not to run for the second term, citing health reasons. Jimmy's daughter Grace Meng sought to succeed him, but Ellen Young, another Chinese American woman who had worked as John Liu's district administrator, successfully discouraged Young from running (Harlan 2006) and eventually won the 2006 general election.

In New England, Chanrithy (Rithy) Uong was elected to the city council in Lowell, Massachusetts, in 1999, becoming the first Cambodian American in the United States to occupy an elected office (Kiang and Tang 2006). Along with Long Beach, California, Lowell is one of the major population centers for Cambodian Americans. In Boston, professors and students in the Asian American Studies program at the University of Massachusetts, Boston, have joined with community organizations to promote voter education, registration, and mobilization for the large number of Vietnamese in the city (Kiang and Tang 2006). In 2005 Sam Yoon, a Korean American, was elected to be a Boston city council member. Yoon had worked in Boston's large Chinatown as development director for the Asian Community Development Corporation (ACDC), a non-profit organization aimed at providing affordable housing and preserving Chinatown (Yoon 2006).

Why are Asian Americans Under-represented?

Why have Asian Americans not been able to achieve a level of representation that matches their population level? History, demography, internal complexity, political structure, and cultural biases appear to be the most important reasons. One frequently cited reason, characteristics of Asian American culture, seems less likely, however.

The Myth of an Anti-political Culture

A popular explanation is a cultural one: Asian Americans do not engage in politics because their cultural background discourages them from doing so. According to this argument, Asian parents encourage their children to become doctors, engineers, and lawyers – to choose a profession that is well regarded and allows for independent practice. Moreover, according to this explanation, Asians generally regard politics as dirty work to avoid. Asian education stresses modesty and self-restraint while downplaying the self-expression and assertion which seem necessary to run for elective office. Finally, Asian Americans tend to avoid risks, according to this view.

While this explanation is widely accepted by non-Asians,[6] the evidence contradicts it (Takeda 2001, 89–92). Asians, both in Asia and in the Americas, have engaged in a variety of political activism. Examples of protests and rebellions abound in the history of modern Asia, from Japan to Korea to the Philippines to the Indian subcontinent. After immigrating to the United States, Asians continued to be politically active, contacting political officials, forming their own political organizations, and beginning new political movements. Additionally, some Asian immigrants have been politically active in home country politics, in the U.S., or in efforts that span their home countries and the United States. Many Asian ethnic groups have been active in transnational politics since the early days of their large-scale immigration to the U.S., and some still are today (see chapters 4 and 8).

Second, a number of Asian American individuals did run for Congress and state legislatures, although many of them did not get elected (so we do not see their names in tables 5.2 and 5.3). Asian Americans ran for Congress, albeit unsuccessfully, from "unexpected" states far from their population centers, such as Delaware (Jan Ting, a Chinese American Republican, for the U.S. Senate in 2006), Colorado (Stan Matsunaka, a Japanese American Democrat for the U.S. House 4th district), and Oregon (John Lim, a Korean American Republican, for the U.S. Senate in 1998). Cho (2002, 359–60) identifies twenty-one attempts by twenty individuals who ran for congressional seats outside of Hawai'i and California in the two decades between 1978 and 1998.[7] Although only one of them, David Wu (D-OR), was eventually elected to be member of Congress, the list of those who "gave it a try" includes notable Asian Americans such as S. B. Woo, a former lieutenant governor of Delaware. Woo lost elections for the U.S. Senate in 1988 and for the at-large (statewide) House district in 1992 (and is now the leader of the 80–20 initiative; see chapter 4).

Historical Explanations

Asian American under-representation is more plausibly explained with a historical rather than cultural explanation. In chapter 1, we saw that almost all Asian ethnic groups were prohibited from immigrating to the U.S., and those who had arrived before the bans were kept from naturalization. These chapters in history had a negative impact on participation of Asian Americans in the electoral arena. Lacking U.S. citizenship, first-generation Asian immigrants could not run for election for many decades. Severe legal and social discrimination kept second-generation Asian Americans from running for office, at least until after World War II. Even if they had run, their ethnic support would have been undermined, because their first-generation co-ethnics were not allowed to vote. These "legal barrier[s] delayed the development of electoral participation and representation by Asian Americans in California and elsewhere until the second and subsequent generations during the post–World War II period; over a hundred years after their initial immigration" (Nakanishi 1998, 9). For Asian Americans, there were no "machine bosses" like those in Tammany Hall who would help them naturalize and vote. Like Asians, Mexican Americans have also been targets of racial discrimination for a long time (and in the worst cases during the Great Depression in the

1930s, repatriated from the U.S.). But, not subject to the same immigration and naturalization bans imposed on Asians, Mexicans were able to begin to vote and run for elective offices earlier than Asians did. When Asian immigrants were beginning to naturalize in the 1950s, Mexican Americans were already electing their own representatives to local and state offices. The future prominent member of the U.S. House of Representatives Henry Gonzalez was a member of San Antonio, Texas, city council in 1953–56, and Edward Roybal was a member of Los Angeles city council in 1949–62 (Schulz et al. 2000b, 462, 513).

Demographic Patterns

Perhaps the greatest reason for the current under-representation of Asian Americans is demographic patterns. Partly due to ethnic and other diversity, Asian Americans do not live in concentrated areas. Japanese and Cambodian Americans do not live next to each other just because the Census Bureau places them in the same racial category. Asian Americans are less likely to form population centers than Latinos and African Americans and, as a result, are not likely to create electoral districts where Asian Americans are the majority. Moreover, among Asian Americans no group dominates numerically in the way that Mexican Americans predominate among Latinos.

Reflecting this, there are no "Asian majority" congressional districts outside Hawai'i. Among the 435 districts for the U.S. House of Representatives there are nine districts with 20 per cent or more Asian American population, thirty-nine districts with 10 per cent or more Asians, and 89 districts with 5 per cent or more Asians (calculated with the 2000 census data for the 110th Congress (2007–8)). Table 5.4 lists the top twenty districts on Asian American proportion in the district. We can see that most of these districts (except those of Honda, Hirono, and Matsui) are represented by non-Asian members. Many of the districts are majority white and represented by white members. When Hispanics are the largest group, the district is represented by a Latino/a member (such as Hilda Solis, Nedia Velazquez, and Loretta Sanchez).

Such a situation for Asian Americans stands in stark contrast to African Americans and Latinos. African Americans are the majority (that is, exceeding 50 per cent of total population) in twenty-four districts, and Latinos are the majority in another twenty-four districts during the 110th Congress. Drawing district lines is a political act in which various partisan and racial interests collide (Saito 1998, 2001). The "majority-minority districts" for African Americans and Latinos (see below, p. 111) reflect effective wielding of their interests.

Mainland Asian Americans, however, lack the large and dense population clusters which would make it easy to draw a congressional district where they comprise a majority. Depending on a state's population, 500,000 to 900,000 people are necessary to create one House district. Only in Hawai'i does Asian

TABLE 5.4 Top 20 House districts with largest percentage of Asian Americans, 110th Congress (2007–8)

District	White alone (%)	African Am. alone (%)	American Indian alone(%)	Asian Am. alone (%)	Pacific islander alone (%)	Hispanic (any race) (%)	Member representing the district
1 District 1, Hawai'i	18.8	2.0	0.2	54.3	6.8	5.4	Neil Abercrombie (D, white)
2 District 15, California	54.7	2.5	0.6	29.4	0.3	17.2	Mike Honda (D, Asian)
3 District 8, California	49.4	8.8	0.5	28.9	0.6	15.7	Nancy Pelosi (D, white)
4 District 2, Hawai'i	29.8	1.6	0.4	28.8	11.9	9.0	Mazie Hirono (D, Asian)
5 District 12, California	55.5	2.6	0.4	28.7	0.9	15.7	Tom Lantos (D, white)
6 District 13, California	47.5	6.5	0.7	28.4	0.9	21.1	Fortney Stark (D, white)
7 District 5, New York	55.7	5.8	0.3	24.6	0.0	23.5	Gary Ackerman (D, white)
8 District 29, California	51.2	6.1	0.5	23.9	0.1	26.1	Adam Schiff (D, white)
9 District 16, California	45.8	3.6	0.9	23.6	0.4	37.6	Zoe Lofgren (D, white)
10 District 32, California	41.2	2.8	1.2	18.7	0.1	62.3	Hilda L. Solis (D, Latina)
11 District 14, California	67.4	3.1	0.5	16.1	0.7	17.5	Anna Eshoo (D, white)
12 District 42, California	66.1	3.0	0.5	16.0	0.2	23.8	Gary Miller (R, white)
13 District 12, New York	39.5	10.9	0.7	16.0	0.1	48.5	Nydia M. Velazquez (D, Latina)
14 District 40, California	62.9	2.4	0.7	15.8	0.4	29.6	Ed Royce (R, white)
15 District 9, California	42.2	26.4	0.6	15.5	0.5	18.7	Barbara Lee (D, African)
16 District 46, California	70.8	1.5	0.6	15.5	0.3	16.9	Dana Rohrabacher (R, white)
17 District 26, California	64.2	4.6	0.6	15.3	0.2	24.4	David Dreier (R, white)
18 District 5, California	50.9	14.8	1.3	15.1	0.9	20.8	Doris Matsui (D, Asian)
19 District 9, New York	71.0	4.4	0.2	14.6	0.0	13.6	Anthony D. Weiner (D, white)
20 District 47, California	43.3	1.8	1.1	14.0	0.4	65.3	Loretta Sanchez (D, Latina)
NATIONWIDE	75.2	12.2	0.9	3.6	0.1	12.6	

Source: Compiled by the authors from "P3 Race" and "P4 Hispanic or Latino, and not Hispanic or Latino by Race (Total Population)" of 110th Congressional District Summary File (100-Percent), Custom Table, American Fact Finder, 2000 Census Summary File 1.

American population density make this easy to achieve. Another obstacle is that when Asian American population density is high, it tends to be in areas where a large number of Latinos live. Quite often, Asian Americans are packed into majority-Hispanic districts, and as a result are outnumbered by Latinos. Sunset Park, Queens, one of the "new Chinatowns" of New York City, is located in a district (NY-12) represented by Nedia Velazquez; Koreatown in Los Angeles is in a district (CA-31) represented by Xaiver Bacerra. Probably one of the persons who best knows what it is like to run as an Asian American in a Latino-majority district is Judy Chu. Having been elected council member of Monterey Park (which became the first Asian-majority city on the mainland; see chapter 6) from 1988 to 2001, Chu ran unsuccessfully for the California Assembly 49th district in 1994 and 1998. Both times she was defeated in the Democratic primary by a Latina candidate who would become a winner in the general election (Saito 1998, 108; California Secretary of State, various years). A close study of her 1994 bid reveals that Latinos and Asians, especially those living in concentrated areas, heavily voted for candidates of their own races rather than crossing racial lines (Lai 1998–9). When Gloria Romero, who had defeated Chu in the 1998 primary, left the assembly seat to become a state Senator, Chu finally won the seat in a special election, defeating Latino candidates this time. By that time, Chu had built a network of support from Latino voters and officials in the area, including Latina members of Congress (Saito 2006, 136).

Internal Complexity

The widespread diversity among Asian Americans makes it difficult to build the panethnic coalition which could boost the prospects of candidates. Several studies have shown that when Asian American candidates run, they may struggle to win votes and financial support of Asian ethnic groups other than their own. In the places on the mainland where Asian Americans are a substantial portion of the population, different Asian ethnic groups often end up running their own candidates and competing against one another. For example, in a 1991 special election for a California State Assembly seat in the 46th district, a Korean American (T. S. Chung), a Filipino American (Joselyn Geaga Yap), and a Japanese American (Keith Umemoto) ran in the primary. The district, which included Koreatown and Filipino Town in Los Angeles, was 16 per cent Asian American. James Lai's (2000) analysis of the primary shows that the three ethnic groups cast their votes and made financial contributions largely along the ethnic line. Chung, Yap, and Umemoto finished in second, third, and fifth place, but the combined votes of the three candidates were much larger than those of the winner.

Similarly, in a 2004 primary election for a California State Assembly seat that opened up due to term limits (in the 20th district), an American of Bolivian and Japanese descent (Alberto Torrico), a Japanese American (Dennis Hayashi), a Filipino American (Henry Manayan), and a South Asian American

(Ash Bhatt) ran. The district, which included the cities of Fremont and Newark in Alameda County and Milpitas in Santa Clara County was 24 per cent Asian American (Walker 2004). The Silicon Valley Asian Pacific American Democratic Club, which had helped elect a number of Asian Americans to local offices such as in Sunnyvale and Cupertino, supported Manayan (Kang 2004). In the end, Torrico barely beat a non-Asian candidate who finished second, while Hayashi, Manayan, and Bhatt finished in third, fourth, and fifth place. Torrico was then elected to the assembly seat in the general election, but the election results show that Asian Americans could have lost a chance to elect an Asian member due to the four candidates dividing the Asian American vote.

The difficulty of achieving panethnic unity is pointed out in other studies as well.[8] Cho's (2002) analyses of campaign contributions to Asian American candidates for Congress shows that a predominant portion of donations from Asian American individuals come from Asians of the same ethnic group as candidates. Cho and Lad (2004) found an even clearer pattern of this among contribution of Asian Indian candidates for Congress. Srikanth's (1998) case study of a half-South Asian candidate for Congress reached similar conclusions. Srikanth's analyzed the campaign of Ram Yoshino Uppuluri, who ran for the U.S. House of Representatives from the fourth district of Tennessee in 1994. Since Uppuluri is half-Japanese, as indicated by his middle name, his campaign was a good test of whether two Asian ethnic groups that are culturally very different can work together. Srikanth found that Uppuluri received wide support from South Asians all over the country, but very little attention from Japanese American communities.

Cultural Biases and the Need for Deracialization Campaigns

Another obstacle is the biases of other Americans. As we will see further in chapter 7, Asian Americans are frequently assumed to be foreigners, no matter how many generations their families have been in America. This "forever foreigner" image plagues Asian Americans who run for elections. Even when they speak perfect English (as many do), their "Asian" look and family names are frequently used by their opponents and the media to imply that they are foreign or to question their loyalty to the United States. For example, Matt Fong, a fourth-generation Chinese American who won the 1998 California Republican Senate primary, was once asked by a reporter which country he would support if America and China went to war against each other (Fong 1999). Similarly, when Swati Dandekar, a naturalized Asian Indian, ran for an Iowa State House seat in 2002, her opponent "questioned Dandekar's background," sending out an e-mail "cast[ing] doubt on Dandakar's ability to represent Midwestern values and core beliefs. [She] would go on to express her concern and desire to have a native-born opponent, feeling that she would rather have a fellow citizen representing the district" (PBS n.d.).

Due to the scarcity of majority Asian districts on the mainland, Asian Americans have to run from predominantly white districts or from multiracial districts where Asians may be 10 or 20 per cent of the population at most but are not a plurality (that is, they are not the largest ethnoracial group). When running in these districts, successful Asian American candidates have to develop a "de-racialized" campaign (Saito 2006, 137–8), de-emphasizing racial issues and stressing their desire to represent all people, regardless of race and ethnicity. White candidates running in racially diverse districts may do the same, but Asian American candidates often feel particular pressure to prove their connection to voters of different racial backgrounds. Thus, when David Wu ran for a seat for Congress in Oregon 1998 (which he won), his campaign website made a special reference to the fact that his wife was a sixth-generation Oregonian. The website mentioned Wu's ethnic background (he immigrated from Taiwan in his childhood), but it was presented as a typical immigrant "American Dream" story with emphasis on his hard work in education, without focusing on his Asian heritage (David Wu for Congress, n.d.). Another Asian member of Congress, Bobby Jindal, did not mention his South Asian heritage at all in the biography section of his official website. His bio began with the sentence, "Louisiana native Bobby Jindal is proud to represent Louisiana in Congress," and emphasized his birthplace (Baton Rogue) and his education in Louisiana Public School System (Jindal n.d.). Jindal's de-racialization in his presentation of self could be understood as a reflection of his district characteristics (predominantly white with 1.5 per cent Asians), as well as of his Republican partisanship (he was not a member of Congressional Asian Pacific American Caucus).

In contrast, Latino or African American candidates often run in districts where their co-ethnics make up a plurality or majority of voters. In those circumstances, the campaigns can focus on issues of particular concern to their ethnoracial community.

Political Structure

Political structure can also influence Asian American prospects. The size of state legislatures and city councils varies across the country. Some states with a large population have a smaller legislature than states with far fewer people. For example, Minnesota has 201 legislators for 4.9 million residents, while California has only 120 legislators for 33.9 million people, making Californian legislative districts vastly larger than Minnesotan ones.

The size of districts can make a big difference. A smaller electoral district may work in favor of Asian Americans, making it easier for face-to-face campaigning to comprise a substantial part of the campaign, and reducing the need for expensive media campaigns. Face-to-face contacts can provide a much more effective way to overcome stereotypical racial images often attached to candidates.

In fact, in Minnesota's relatively small legislative districts, successful candidates usually spend considerable time "doorknocking," going door-to-door and meeting voters one at a time. Mee Moua, the first Hmong in the nation to be elected to a state legislature (in 2002), won her state Senate seat in this fashion, distributing leaflets on street corners and campaigning door-to-door (Yoshikawa 2006). Moua's direct contact with voters was particularly effective because she was running in a special election, where turnout is usually lower than in regular elections. Candidates can succeed if they can convince a relatively small number of dedicated voters, since victory usually requires a much smaller number of votes than in regular elections. Moua won the Democratic-Farmer-Labor primary with only 1,751 votes (versus 1,581 for her opponent), and then won the general election with only 3,055 votes, a tiny percentage of the tally needed to win a legislative seat in California.

Asian American Representation in the Executive and Judicial Branches

Whether Asian Americans are under-represented in the executive branch is not easy to judge. Because only one person can occupy a seat in many high-ranking positions in the government, it is more difficult to measure under-representation. What is clear is that that neither women nor African Americans have ever been elected to the presidency, although the 2008 presidential campaign (still underway at this writing) will see one or the other become the Democratic nominee. Unknown to most people is that the Japanese American Patsy Mink ran for the Democratic nomination in 1972 (the year when an African American woman Shirley Chisholm also ran). Mink received only 1,200 votes in the Wisconsin primary and collected a smaller number of voters in several other states (*Congressional Quarterly* 1995, 182–4), but she is remembered as the first Asian American who ran for the nomination of one of the major political parties.

Two Asian Americans have served in a president's cabinet so far. The first was Norman Mineta, a Japanese American who had served in the House of Representatives for two decades. Mineta was appointed to be Secretary of Commerce in 2000, the last year of the Clinton administration. Although he was a Democrat, Mineta stayed on in George W. Bush's cabinet as Secretary of Transportation, a position that was relatively nonpartisan. In his first year as head of Transportation, the 9/11 terrorist attacks happened, putting Mineta in the difficult position of having to handle issues such as the use of race in safety screening at airport gates. Nonetheless, he remained in the position until 2006, when he left the post voluntarily.

The second is the first Asian American woman to serve in the Cabinet, Elaine Chao. A Chinese American, Chao served as Secretary of Labor under the George W. Bush administration. With the resignation of Defense Secretary Donald Rumsfeld after the Democratic victory of the midterm election in 2006, Chao became the longest serving secretary in Bush's cabinet. As a Republican, Chao has often become the target of criticism from progressive Asian American grass roots organizations which support affirmative action. Nevertheless, Chao and Mineta were two important "firsts" in Asian American history. Whether future presidents will feel obliged to include an Asian American in the cabinet remains to be seen, however.

On the state level, several Asian Americans have become governor. The first was in Hawai'i, where George Ariyoshi, a Japanese American Democrat, served from 1975 to 1986. Ariyoshi was succeeded by Democrats John Waihee (Native Hawaiian, 1987–94) and Benjamin Cayetano (Filipino American, 1995–2002). After Cayetano, Republican Linda Lingel, a white woman, defeated the female Democratic candidate, Mazie Hirono. Two Asian Americans have served as governor of mainland states. The first was Chinese American Democrat Gary Locke, who was initially elected in 1996 and served as governor of Washington until 2004. Three years later, in 2007, South Asian American Bobby Jindal won the Louisiana gubernatorial election.

Moving below the top positions, the level of descriptive representation of Asian Americans in the executive branch can be more easily measured. Examining professionals and employees in the government, Wu and Eoyang (2006, 40) report that "about 4.8 per cent of the civilian workforce in the executive branch" are Asian Pacific Americans. They note, however, that statistics show that Asian Americans are under-represented in high-ranking managerial positions in the federal government. In order to address this problem and "to promote, support, and expand Asian Pacific American leadership in federal, state, and local governments" (Wu and Eoyang 2006, 47), the Asian American Government Executive Network (AAGEN) was founded in 1994. Asian Americans are also under-represented among municipal employees in Californian cities with large minority populations. A study of eleven Californian cities found that the level of Asian American employment was lower than the percentage of the Asian American voting age population in every city, except for San Francisco and Richmond (Browning, Marshall, and Tabb 2003, 39–42).

Asian Americans are under-represented in the judicial branch as well. Although there was considerable publicity for Judge Lance Ito, who presided over O. J. Simpson's criminal trial, Asian American judges are under-represented in both federal and state benches. Graham (2004) reports that Asian Americans comprised only 1.1 per cent of the federal Court of Appeals (two judges out of 179) and 0.9 per cent of federal District Courts (six out of 665) of the federal government in 2001. In most state courts, including California, the share of Asian American judges does not match their percentage of the state population. Only two states were exceptions to this pattern: Hawai'i and Vermont, although in Vermont it only requires one Asian American judge for the proportion of Asian American judges to exceed the state's percentage of Asian Americans.

The Consequences of Asian American Under-representation

In this chapter we have seen that Asian Americans are in Congress and state legislatures at lower percentages than their numbers in the general population. Although the numbers are growing, Asian Americans living in most places have to expect to be represented by non-Asians. Are their interests and concerns well taken care of by non-Asian representatives? We need more thorough studies of substantive representation of Asian Americans to answer that question. Until then, it would seem to be in the interest of Asian Americans to consider ways to increase their descriptive representation. In part, this could come about through stronger coalitions between Asian Americans and other ethnoracial groups, which is the topic we address in the next chapter.

CHAPTER SIX

Conflict and Cooperation with Other Minority Groups

March 16, 1991. Soon Ja Du is working at the cash register at the Empire Liquor Market in South Central Los Angeles, when Latasha Harlins comes in to buy some juice. As Harlins approaches the counter, money in hand and juice in backpack, Du grabs Harlins's backpack and accuses her of attempting to steal the juice. Harlins punches Du, knocking her down, then heads toward the door. Du grabs a gun from under the counter and fires. Harlins falls dead.

In the ensuing weeks, Korean grocers are attacked, and two are killed. One assailant reportedly says "This is for Latasha." For many weeks, African American and Korean American leaders struggle to keep the peace, but find themselves constantly fighting media images which portray this as a battle between African and Korean Americans. Leaders on both sides found themselves subject to withering criticism if they encourage their followers to seek common ground, and the Black–Korean Alliance dissolves under the pressure.[1]

The tragic events in Los Angeles epitomize the challenges of intergroup relations. How can tensions be managed? Why do some groups find themselves in situations where they come into conflict? Such questions illuminate critical aspects of the politics of identity.

A little over a year after the Latasha Harlins shooting, South Central Los Angeles erupted into a maelstrom of destruction and violence. Korean and African Americans played central roles, but the conflict extended well beyond them. By the time it was over, when Rodney King made his poignant plea – "Can we all get along?" – it was painfully clear that coalition-building and tension-bridging was a critically important task for all of America. In this chapter you will learn about:

1 Why cooperation and conflict between communities of color matter.
2 How different ethnoracial minorities perceive each other.
3 How people may respond to growing ethnoracial diversity in their community.
4 What factors affect coalition-building.
5 How actual alliances and conflicts have developed.
6 Where Asian Americans fit in minority coalition-building.

Why Focus on Communities of Color?

In chapters 4 and 5 we looked at broader efforts of Asian Americans to win support from non-Asians. In this chapter we focus specifically on Asian Americans' success at building coalitions with other ethnoracial minorities. What is so important about relations between communities of color? Why should we be concerned specifically about coalitions composed of ethnoracial minorities? We devote extra attention to this topic because of the history of race in the United States. As we have explained, people defined as nonwhite have always had to continually struggle for equality and a fair share of political and economic power. For Asian Americans, this has meant in part a struggle to be accepted as citizens, and to be accepted as "full" Americans. That struggle continues to this day. If people of color join together, their prospects can improve greatly.

Cooperation is not assured, however. Some groups might feel that they can benefit at the expense of other groups. In the mid-nineteenth century, for instance, many Irish Americans took steps to improve their situation at the expense of African Americans. Although revolutionaries from their home country had recognized that Irish and African Americans suffered from the same oppression, many of the Irish in America decided that they could gain greater acceptance if they enthusiastically cooperated in the mistreatment of blacks (Ignatiev 1995).

The New Minority Politics

A separate chapter on relations among ethnic minorities is also justified because of the dramatic demographic transformation of the United States. Immigration since 1965 has brought far more people from Latin America and Asia, greatly increasing their proportion of the U.S. population. Much smaller but not insignificant growth has also occurred in African immigration, and from Caribbean nations that have large numbers of African-heritage citizens. According to Census Bureau estimates, non-Hispanic whites made up about two-thirds of the population in 2005.[2] Projections suggest that this will drop to about 50 per cent by 2050, leading some to say that the U.S. will become a "majority-minority" country: that is, African Americans, American Indians, Asian Americans, and Latinos will collectively make up more than 50 per cent of the population. While there are good reasons to question this prediction, it does highlight the degree of change the U.S. is experiencing.

This demographic transformation has produced what might be called the "new minority politics." For years, "minority politics" meant the politics of African Americans. Books and articles that used the term "minority politics" rarely had more than a brief reference to Latinos or Asians, and most often focused exclusively on African Americans. However, the huge wave of immigration after 1965 has dramatically changed the ethnoracial minority population in the U.S.

Although it is impossible to be certain about the political consequences, communities of color could play an increasingly important role in the politics of the twenty-first century. In large cities, political success already often depends on putting together a coalition of ethnoracial groups. With the rapid growth of Latino and Asian American populations, the old biracial calculations are being replaced by a more complex, multi-group calculus.

Possible Ethnoracial Coalitions

Because Asian Americans still make up a relatively small percentage of the population, they also need to work within larger coalitions. Although Asians make up a plurality or even a majority in a few regions, this is a rare occurrence, as we explained in chapter 5. Because of that, most Asian American candidates need to draw support from a multiracial coalition of voters.

Whether they can do so can tell us much about what we have called the politics of identity. Alliances can give us insight into the "social location" of a group – that is, how others see that group as fitting into society. For a subpopulation such as Asian Americans, who have long been pushed to the margins and denied important rights, this is a critically important issue.

What type of ethnoracial coalitions might Asian Americans enter? Below, we consider some of the logical possibilities, and consider what they would suggest about the social location of Asian Americans.

A "Rainbow Coalition"

The term "rainbow coalition" was made famous in Jesse Jackson's 1984 presidential campaign and denotes a kind of inter-ethnic collaboration that would bring together African Americans, American Indians, Asian Americans, Latinos, gays and lesbians, and liberal whites. Such a juggernaut would be as politically overwhelming as it is unlikely. We examine reasons for our skepticism later in this chapter. Still, even if Jackson's dream of a national rainbow coalition was highly improbable, there are nevertheless realistic prospects for some smaller coalitions of this type, drawing together people of many ethnicities who share common experiences and interests. The greater the number of groups that can be brought together under one banner, the more likely their coalition will become, and the greater their ability to effect political change.

If peoples of color could establish enduring patterns of collaboration, that would strongly suggest that the color line between white and nonwhite still has a significant effect on the lives of Americans: that there are still significant disadvantages to being perceived as "nonwhite" in America. Otherwise, groups would organize along other lines – perhaps economic, geographic, or educational – the same kinds of lines that limit access to power for some white Americans.

Asian Americans would not be the major players in a rainbow coalition. Their numbers are simply too small. Because the stunning growth of the Latino population has made them the largest minority group, Latinos and African Americans now would have the most clout in such a coalition. However, although they are many fewer in number than blacks or Latinos, the

Asian Americans may be able to wield disproportionate influence because of their heavy concentration in California. California's tremendous importance – it has 20 per cent of the electoral votes needed to win the presidency, for example – guarantees that national political leaders cannot afford to ignore it. Much like Jews in New York, or Cubans in Florida, Asian Americans in California have the good fortune to cluster in a state where their their political influence is magnified.

Ethnoracial Pluralism

A very different scenario from Jackson's rainbow coalition would be one where ethnoracial groups move in and out of ever-changing alliances as they confront different issues. Shifts in alliance can be motivated in many different ways. Groups might shift alliances as their interests dictated, and strong tensions might make it difficult for groups to sustain cooperation with each other for extended periods of time.

The waves of tension and conflict that sweep communities of color can tell us important things about the racialization projects that have shaped America. Some (e.g. C. Kim 2000) argue that ethnoracial minorities have often been drawn into societal arrangements that pit them against each other, to the benefit of whites and the disadvantage of those perceived to be nonwhite. For example, in their analysis of the consequences of the South Central Los Angeles civil disturbances, Nancy Abelmann and John Lie argue that Asian Americans and African Americans have been implicitly pitted against each other, thanks to their respective images as the "model minority" and the "urban underclass." As we noted in chapter 2, the model minority image has been used to belittle the demands of disadvantaged groups beyond the Asian American community, because it carries the implication that, since Asian Americans have overcome prejudice without assistance, other groups should be able to do so as well. Ablemann and Lie argue that a dominant version of the "underclass" myth has perpetuated the notion that able-bodied individuals create problems for themselves and society at large by taking advantage of government assistance and behaving in deviant ways. This image implies that the problem with the underclass is that they have made bad choices – the polar opposite of the responsible choices made by the model minority. Abelmann and Lie believe that these contrary images – model minority and urban underclass – serve to obscure the powerful role the social structure plays in creating inequalities, and to minimize the continuing power of racial discrimination (Ablemann and Lie 1995, ch. 6).

Conflicts between communities of color hurt all involved. The only beneficiaries are the groups holding power to start with, since ethnoracial minorities will find it much more difficult to challenge the structures that render them powerless if most of their efforts are channeled into battling other nonwhite groups.

"UPRRISING" OR "RIOT"?

In April of 1992, Los Angeles was rocked by prolonged and severe civil disorder. Asian Americans – especially Korean Americans – were profoundly affected. The event was of such magnitude that we describe it further in a text box later in this chapter. Here, we examine one revealing question arising out of that unrest: how should it be named?

Some, particularly those with more left-leaning political views, believe that the proper name is "uprising" (e.g. Gooding-Williams 1993) or "rebellion" (e.g. "The Rebellion in Los Angeles" 1992). From this perspective, the disturbances were the actions of an oppressed people rebelling against a society which had treated them very unfairly. A similar view could be found of disturbances in Los Angeles a quarter-century earlier, which some described as the "Watts rebellion." From this perspective, to call this event a "riot" is to dismiss it as an apolitical act of violence.

For some, "riot" may simply be a term of convenience, not judgment. Nancy Abelmann and John Lie, who explicitly aimed to offer an alternative to the mainstream view of the Los Angeles unrest, use the label "L.A. riots" because that is the term most often used. Abelmann and Lie stress that they "do not assume that 'riot' refers to apolitical or senseless action; to call a civil disturbance a riot does not deny its political character" (Abelmann and Lie 1995, xiii).

Nevertheless, the question of the proper term is a controversial one. Offering an adequate assessment of the disturbances is beyond the scope of this book, so our goal is to use the most neutral terms possible. Consequently, we generally refer to the events as "civil disturbances" or "unrest," although we refer to other works which use the term "riot."

"Honorary Whites" and "Black Exceptionalism"

Another prospect for the future of ethnoracial coalition building is that some ethnoracial minorities will escape their "minority" status altogether and become "white." As we explained in the opening chapters, becoming "white" has little to do with skin tone and everything to do with social status. After all, although Asian Americans are defined today as "nonwhite," some have skin tones lighter than that of some European Americans. Some have argued that Latinos and Asian Americans are pursuing this model, leaving African Americans on the other side of the color line as they seek and find growing acceptance in white society. Given the long, shameful history of treatment of African Americans, it is hard to be enthusiastic about this scenario, but it cannot be dismissed. Already some observers have noted that Asian Americans seem to be on their way to becoming "honorary whites" (Tuan 2001; Liu 1998), others (e.g. Yancey 2003) have suggested the same trend underway for Latinos. (We discuss a related image, the "model minority," in chapter 8.)

Although we doubt that Asian Americans are currently viewed as "white," there is some evidence that African Americans face greater barriers than other ethnoracial minorities. Consider residential segregation, for instance. Today, demographers recognize different types of segregation (Massey and Denton 1988), and if a group is highly segregated on several of those measures, it is often referred to as "hypersegregated" (Massey and Denton 1993). Using data from Census 2000, a study of metropolitan areas found that African Americans were hypersegregated in twenty-nine metropolitan areas, while Latinos were hypersegregated in just two. Asian Americans and American Indians were not hypersegregated in any metropolitan areas in 2000 (Wilkes and Iceland 2004). Another revealing measure is intermarriage rates – the percentage of an eth-noracial group that is married to someone of a different ethnoracial group. Asian Americans and Latinos had intermarriage rates approximately twice as high as those of of African Americans in 2000. In 2000, for adults under 30, whose rates are likely to reflect current norms, 20 per cent of Asian Americans were intermarried, compared to only 12 per cent of African Americans. Large numbers of Asian Americans are immigrants, who we would expect to be less likely to intermarry, making this gap even more striking. Indeed, when look-ing only at U.S.-born individuals, we find enormous differences, especially among women: 44 per cent of U.S.-born Asian American women were inter-married, compared to only 4 per cent of U.S. born African American women (Lee and Edmonston 2005).

These statistics do not prove that Asian Americans are on their way to being accepted as "white," but it does suggest that they are more likely to gain accep-tance than African Americans, at least in some key areas. While they continue to be hampered by the "forever foreigner" image, Asian Americans may find that image less debilitating than the "urban underclass" image that can plague African Americans, particularly young black men. It should not sur-prise us if some African Americans, most of whom are from families who have been in the U.S. for many generations, express some frustration at seeing yet another group of relative newcomers bypassing blacks on the path across the color line.

Intergroup Perceptions

Evidence about ethnic groups' perceptions of each other suggests we should not expect the formation of a rainbow coalition any time soon. In 1997, five years after the civil disturbances in South Central Los Angeles, the *Los Angeles Times* polled Southern Californians about their impressions of whites, blacks, Latinos, and Asians (*Los Angels Times Poll*: 1997a). Not surprisingly, the *Los Angeles Times* survey showed that groups tended to have the most positive impression of their own ethnic group. Beyond that, each group's impressions of other peoples of color were mixed. The majority of all three groups – Latinos, blacks and Asian Americans – felt that whites were the most prejudiced, but almost a quarter of African Americans felt that Asian Americans were most preju-diced. Latinos were more likely to see African Americans than Asian Americans as most prejudiced. Interestingly, four out of every ten Asian American respondents said that they did not find any group to be the most prejudiced.[3]

TABLE 6.1 Which group is easiest to get along with?

	% of Asian respondents who felt that	% of White respondents who felt that	% of Latino respondents who felt that	% of Black respondents who felt that
Asians are easiest to get along with	2.9	3.7	4.1	4.5
Whites are easiest to get along with	3.9	3.2	3.7	4.2
Latinos are easiest to get along with	3.6	3.6	2.8	3.7
Blacks are easiest to get along with	4.1	3.8	4.4	3.4

Note:
Question wording: "Next, for each group I want to know if you think they tend to be easy to get along with or tend to be hard to get along with. Where would you rate (GROUP) on this scale, where 1 means tends to be easy to get along with and 7 means tends to be hard to get along with . . ."
   To see how each group perceived the others, read down (i.e., read the columns). To see how each group was perceived by others, read across (the rows). A lower number means that the respondent felt the group was easier to get along with.

Source: LASUI in Bobo et al. 2000.

Although this survey was limited to Southern Californians, it suggests that a rainbow coalition is far from a certainty, at least on a large scale. Many African Americans seem to have positive views toward Latinos with regard to their degree of prejudice, but Latinos are more likely to view Asian Americans than African Americans positively on the question of prejudice.

The Metropolitan Study on Urban Inequality investigated similar perceptions, with surveys in four major cities. We focus on the survey in Los Angeles (the Los Angeles Study of Urban Inequality, or LASUI, for short), since it was the only one with a sufficiently large Asian American pool of respondents to draw any conclusions. One question on the LASUI asked respondents to rank how easy it was to get along with each ethnoracial group (Table 6.1). Not surprisingly, respondents tended to choose their own group as the easiest to get along with, but, after that, Asians chose Latinos and whites, while whites ranked Latinos and Asians about equally. African Americans ranked Asian Americans the most difficult to get along with, and Latinos easiest.

Again, this measure suggests that African Americans may view Latinos most positively of all groups, but Latinos reserve their most positive perceptions for whites and their least positive for blacks (not counting their views toward their own respective group). No clear pattern emerges, but it is noteworthy that Asians were ranked only the third or fourth on the question "which group is easiest to get along with?" by their potential coalition partners, Latinos and African Americans.

In addition to providing evidence about groups' perceptions of each other, surveys have also indicated how different groups assess the circumstances of other groups. The April 1997 *Los Angeles Times* poll asked respondents which group they believed faced the most discrimination. Very few members of any group – less than 10 per cent in each case – felt that Asian Americans faced the most discrimination (*Los Angels Times Poll*:1997a). These results echo findings in other *Los Angeles Times* polls that asked which Americans faced the most discrimination. These results also parallel evidence from the LASUI, which found that few Asian Americans reported experiencing personal discrimination in the workplace, although Lawrence Bobo and Susan Suh suggest that this may be due to the fact that Asian Americans are more likely to work in "ethnic enclaves" where they are often surrounded by other Asian Americans (Bobo and Suh 2000, 527). Notably, a majority of every group agreed that African Americans were among the groups facing the most discrimination, although Latinos were more likely to say that they faced discrimination. Asian Americans were equally likely to choose African Americans or Latinos as the groups facing the most discrimination.

Other evidence of intergroup relations suggests the same murky picture: ethnoracial groups' views of each other do not seem likely to foster the creation of a rainbow coalition, but nor do they suggest that the society is deeply fractured along racial lines. The pattern of the new minority politics remains uncertain.[4]

Bases of Cooperation and Conflict

What factors might influence the direction that minority politics takes in the future? We examine five factors that affect the chances of cooperation or conflict: *large-scale political and economic developments* (which set the context for ethnic groups' interactions); *interests*, *ideology*, and *leadership* (which influence the formation and maintenance of specific alliances – Sonenshein 2003); and, finally, *organized groups*, which can provide resources and social structures that can provide the scaffolding for the building of alliances.

Large-scale Political and Economic Developments

Large-scale political and economic developments like poverty, war, and shifts in national and international economies set the context for ethnoracial interactions. The ways that individuals respond to such large-scale developments beyond their control create conditions that may foster either cooperation or conflict among ethnoracial groups. One significant impact of large-scale political and economic developments has been on patterns and rates of immigration.

U.S. foreign policy is one large-scale development that has had a considerable impact on Asian immigration. "In pursuit of markets, raw materials, military bases, or lost souls, the United States' Pacific crossings have had a substantial impact on shaping both Asia and the U.S." (Watanabe 2001, 639). Immigration from Asia has often been fueled by connections forged through U.S. foreign initiatives. Immigration from the Philippines, for instance, was substantially boosted by the U.S. control over the islands in the first decades of the twentieth century. Korean and Southeast Asian immigration was sparked by wars the U.S. fought in those regions. In the nineteenth century, Chinese, Japanese, and then Filipino immigrants were drawn by the plantation economy in Hawai'i, just as highly skilled Asian immigrants today are swept into an increasingly globalized economy where well-trained workers cross national borders to go where their skills are in high demand (Ong et al. 1994; Takaki 1998, ch. 4). As we will discuss later in this chapter, another way that the large-scale context has affected patterns of conflict and cooperation involves economic developments: Sweeping economic changes in American cities have channeled Asian Americans into positions that create tension. Within large cities, for instance, many African Americans have seen their financial security undermined as industries have taken flight from major urban centers, while at the same time some Asian immigrants have found economic opportunity in these circumstances.

Interests

Common interests can provide a strong incentive for cooperation. To what extent do Asian Americans share interests with other communities of color? Given the vast array of issues in American politics, it would be almost impossible for there *not* to be some shared interests. However, the more pertinent question is whether the shared interests outweigh the competing ones, because, given the vast array of issues, there are also going to be times where Asian Americans will be in competition with other ethnoracial minorities. For example, Asian Americans may sometimes find themselves pursuing the same jobs or housing sought by other ethnic groups. Since the 1960s, the U.S. has undergone extensive economic restructuring. The massive flight of industry from central cities has resulted in the loss of millions of good jobs and considerable economic hardship for workers with lower levels of education. Low-skilled immigrants willing to work for very low wages can compete with native-born workers, many of whom are African American. Although economists disagree over whether immigrants ultimately cause economic hardship to low-skilled native-born Americans, even the appearance of immigrant competition can create considerable tensions between the native-born and the newcomers (Johnson and Oliver 1989).

Of course, Asian Americans themselves have different interests. There is tremendous diversity among Asian Americans, as we described in chapter 2. Although widespread agreement exists on a few positions, such as opposition to anti-Asian violence, considerable variation in political orientations and ideology persists (Lien et al. 2004, ch. 3).

Ideology

Ideology – attitudes and beliefs – also influences patterns of conflict and cooperation. Shared ideology can help calm tensions over competing interests, and can boost cooperation when interests are shared. Enduring coalitions are more likely between groups that share both interests and ideology, but common interest on a specific issue is, by itself, a fragile basis for an alliance – once attention turns to another issue, the coalition is likely to dissolve. For example, a variety of different groups share an interest in opposing free trade with other countries, but those same groups can disagree sharply over issues such as environmental protection or military spending. On the other hand, ideologies are more enduring; shared views on broader political principles can help hold alliances together even when attention shifts to another concern. A shared ideology means that people are more likely to interpret and respond to new issues in the same way.

Coalitions can form around a shared ideology even without shared interests African Americans, for instance, had little direct interest in the issue of repa- rations for Japanese Americans interned during World War II, but because of their ideological support for victims of racial injustice some black groups ral- lied to support this cause, even though African Americans were not directly affected (Hatamiya 1993).

Leadership

Leadership is an essential catalyst for coalition-building, even when people share the same interests and ideology. Given the many pressures and priorities that most people have in their lives, there is no guarantee that people will take the active step of working with other like-minded individuals unless a leader prods them into action. Favorable conditions alone cannot guarantee that coalitions will form.

Not everyone will have the skills required for effective leadership. Successful leaders need to be able to inspire people, of course, but they also usually need considerable organizational and administrative skills, or, at least, trusted assistants who have those skills. It is not enough to be able to motivate hun- dreds or thousands of people to sign up to volunteer for a political campaign – you also need someone who can keep track of those who signed up, inform them of their shifts, call with reminders of when they agreed to help, and orga- nize them so that they have useful work to do when they show up.

The necessity of having effective leaders was tragically demonstrated in Chicago in the late 1980s. Harold Washington had used his considerable polit- ical skills to put together an electoral coalition that had made Washington the city's first African American mayor in 1983. Washington was re-elected in 1987, but died shortly after the election, and his electoral coalition died with him (Sonenshein 2003, 347–8). As of this writing, no other African American has again been elected mayor of Chicago, although groups mobilized during Washington's time have remained active, and blacks have been able to win countywide and statewide positions since his death (Pinderhughes 2003, 162–3).

Social Structure and Organizations

Another important factor that can help foster the formation of alliances is the existence of formal organizations. Organized groups are essential to coalition-building, although they can also help to foster conflict. We often refer to organized groups as part of the social structure. Social structure is

> the framework of society that exists above the level of individuals and provides the social setting in which individuals interact with one another to form relationships. The concept of structure is important because it implies a patterned regularity to the way societies work. . . . [Social structure is] the social institutions, organizations, groups, statuses and roles, values, and norms that add order and predictability to our private lives. (Newman 2000: 264)

Social structure can influence group interaction the way that neighborhood or housing design can influence individual interaction. For instance, some have argued that architecture can increase or decrease contact between neighbors (Jacobs 1961). Suburban styles of housing often feature attached garages and small entryways. Residents can drive into their garage and go directly into their house, without ever coming within eyesight of their neighbors. The lack of front porches and the proliferation of backyard decks can further lead people to spend more time in the private spaces of their homes, decreasing neighborhood interaction even more. Finally, the lack of sidewalks typical in most suburban areas can discourage strolling through the neighborhood, completing the circle of isolation.

Just as sidewalks and porches can lead neighbors to interact more, entire communities can have features that increase or decrease interaction, or raise or lower the chances of conflict. A community that has a large number of voluntary organizations – youth sports teams, book clubs, bowling leagues, and many other types of groups – will offer far more opportunities for people to communicate. People can use these settings to discuss problems they encounter, even if the group was created for other purposes. For example, parents watching their children play soccer might talk to each other about traffic problems that have been growing in the neighborhood.

We can see a good example of this in anthropologist Roger Sanjek's (1998) study of race relations in Queens, New York City. In Elmhurst-Corona, the community that Sanjek studied, whites, African Americans, Latinos, and Asians live side by side, without making their own enclaves. The neighborhood, located within half an hour's subway ride from Manhattan, is a densely populated urban area where people live in high-rise apartment complexes or small houses without gardens. In this setting, people of different races naturally meet and recognize one another in apartment hallways, sidewalks, and subway stations (after all, most people walk, not drive). Sanjek observed the development of multiracial cooperation through school activities, block and tenant associations, inter-cultural festivals, and religious activities.

Formal organizations can provide regular opportunities for people to meet. Hundreds or even thousands of people might be interested in an issue, but little discussion may take place if there is not an institution which can coordinate and provide a common place and time for them to interact. Political organizations offer an opportunity for people to discuss political concerns and possibly find common ground.

Organizations can provide valuable resources. One important example is the Asian American Studies Center (AASC) at UCLA. Widely regarded as one of the most important institutions for the study of Asian Americans, the center has provided valuable technical expertise and training to activists in Southern California and elsewhere. Their voter surveys and analyses of voting data are resources for coalition-building that many activist groups would find difficult or impossible to develop on their own.[5]

The existence of organized activist groups can render ethnic populations more effective as coalition partners. As groups organize, gaining resources and sophistication, they become more effective and have more to bring to an alliance.

Interaction and Intergroup Relations

Much of what we have discussed in the previous section refers to political activists, but most people are not activists. What happens when individuals from different ethnoracial groups interact with each other in less formal settings? Does incidental everyday contact among more typical individuals produce more positive perceptions, or, does it lead to more negative ones? Interaction among people from different backgrounds can help overcome negative stereotypes, and help us to see others as real human beings, rather than the caricatures sometimes portrayed in popular culture. However, interaction can also have the opposite effect, increasing tensions and negative views. Contact among people from very different backgrounds can lead to minor clashes over small differences, and, over time, these many small clashes can snowball into major hostility. Greater contact does not by definition lead to more positive relations.

There has been considerable research on the question of how interaction influences interethnic relations. Some studies have found greater hostility and some have found greater understanding. Most have focused on black–white relations, but a few have included Asian Americans and Latinos.

Interaction Increases Conflict: The "Threat Hypothesis"

One body of research concludes that greater contact produces greater *conflict*. This view, which was pioneered by V. O. Key's classic study of Southern politics

(Key 1949), is sometimes referred to as the "threat hypothesis." According to this hypothesis, the level of threat that people of one group perceive from another group is likely to grow as the number of newcomers from the "other" group in their communities grows. Thus, Key found that in the community he studied, as numbers of ethnoracial minorities grew, whites felt a growing sense of racial threat. Why would the increase in the population of newcomers of another ethnicity cause an individual to feel threatened? After all, most people are not be directly affected by such immigration.

One of the most influential views of why this happens focuses on group perceptions. According to this view, racial prejudice is shaped not simply by an individual's perception of her or his situation, but by individuals' perceptions of their *group's* position. In other words, how you believe your group is doing will have a strong influence on how you feel toward other groups. If you believe that another group threatens your group's position in some way, you are likely to feel greater fear and hostility toward the other group, no matter what your individual circumstances are (Blumer 1958). A number of studies have shown that if the black population in an area grows, white prejudice toward African Americans grows as well (e.g. Fossett and Kiecolt 1989; Quillian 1996), although Key's study found that it was not the population size alone that generated increased white hostility but the white people's sense of economic vulnerability.

Many of these findings have been based on research on relations between blacks and whites. We cannot assume that the experiences of Asian Americans (or Latinos) will be identical. In fact, a nationwide study that showed that white prejudice increased when the percentage of blacks increased did not find similar results when populations of Asian Americans or Latinos increased (M.C. Taylor 1998, 528–31). Other research has similarly suggested that whites' views toward African Americans differ from their views of Latinos or Asian Americans (Bobo and Hutchings 1996; Link and Oldenick 1996). However, if the patterns associated with the "threat hypothesis" were to hold for Asian Americans, dramatic increases in Asian American population growth could pose a difficulty for interethnic coalition-building.

Interaction Reduces Tensions: The "Contact Hypothesis"

There are a number of studies which have reached the opposite conclusion: that increased interracial interaction leads to *less* racial hostility (e.g. Allport 1954; Sigelman and Welch 1993; Welch et al. 2001). Although studies making this argument have also largely focused on black–white relations, more recent ones have sometimes included Asian Americans.

Reviewing these studies, J. Eric Oliver and Janelle Wong argue that residential integration does reduce negative perceptions of other ethnoracial groups (Oliver and Wong 2003). They conclude that the contradictory findings of increasing hostility as groups interact are the outcome of inappropriately large-scale methods of analysis, The studies that have found an association between increased contact and negative views have generally focused on large areas, such as counties or metropolitan areas. At such a broad scale, it is only possible to establish the growth in the percentages of ethnoracial minorities in an area, but growing ethnic diversity does not necessarily translate into actual greater contact among members of different ethnoracial groups. A metropolitan area with growing numbers of African Americans, for instance, might be highly segregated.

Oliver and Wong find that increasing racial diversity at the *neighborhood* level does indeed seem to lead to a decrease in negative views of other ethnoracial groups (Oliver and Wong 2003). Further supporting this notion is their finding that negative perceptions are most likely in neighborhoods that are more segregated. Interestingly, this general pattern does not hold for Asian Americans, although it does hold for native-born Asian Americans, who are also more likely to hold negative stereotypes of other groups if they live in predominantly Asian neighborhoods. The survey they use was conducted shortly after the disturbances in South Central Los Angeles in 1992, however, so it is unclear whether Asian American attitudes were skewed by those traumatic events.

These studies have important implications. The evidence suggests that where metro-wide racial diversity is growing, racial segregation (also called "racial isolation") has a greater impact. So, in areas of growing diversity – a description which fits most U.S. metropolitan areas today – highly segregated neighborhoods are likely to produce greater racial tensions.

Asian Americans' perceptions of other groups may be a little more complex, however. Among Asian American immigrants, living in largely Asian neighborhoods may mitigate prejudicial attitudes that immigrants bring with them to the U.S. For later generations, Oliver and Wong's analysis suggests the same pattern as for other groups: greater segregation of Asian Americans leads them to hold more negative attitudes toward other ethnoracial groups. However, as Leland Saito notes, "racial and ethnic relationships are highly fluid and influenced by local circumstances" and other factors (Saito 1998, 128). Because of this, it helps to look at actual examples of cooperation and conflict.

Examples of Cooperation and Conflict

Asian Americans have had both cooperative and conflictual relations with other ethnoracial minorities. Conflict, bloodshed, accidents, and other spectacularly bad news tend to get our attention. Quieter, more productive cooperation often has to take a back seat. We try to counter that unfortunate reality by first describing substantial cases of cooperation in the Monterey Park area. We then turn to the well-publicized and somewhat distorted cases of conflict between African and Korean Americans in New York City and Los Angeles. Finally, we turn to consider possible sources of economic conflict.

Monterey Park and the San Gabriel Valley Region

One of the best-studied settings for Asian American relations with other eth-noracial groups has been Monterey Park and the surrounding San Gabriel Valley region in California. Monterey Park was the first majority Asian American city on the mainland. Only about ten miles east of Los Angeles, it provides a fascinating case of the challenges created by rapid population change. Mirroring much of the larger Los Angeles area, Monterey Park had been largely white in the 1960s, then gradually attracted middle-class Mexican Americans by the end of that decade, as well as Chinese Americans moving out from the nearby Chinatown. Immigration began to transform the suburb in the 1970s, and by the time of the 1980 census, whites had gone from 85 per cent of the population (in the 1960s) to 25 per cent, outnumbered by both Latinos (39 per cent) and Asian Americans (35 per cent), with African Americans making up only a little over 1 per cent. The white share of the population continued to drop, sinking to 12 per cent in 1990, although it bounced back to 20 per cent in 2000 (Horton 1995, 10–11). The number of Asian Americans, meanwhile, grew to slightly over 60 per cent of the population by the end of the century, with Latinos dipping to a little under 30 per cent, and African Americans making up less than 1 per cent of the population, according to Census 2000. Some refer to it today as a suburban Chinatown, reflecting the changing architecture and growing presence of properties owned by Chinese Americans. These changes were not without controversy.

Many long-time residents were unhappy with the rapid development of their city, and a slow-growth movement emerged. Reflecting the complexities of Monterey Park, the movement united liberals opposed to the business-driven changes in a coalition with residents hostile toward nonwhite immigrants. As the percentage of immigrants grew, a movement emerged to make English the official language of the city, triggering further controversy. Progressives responded with their own organizations, and eventually began to win city elections. Asian Americans found themselves squarely in the middle of these political battles, as residents maneuvered to advance their vision for the city. Interests, ideology, leadership, and organizations all played important roles as alliances formed over the future of Monterey Park.

Formal organizations played an important role in coalition-building in Monterey Park. An early example was the slow-growth group known as the Residents Association of Monterey Park (RAMP), formed in 1981. However, although Asian Americans and Latinos were among those concerned with rapid growth, RAMP was dogged by charges of racial motivations. Its leadership was primarily white and middle-class, and some of its supporters seemed concerned more about the ethnoracial aspect of the changes – the fact that much of the new development had a Chinese character – than the specific problems created by rapid growth (Horton 1995, ch. 4).

Supporters of greater cultural diversity came together to form the Citizens for Harmony in Monterey Park (CHAMP) in 1986. CHAMP initially included more conservative businesspeople, but they later split off to form their own organization, A Better Cityhood (ABC), leaving CHAMP with a multicultural group of left-leaning leaders (Horton 1995, 101). CHAMP played a leading role in opposing a resolution to make English the official language of Monterey Park, which they saw as an anti-immigrant statement. Council member Judy Chu was a leader in these efforts, joined by leaders of local Asian American and Latino organizations (Saito 1998, 72–3, 145–6).

Another organization that has promoted inter-group alliances is the West San Gabriel Valley Asian Pacific Democrats Club. Created in 1985, the club was started with the explicit political purpose of building panethnic support for Asian American candidates for office, but it has also supported Latino candidates, and has worked with Latino political groups (Saito 1998, 76–7).

Coalitions are always subject to new stresses, but they also can become more resilient over time. In the early 1990s, for example, local high schools in the Alhambra district in the San Gabriel Valley were witnessing conflict between students of different ethnoracial groups. The Chinese American PTA and the local chapter of the League of United Latin American Citizens (LULAC) pressed the school board to deal with the violence, and tensions simmered between the Asian and Latino parents. However, leaders of the groups worked hard to find common ground, assisted by organizations such as the Los Angeles branch of the Mexican American Legal Defense and Education Fund (MALDEF) and the Asian Pacific American Legal Center. Working together, they formed what eventually became known as the Multi-Cultural Community Association, which succeeded in getting the district to adopt more effective policies for dealing with the student conflicts (Saito and Park 2000).

Asian Americans and Latinos in Southern California

Common interests have long brought Asian Americans and Latinos together in California. As far back as 1903, Japanese and Mexican farm workers joined in a strike for higher wages on beet farms in the Oxnard area in Ventura County, and they formalized their alliance by creating the Japanese–Mexican Labor Association (S. Chan 1991, 86). In 1965 Filipino farm workers mounted a strike that attracted the support of labor leader Cesar Chavez, leading to the formation of the United Farm Workers (UFW), which helped vault Chavez to national prominence (Saito 1998, 130).

Interests and ideology sometimes have divided Asians and Latinos. In the early 1970s, the UFW attempted to organize Mexican workers on Japanese American-owned farms. The predominantly second-generation farm owners created the NFL–Nisei Farmers League ("Nisei" being the Japanese word for second generation) – which sought the support of other Japanese Americans in opposing the UFW efforts. Although the UFW had a largely Mexican

American membership, it also solicited support from Japanese American groups (Saito 1998, 132). Japanese Americans often split along ideological and generational lines, with more business-oriented and second-generation individuals favoring the NFL, while left-leaning and third-generation Japanese Americans often sided with the UFW (Fugita and O'Brien 1977).

Ideology can also bring groups together even when interests might not always coincide. The congressional redistricting efforts of 1990 serve as a good example. Every ten years, the census provides new official population figures, and governments must redraw boundaries so that each legislative district has about the same population. The consequences can have a very big influence on who is likely to win, because legislative district boundaries can be drawn to favor one type of candidate over another. Ethnoracial minority groups have taken a great interest in this redistricting, since it offers one of their best chances to increase the small number of ethnoracial minority elected officials. However, because of the nature of redistricting, the gains of some groups often come at the expense of others, making conflict almost inevitable.

Nevertheless, Asian American and Latino organizations agreed to work together on redistricting in California, motivated in part by a shared ideological commitment to increasing the power of disadvantaged groups. In addition, leaders of these organizations had built close ties through years of cooperation (Saito 1998, 140–3). Prominent Latino groups included the Mexican American Legal Defense and Educational Fund (MALDEF) and the Southwest Voter Registration and Education Project (SVREP), while Asian American interests were represented by the Asian Pacific American Legal Center of Southern California (APALC).

Historically, political leaders have played an important role in bringing Latinos and Asians together for such collaborations in Southern California. Edward Roybal was a pioneer in building electoral coalitions that included Asian Americans and Latinos, as well as African Americans and whites. In 1962, Roybal was elected to the U.S. House of Representatives, becoming the first Latino elected to Congress from California since the late nineteenth century. About a quarter-century after Roybal was first elected to Congress, Judy Chu was elected to the Monterey Park city council by also building a diverse electoral coalition. Although Asian Americans were Chu's strongest supporters in the 1988 election, she also drew substantial support from other Latino and Anglo voters, in a victory that surprised many observers (Horton 1995, 113–21).

Black–Korean Relations in Los Angeles and New York

Of all the relations between Asian Americans and other ethnoracial groups today, perhaps none is as infamous as those between African Americans and Korean Americans. Claire Jean Kim remarks that it "has become part of American urban mythology" (C. Kim 2000, 1). In the nation's two largest cities, on opposite sides of the country, there have been widely publicized tensions and violence, including the 1992 conflagration noted in the text box below. Although students of black–Korean relations have argued that the tensions have been exaggerated by the media, there is no question that African Americans and Korean Americans have found themselves on opposite sides of some tense situations in New York and Los Angeles (Chang and Diaz-Veizades 1999). We consider the "black–Korean conflict," not only because it has attracted a great deal of attention, but also because it helps to illuminate important factors that influence cooperation and conflict between Asian Americans and other communities of color.

A central question asked by those who have studied these conflicts is the extent to which the conflict is real. Two leading studies have suggested that the clashes have been misrepresented.

Los Angeles – Clashing Ideologies

Black–Korean tensions in Los Angeles have been fueled by conflicting ideologies and interests, as well as by larger economic, political, and social forces. Nancy Abelmann and John Lie (1995) argue that Korean immigrants are pursuing the American dream of economic gain, while African Americans are seeking greater political empowerment. In their pursuit of economic success, Korean Americans moved into economic niches that had the potential to bring them into conflict with African Americans (Johnson and Oliver 1989; Freer 1994).

Black Americans epitomize a subpopulation that has been buffeted by large-scale political and economic developments. The long history of racial discrimination in America has left them more segregated than any other ethnoracial group (Massey and Denton 1993), and has also contributed greatly to the high levels of poverty among African Americans. The combination of segregation and limited access to opportunity has produced areas where very high percentages of the residents are poor. Investors have largely abandoned these areas, and many retail services have moved out over the years.

Meanwhile, other large-scale forces have brought Korean immigrants into these neighborhoods. Korean immigration accelerated in the wake of U.S. involvement in the Korean War. Korean immigrants in the 1950s and 1960s found a changing U.S. economy that offered fewer opportunities to newcomers with limited or no English skills, so they sought niches where they could succeed despite these limitations. They found one major opportunity in the very neighborhoods where poor African Americans tended to live, neighborhoods that, thanks to sweeping changes in urban demographics, were in great need of basic retail services (Min 1995, 204–6).

While these large-scale forces brought Korean and African Americans into contact, different ideologies and interests created the potential for tensions. The two groups often had very different views of the poor neighborhoods where they

Los Angeles, April 1992

One of the most devastating cases of conflict between ethnoracial groups took place in Los Angeles in April 1992. Four police officers had been on trial for beating Rodney King, an African American, as they were taking him into custody. A resident had video-taped the officers attacking King, and the footage had been repeatedly shown on tele-vision throughout the U.S. Despite the video, which appeared to show the officers engaged in a prolonged beating of King as he lay on the ground, on April 29, 1992, a suburban Los Angeles jury, ten of whom were whites, acquitted the officers of assault.[6] The South Central area of Los Angeles erupted into a swirl of protest, loot-ing, and assaults. There has been deep disagreement over how to interpret those events, with different views reflected in different names: "the Los Angeles uprisings" versus "the Los Angeles riots." Advocates of the former see the events as a reaction to deep social injustices, while others saw the disturbances as an extreme case of law-less behavior and opportunism. This debate replicated the different views of the unrest in the 1960s, particularly the violence in a Los Angeles neighborhood known as Watts. In 1965, when Watts erupted, some had labeled it a "rebellion" or "insurrection" (Sears 1994, 238), while others referred to it as "rioting for fun and profit" (Banfield 1970).

By that afternoon of April 29, there were reports of attacks on vehicles in South Central Los Angeles. Motorists and pedestrians were assaulted, and looting of stores began. At 6.30 that evening, truck driver Reginald Denny was pulled from his vehicle and severely beaten, as television cameras broadcast the images to a national audience. Denny, a white man, was eventually saved by several black men and women who man-aged to get him to a hospital. By later that evening, the violence was spreading, and Latino residents had joined in the burning and looting.

The next day, looters destroyed the Watts Labor Community Action Committee Center, a place that had provided many services and jobs to impoverished community residents. Cars of young men were reportedly seen headed to Koreatown, and, although Korean Americans had built barricades and posted guards around their prop-erty, much of the community was burned and looted. One young Korean man was shot to death.[7] The effects had a profound effect on the Korean American commu-nity, symbolized by the stark name given to the April 29 devastation: "sa-i-gu" ("4-2-9"). By May 5, when the violence had faded, a good deal of Koreatown was devastated.

The evidence collected to date suggests that the black–Korean conflict was exagger-ated in media reports. For example, as John Lie has pointed out, while there was substantial property damage to Koreatown businesses, two-thirds of the businesses suffering damage were not Korean-owned (Lie 2004, 309). Also, the emphasis on African American attacks on Korean American property ignored the substantial pres-ence of Latinos in the looting and violence. Nevertheless, *sa-i-gu* provided dramatic evidence that black–Korean relations, already raw from the Latasha Harlins incident, continued to be deeply troubled.

came into contact. There were other causes of conflict as well, but this different perspective played an important role in fueling misunderstandings.

In their conversations with Korean Americans, Abelmann and Lie found that the shop owners saw the poor neighborhoods as a chance "to achieve their personal American dreams" (Abelmann and Lie 1995, 155). For them, their stores were personal economic opportunities, and their interest lay in profiting personally from those opportunities. Korean American store owners hoped in time to move on to better opportunities elsewhere.

Many African Americans, however, viewed their segregated neighborhoods as potential bases of solidarity and power" (C. Kim 2000, 61). From this point of view, local businesses existed to serve the community good and to provide employment to local African American residents. For many years, "black nationalists" had called for African Americans to take control of their fate by taking control of their communities, through ownership of local businesses and support of African American-owned stores. From this perspective, the Korean American store owners "exploited the community" by failing "to use some of their profit for community betterment" (Abelmann and Lie 1995, 155). As Korean-owned businesses proliferated in heavily black areas, they became increasingly obvious targets for African American activists seeking to increase community control. In addition, Abelman and Lie argue, "[S]ome African Americans' political efforts target the nearest group of 'successful' newcomers. It is possible to read U.S. history as a series of new immigrants benefiting from the systematic disadvantages facing African Americans" (Abelmann and Lie 1995, 156). Although relations were sometimes inflamed by the negative stereotypes some Korean Americans had of African Americans, we want to be cautious not to exaggerate these. Abelmann and Lie found many cases of friendship between Koreans and blacks. They argue that what the media came to portray as an ethnic conflict between African Americans and Korean Americans was more a clash between different visions of how to win access to opportunity, only partly involving racial animosity. In their discussions with Korean Americans, Abelmann and Lie found that every respondent agreed that the "'black–Korean' conflict was not at the roots of the riots" (Abelmann and Lie 1995, 152), and "some working-class Korean Americans stressed their solidarity with African Americans" (p. 154).

The developments in South Central Los Angeles illustrate how larger social and political developments, ideological differences, and different interests can contribute to tensions between ethnoracial groups. We deliberately write "tensions between ethnoracial groups" rather than "ethnoracial tensions" because we emphasize that many of the sources of conflict were not tied to race or ethnicity. Even if the Korean immigrants and African Americans had been of the same ancestry, they would probably have experienced tensions because of the different experiences and perspectives of each group.

New York and the Role of Leaders

The Korea/African American conflict in New York demonstrates the important role of leadership. The disturbances in South Central Los Angeles developed too quickly for leaders to exert much, if any, influence. The conflict in New York, in contrast, centered on an organized, intentional event – much of the conflict was initially centered around a boycott of two Korean American-owned produce stores – providing much more opportunity for the influence of leadership.

The large-scale economic and political forces at work in the two cities were very similar: Korean immigrants had moved into retail shops in poor black neighborhoods that had few black-owned businesses. As in Los Angeles, some tensions would have been likely regardless of the ancestry of the owners and residents, and in both cities the first tensions flared over incidents involving family-owned stores.[8] The ethnoracial makeup of the two cities was somewhat different, however. New York has seen substantial flows of people from the Caribbean – including Haiti, the Dominican Republic, and Puerto Rico – as well as other parts of the world. The boycott of the produce stores in Brooklyn initially involved Haitian and Korean Americans, although it was often depicted simply as a "black–Korean" conflict.

The precipitating incident came in January 1990, when the manager of the Family Red Apple store, Bong Ok Jang, got into a dispute with a Haitian American customer, Ghiselaine Felissaint. Accounts vary, with Felissaint accusing the Korean American workers of assaulting her, while the store employees denied the charge and alleged that Felissaint was the only one who acted aggressively. In any case, hard feelings emerged, and a community boycott targeted the Family Red Apple and the Church Fruits store across the street (the boycott is often referred to simply as the "Red Apple boycott") (C. Kim 2000, 117).

Ideology played an important role. Claire Jean Kim's study of the boycott led her to conclude that the boycott was part of a battle against continuing white dominance. Her interviews with numerous participants in the conflict found that

> the boycott leaders believed . . . that Korean merchants as a group were frontline representatives of the White power structure, and that individual Korean merchants who showed overt disrespect for Blacks rendered themselves legitimate targets of protest. In their worldview, Korean merchants were not pawns or proxy targets, but active participants, along with Blacks and Whites, in an ongoing racial war. (C. Kim 2000, 110)

A black nationalist perspective had gained support after ugly racial incidents in the late 1980s, when black men had been killed in Brooklyn and Queens, primarily, it appears, because they ventured into white neighborhoods. The Red Apple boycott offered an opportunity for black nationalist leaders to gain the support of Haitian and other immigrants, who often did not see themselves sharing the goals of Black Power movements. From the perspective of many black nationalists, closure of the Korean-owned stores was the appropriate response (C. Kim 2000, ch. 4). This demand, however, made it difficult to find a compromise.

Some of the boycott supporters stressed that their focus was not on Koreans in general, but on those who they believed had shown disrespect and had expressed racist attitudes. Similar to Abelmann and Lie's findings in Los

Angeles, Kim found that many of her respondents explicitly denied that black–Korean hostility was at the base of the conflict (Kim 2000, 128–33). As in Los Angeles, there was undeniable racial hostility, but boycott leaders emphasized other factors. Once again, however, the media stressed racial conflict, missing the more complex underlying causes (C. Kim 2000, ch. 6).[9]

More moderate African American leaders focused on changing behavior rather than shutting down stores. While they felt that Korean Americans had treated black shoppers poorly, these leaders tried to avoid escalating the tensions. Some black leaders even opposed the boycott, and organized trips to cross the picket lines and shop at the stores (C. Kim 2000, 152–5).

Korean American community leaders decided to respond forcefully to the boycott. Although they had settled previous disputes with quiet negotiation, they seemed determined to take a stand this time. Like African American black nationalists, many Korean American leaders came to see the boycott in stark terms, as a racially motivated attack. This viewpoint also made it more difficult to find common ground (C. Kim 2000, ch. 5).

However, some Korean American groups favored a more moderate position. As in the black community, there were Korean Americans who wanted to avoid aggressive responses to the boycott and who felt that each side had some valid points (C. Kim 2000, ch. 5). On each side, however, those supporting stronger responses seemed to have the upper hand.

Eventually, the boycott faded, but not for almost a year and a half. Bong Ok Jang was acquitted after a surprise witness – an African American customer who had been in the store at the time – testified Felissaint had thrown items at the employees, and that the employees had not assaulted her. The acquittal did not deter the boycott, however, and the Family Red Apple store was sold to other Korean owners, who changed the name to Caribbean Fruits and Grocery. "Two weeks later, the protesters disappeared" (Zia 2000, 105–6).

The New York City conflict underscores the role leaders can play in shaping conflicts. Guided by different ideologies, the most prominent African and Korean American leaders encouraged their followers to pursue approaches which made compromise almost impossible.

Economic Competition

Tensions over competing economic interests have a long history. In the nineteenth century, Asian immigrant workers were exploited to combat labor organizers. In the years after the Civil War, Chinese workers were brought to Mississippi to create competitive pressures against newly freed black workers. In North Adams, Massachusetts, a factory owner used Chinese workers in 1870 to undermine unionizing efforts, while the union made an attempt to organize the Asian laborers, without success (Takaki 1998, 94–6). Today, immigrants and native-born workers continue to compete for jobs, although the effects are probably not evenly distributed throughout society.

There is fairly widespread agreement that middle- or upper-income households are unlikely to be hurt by, and often benefit from, immigration (Bean and Stevens 2003). Although there are individual exceptions, non-poor households collectively benefit from the work of low-skilled immigrants, who work in a wide range of sectors, such as food service or home repair. If employers had to pay higher wages, prices would eventually go up, resulting in consumers paying more and having less additional money to spend. By paying less for groceries, or fast food, or a new roof, households can have more money left to buy other things. For those with more income, immigrant labor is likely to be a net benefit, because it helps to keep prices lower.

For low-skilled native-born workers, the consequences may be different. Some argue that poor African Americans are likely to be hurt economically when immigrants are willing to work for very low wages. If immigrant workers are willing to do a job for the minimum wage, a low-skilled native-born worker may find it difficult to earn a higher wage for the same job, since the native-born worker could be replaced with a lower-paid immigrant laborer. Economists continue to debate whether immigrant labor is indeed having these negative effects, but perceptions matter as much as reality for intergroup relations. If immigrants are believed to hurt U.S.-born workers, that perception can promote hostility between immigrants and the native-born, regardless of the reality.

Immigration can hurt U.S.-born workers in other ways. A combination of cultural differences and racial stereotypes may lead employers to favor immigrants over native-born blacks. A study of employer preferences found that immigrants are often seen as more cooperative, and appear to be more likely to be hired, at least in suburban settings, than native-born African American workers (Moss and Tilly 2001).

Asian Americans also might find themselves divided from other communities of color because of different economic positions. In chapter 1, we presented data showing how Asian Americans have a socioeconomic profile considerably higher than other ethnoracial minorities. As we stressed in that chapter, that profile is misleading, as it hides a tremendous diversity which includes considerable poverty and low levels of educational attainment. However, it does mean that large numbers of Asian Americans are in circumstances where they are not likely to be beneficiaries of programs to assist the disadvantaged. This does not mean that all financially secure Asian Americans will oppose policies that would help poorer households, but it does create another source of possible division between them and ethnoracial groups that have far higher percentages of members in poverty.[10]

Where do Asian Americams fit in Minority Coalitions?

Where might Asian Americans fit within minority coalitions? The data we examined earlier in this chapter suggests that different ethnoracial groups do not necessarily fall into the same political alignments. Latinos and African

Americans share some concerns about poverty and educational opportunity, but they differ greatly in their orientations to the United States. Latinos include large numbers of immigrants, while most African Americans are from families that have been in America for many generations. Asian Americans and Latinos share concerns about reunification of immigrants and family members still in other countries, but they are increasingly cast on opposite sides of affirmative action policies, and their socioeconomic profiles are quite different. Interests are likely to align on some issues but clash on others.

In the mid-1990s, Gary Okihiro asked, "Is yellow black or white?" (Okihiro 1994). What Okihiro was suggesting was that there continues to be a fundamental distinction between white and nonwhite in American society. For years, "nonwhite" was simply "black," but now the picture has grown more complex. Asian Americans are confronted with the question of where they are situated – and where they might like to be situated – along that color line. When Asian immigrants first faced that question, in the late nineteenth century, they strove to be placed on the white side, in recognition of the enormous benefits given to whites. In most cases, however, their efforts failed, as we saw in chapter 1.

At the end of the twentieth century, Okihiro argued, Asians were still faced with the question of where they stood. With the tremendous legal discrimination of the nineteenth century now abolished, Okihiro called on Asians to join with blacks in efforts to eradicate other forms of discrimination that persisted. But, although he wanted Asian Americans to side with African Americans, Okihiro argued that "yellow" was neither black nor white.

Our review of conflict and cooperation echoes his conclusion. Although there are many opportunities for cooperation between Asian Americans and other peoples of color, there may be as many possibilities for conflict. Asian Americans, African Americans, Latinos, and American Indians all continue to operate within a society where white Americans usually hold the most power, economically, politically, and socially. The benefits of alliances with communities of color must be weighed against the benefits of potential alliances with whites, which may offer more immediate rewards. Further complicating the picture is the fact that each subpopulation is very diverse. Class, nationality, nativity, gender, and other differences increase the number of possible coalitions, and the potential for conflict.

Are Asian Americans black, white, or neither? This question challenges activists and advocacy groups when they try to build or join multiracial coalitions. According to Claire Kim's (2004) research, Asian American community leaders feel that white, African American, and Latino civil rights leaders are uncertain about whether Asian Americans should be classified as a minority group at all, and whether they should be counted as coalition partners. Some of them had to deal with African American activists who believed that, as newcomers, Asian Americans were exploiting the fruits of the civil rights movement. Others experienced being treated as a junior partner in a coalition due to their smaller number and the perception that they were too ethnically diverse.

Our exploration of the place of Asian Americans returns us to the issue that runs throughout this book: the question of identity. Asian Americans' place in larger coalitions will depend in part on how they are perceived. Throughout their history, Asian Americans have struggled against images not of their making. We look at that in our next chapter.

CHAPTER SEVEN

Images of Asian Americans and their Political Consequences

Asian Americans today encounter a wide range of images of themselves. Some of these images seem to gush with praise, while others spew hatred. In this chapter, we examine those depictions and their consequences.

Over forty years ago, for example, a *New York Times Magazine* article exemplified the praise: "By any criterion of good citizenship that we choose, the Japanese Americans are better than any other group in our society. . . . Every attempt to hamper their progress resulted only in enhancing their determination to succeed" (Peterson 1966, 21). On the other hand, Asian Americans continue to find themselves the targets of racists. In his research in Southern California, Leland Saito talked to an Asian American woman who told him about her encounter with another woman who she had never seen before: "I was just sitting in the store, just looking at stuff . . . She grabbed me [and] she says, 'Go back to China where you belong!' " (Saito 1998, 56).

These images – the ways that Asian Americans are perceived – are stereotypes. Almost a century ago, ago, journalist Walter Lippmann described stereotypes as cultural creations that we use as "a way of substituting order for the great blooming, buzzing confusion of reality" (Lippman 1922/1945, 96). Lippman wrote that a stereotype "precedes the use of reason," and "imposes a certain character on the data of our sense before the data reach the intelligence" (Lippman 1922/1945, 98). In other words, stereotypes can strongly shape perceptions, and those perceptions can persist in the face of strong contrary evidence, because a belief in a stereotype can lead us to ignore or reject contradictory evidence.

Stereotypes such as the model minority or the forever foreigner are cultural creations. They are not the product of any single individual, but the collective combination of many different perceptions and portrayals, similar to what Omi and Winant have labeled a racial project (which we discussed in chapter 1). Although stereotypes are exaggerations with many inaccuracies, they nevertheless influence the way we behave toward and think about those who are stereotyped.

Images of Asian Americans have had a powerful effect on their fortunes. Anyone perceived as nonwhite has had to deal with stereotypes, although the specific stereotypes vary by ethnoracial group. As we explain in this chapter, understanding these stereotypes is important to developing an adequate understanding of Asian American politics. In this chapter you will learn:

1 How Asian Americans are seen both as a *model minority* and as *forever foreigners*.
2 How the model minority and forever foreigner images can coexist.
3 What some of the political consequences of the forever foreigner and model minority stereotypes are.
4 How activists are challenging stereotypes of Asian Americans, and also challenging Asian American invisibility in popular culture.

Model Minority, Forever Foreigner, Invisible Asian

We focus on two stereotypical images of Asian Americans: the "forever foreigner" and the "model minority," because these have played such an important role in the lives of Asian Americans. Asian Americans have long faced the perception that they are foreign, reflecting that fact that the common public perception is that Americans are white or black. A more recent – and seemingly very different – stereotype is that of the model minority. Although there are some positive aspects of this image, it too has some negative political consequences for Asian Americans. We also note another image – or *non*-image of Asian Americans: the invisible Asian.

"Forever Foreigners"

In April 2002 the *Wall Street Journal* ran a story on Vietnam's "dust children," a name given to those born between 1962 and 1976, of American and Vietnamese parentage (Knecht 2002). These children (also referred to as "Amerasian") could get an immigrant visa, the article noted, if they had "American facial features." An unidentified American consulate official explained that "Anyone thought to look like an American" would be approved for a visa. But who "looks like an American"? The clear implication – one endorsed by millions of Americans – was that anyone who appeared to have only Asian ancestry did not "look like an American."[1] You cannot look like an Asian and also look like an American: Asian Americans are forever foreigners.

But, you might wonder, isn't it the case that most Asian Americans *are* foreign-born? Given that, perhaps the "forever foreigner" image is largely a reflection of the current state of Asian America.

While this sounds plausible, two facts argue strongly against it. First, most adult native-born Asian Americans have been asked "where are you from?" (with the implied assumption that they must not be from the U.S.) *after* they have already engaged in conversation. Virtually all people who speak unaccented American English are native-born, and virtually all second- and later-generation Americans speak unaccented English, but almost all of them have still been asked "where are you from?" In addition, many native-born Asian Americans have been asked "how did you learn to speak English so well?" Very rarely would that question be asked of a white American who spoke unaccented English, but many Asian Americans have been asked that question because they are assumed to be foreign.

A second reason why the "forever foreigner" syndrome is unlikely to reflect only an assessment of current demographics is that these questions were commonly asked well before the recent surge of Asian immigration, when the majority of Asian Americans *were* native-born. Because of immigration restrictions discussed in chapter 1, immigration from Asia plunged in the middle of the twentieth century, and the population became increasingly native-born. By the 1960s, only older Asian Americans were likely to be foreign-born, and yet Asian American children and young adults were often asked "where are you from?" and "how did you learn to speak English so well?"

As we noted in chapter 5, Matt Fong, a fourth-generation Chinese American and a Republican candidate for the U.S. Senate in 1998, was asked which side he would support if America and China went to war. Fong later said that his "blood was boiling" when he heard the question, though he tried to "ignore and just laugh off such insensitivity" at that time (M. Fong 1999). Even a conservative such as Fong was assumed to be fundamentally foreign by a media questioner who appeared to believe, as do many Americans, that someone with Asian features could not possibly be fully American.

Nor should there be any doubt about the meaning of that question. Because Fong did not look "American," his loyalty might be in doubt. Many U.S.-born Asian Americans not running for high office have heard the same sentiments expressed in different ways: "go back to where you came from," or "go back to China." For many non-Asian Americans, Asian Americans simply cannot be imagined as an integral part of this nation, no matter how many generations their family has been in America.

The "forever foreigner" image has hurt Asian Americans. Perhaps the most infamous example of this was the World War II internment of Japanese Americans, which we described in chapters 1 and 4. Although key security officials such as FBI Director J. Edgar Hoover did not see most Japanese Americans as security threats, over 100,000 were imprisoned in internment camps in the nation's interior, on the grounds that they might conspire with Japan against the United States. Many of those arguing for their imprisonment claimed that Japanese Americans could never be loyal to the United States: they would forever be foreigners.

The Model Minority

In the nineteenth century, Asians were usually portrayed very negatively, but even then there were some contradictory images. Asian workers were often described as inhuman machines who could not be matched. Over the decades, this image evolved and was not always described so negatively, although it often continued to imply that Asian Americans were fundamentally different in undesirable ways. By the late twentieth century, these images had come to be known as the "model minority myth."

It is impossible to say with precision when the stereotypes of Asian Americans shifted from extremely negative to more positive, but most historians see World War II as a key turning point. With China as an ally of the U.S., many felt it desirable to tone down anti-Chinese rhetoric, although anti-Japanese sentiments grew. There was also concern that blatantly racist policies would undermine the U.S. claim to be fighting for equal rights and democracy. During the war, the heroics of the 442nd Regimental Combat Team helped develop some favorable sentiments toward Japanese Americans, although many Japanese Americans faced withering bigotry after the war.

In the mid-1960s, two watershed articles crystallized the idea of the model minority. One was a *New York Times Magazine* article by William Petersen, entitled "Success Story, Japanese-American Style" (Petersen 1966). In the article, Petersen praised Japanese Americans for their successes, noting that many had been imprisoned in the internment camps, in addition to the many other challenges they faced. While one would expect low educational attainment, high juvenile delinquency, and a number of other problems, statistics pointed to the opposite conditions among Japanese Americans. At almost the same time, *U.S. News & World Report* published an article praising Chinese Americans ("Success Story" 1966). Although neither Petersen nor the *U.S. News* article used the term "model minority," both helped to develop the concept of the high-achieving Asians who could overcome great obstacles and succeed.

Those advancing the idea of a model minority were not necessarily motivated by an admiration for Asian Americans. The *U.S. News* article contrasted Chinese Americans with "other minorities" – presumably African Americans – and found the latter lacking. Two decades later, some critics of multicultural education would again use the success of Asian Americans to criticize other ethnoracial minorities.

The idea of the model minority is an important one for Asian American politics, so it is useful to examine it in some detail. In chapter 1, we looked at the data underlying the image of the highly successful Asian American. We saw how Asian Americans have a high median income and high percentage of highly educated individuals. These figures are some of the key pieces of the model minority image. In addition, the 1966 *New York Times Magazine* article also stressed the low rate of juvenile delinquency among Japanese Americans, noting that we would expect the exact opposite in immigrant groups, particularly those facing the challenges that Japanese Americans experienced.

Even today, the model minority image persists. For example, in a May 2006 article entitled "The Model Student," Nicholas Kristof of the *New York Times* used a version of the model minority thesis to explain why Asian Americans score higher average SAT scores than whites, African Americans, Hispanics, and Native Americans. Kristof first rejected the "genetic selection" explanation,

because, according to him, IQs do not explain why "in Japan, ethnic Koreans lan-
guish in an underclass, often doing poorly in schools and becoming involved in
the yakuza mafia (Kristof 2006)".[2] Instead, Kristof, argued, the answer lies in
culture: "In a Confucian culture, it is intuitive that the way to achieve glory and
success is by working hard and getting an A." He suggested that this holds
"lessons America can absorb," and concluded that "we would be fools not to try
to learn some Asian lessons." While Kristof's claims about the influence of
Confucianism are questionable, the persistence of such arguments demonstrates
the continuing hold the model minority image has on the American mind.

As we explained in chapter 2, the evidence calls the model minority image
into question. For instance, statistical reports of very high median family and
household incomes for Asian Americans are distortions that fail to take into
account the larger families (and greater number of workers per household)
and the fact that Asian Americans are disproportionately located in high-cost
metropolitan areas.

More importantly, we saw that there are enormous variations among Asian
American subgroups. Some, such as Hmong Americans or Cambodian
Americans, face many of the same challenges confronting other ethnoracial
minorities in the U.S. With low income and high poverty levels, they also struggle with the challenges of youth gangs and violence. Their immigrant parents,
often isolated by their limited command of English and mystified by legal
limits on the discipline they can mete out, find it difficult to prevent their children from following the lure of gang life. Rather than model minorities, these
communities could be called modal minorities,[3] experiencing the same problems as have troubled many other immigrant groups.

In these circumstances, the model minority image is a disadvantage. Efforts
to gain help for struggling families can be undermined by the myth of Asian
American success. Programs to help disadvantaged youth may exclude Asians
because of the misperception created by the model minority myth. Programs
designed to help disadvantaged groups sometimes do not include Asian
Americans among the eligible groups, because of the belief that Asians are so
successful. We explore this in more depth later in this chapter.

Some might feel that the model minority image demonstrates the power of
assimilation and the acceptance of Asian Americans. Activists are dubious,
however, because in the minds of non-Asians the model minority also has a
dark side, implying that Asian Americans are machine-like drones, fearful
competitors who live unbalanced lives. Further evidence of continuing negative images of Asian Americans can be found in the other dominant perception: that of the "forever foreigner."

The "Triangulation" of Asian Americans

How can we reconcile the "forever foreigner" image with the "model minority"
myth? The two may be able to coexist because they reflect different ways of

thinking about others. Claire Jean Kim has argued that there are two dimensions used in evaluating ethnoracial groups (C. Kim 1999). Kim suggests that one dimension is constructed "along cultural and racial grounds" (C. Kim 1999, 107). Comparisons along this dimension have generated classic depictions of the allegedly superior culture of certain Asian American groups, and, more recently, praise for Asian Americans' perceived cultural commitment to duty, education, and achievement. Along this dimension, Asian Americans are often compared to African Americans and other ethnoracial minorities and judged superior, a "model minority." The model minority stereotype has been used as a weapon against other ethnoracial minorities and to deny opportunities.

The second dimension for evaluating ethnoracial groups, according to Kim, is an "insider–outsider" continuum. When evaluated in that way, Asian Americans are seen as outsiders, alien and inferior to other ethnoracial groups, including African Americans or American Indians, This continuum generates the "forever foreigner" stereotype.

Political Consequences

We examine these images because they have political consequences. They play a role in shaping debates over public policy, and they can create an atmosphere of suspicion that puts individual Asian Americans at a tremendous disadvantage. The internment of Japanese Americans in World War II was one of the most devastating consequences of the forever foreigner stereotype and racial prejudice. Despite an absence of evidence (and, as we now know, significant contradictory evidence), many Americans saw Japanese Americans as untrustworthy. They would always be loyal to Japan and could never become good Americans, declared prominent leaders. Their consciences relieved by this image of Japanese Americans as inherently alien, government officials were willing to imprison thousands of citizens without trial.

While the internment of Japanese Americans is probably the most dramatic example of the consequences of the "forever foreigner" image, there are many other examples. In this section, we describe more recent cases.

Discriminatory Treatment

One consequence of negative stereotypes can be discriminatory treatment. Because most types of racial discrimination are now illegal, it is hard to find people who will admit to it, but the evidence strongly suggests that it continues.

A good example is the case of Oregon Congressman David Wu, who was denied entry to the Department of Energy (DOE) building, where he was scheduled to give a speech. Guards repeatedly asked him if was an American, even after he showed them his congressional identification card. A DOE spokesperson said that Wu was treated like any other member of Congress, and that it was routine to ask visitors about their nationality. However, a fellow

Wen Ho Lee

Wen Ho Lee was a scientist who suffered serious consequences from the "forever foreigner" stereotype. Lee was working at Los Alamos National Laboratories when the CIA and the FBI became convinced that China had obtained secret information about the W-88 warhead, the most advanced in the U.S. arsenal. In March 1999, when these claims became publicized, Lee was fired from Los Alamos, and then arrested in December of that year.

Although there was a wide array of plausible suspects, Department of Energy (DOE) and FBI officials focused on Lee. The head of intelligence and counterintelligence at the DOE, Notra Trulock, agreed to focus on Chinese Americans, and his primary investigator, Dan Bruno, declined to follow the many leads that pointed to others. Because he had made trips to China and had met with Chinese scientists, Lee became the primary suspect. Unable to get him to confess, the FBI arrested Lee, and convinced a judge to order him held in solitary confinement for nine months.

The government's case was always weak, but Lee's critics seized upon his breach of rules when he downloaded material from a secure computer and transferred it to another machine. Although the other machine was also secure, it was a violation of rules to transfer the data to any other computer. The seriousness of this charge was somewhat undermined, however, when it was revealed that the Director of the CIA, John Deutsch, had also violated rules by transferring material to another computer (unlike Lee, Deutsch was never arrested).

There was no question that Lee was the target of racial profiling (focusing on a group or individual because of their ethnicity or race). However, some conservatives argued that this focus was justified, since China's efforts to gain information were focused on Chinese Americans. But, even if greater attention toward Chinese Americans was justified, it did not explain why DOE and FBI officials failed to investigate the hundreds of other possible suspects (who were not Chinese Americans).

In the end, all but one of the charges (improper handling of data) were dropped. The government no longer claimed that Lee had given away information about the W-88 warhead, and there was considerable debate over whether anyone had given information on the W-88 to the Chinese. Judge John Parker, who had ordered Lee held in solitary confinement, apologized to Lee for his treatment and blasted the government for what Parker called misleading statements about the threat posed by Lee.

Shortly after Parker's apology, the *New York Times* published an unusual editorial, also apologizing for faults in its coverage of the case. The *Times* acknowledged that they had relied too heavily on government sources, and failed to investigate important questions sufficiently.

Why was Lee singled out for arrest and prosecution, while so many other suspects were ignored? Like Japanese Americans during World War II, Lee fell victim to the forever foreigner image, which made it easy to portray him as someone who would betray the United States. As *San Jose Mercury News* reporters Dan Stober and Ian Hoffman noted, he was "a convenient spy."

James Sterngold, "Nuclear Scientist Set Free after Plea in Secrets Case; Judge Attacks U.S. Conduct," *New York Times*, September 14, 2000. Available at www.nytimes.com.
Dan Stober and Ian Hoffman, *A Convenient Spy: Wen Ho Lee and the Politics of Nuclear Espionage* (New York: Simon & Schuster, 2001).
"The Times and Wen Ho Lee," *New York Times*, September 26, 2000. Available at www.nytimes.com.

congressman (not an Asian American) went to test that claim the next day, and found that he was able to enter the building without any questioning (Kamen 2001). It seems very likely that Wu's difficulties reflected the perception of Asian Americans as foreigners. Ironically, Wu was going to the building for a celebration of Asian Pacific American Heritage Month.

A more infamous case is that of Wen Ho Lee, a scientist held in solitary confinement for nine months, from late 1999 to September 2000, largely because of suspicions created by his ancestry (see text box). Just like Japanese Americans during World War II, Wen Ho Lee found that his ancestry made him a target for punishment.

The Wen Ho Lee case highlighted the negative effects of the forever foreigner image. Although Americans of other ancestries have experienced this in wartime, Asian Americans have faced it continuously, regardless of international conditions. German Americans, for instance, had to deal with high levels of hostility during World War I, but few if any third- or fourth-generation German Americans have ever been asked how they learned to speak English so well, and it is unlikely that their children have ever been told to "go back to where you came from!" Nor are Norwegian Americans ever likely to be taunted with ethnic slurs meant for German Americans. Asian Americans, on the other hand, repeatedly see their status questioned, no matter how many generations they have been in this country, and have often been taunted with terms that apply to a different Asian subgroup. For Wen Ho Lee, the consequences were particularly dire, and included a long period of solitary confinement before he was eventually released.

The Campaign Finance Controversy of 1996

Another important example of the costs of negative stereotypes came with the campaign finance controversy of 1996. Like the Wen Ho Lee case, the forever foreigner image led to discriminatory treatment, but with much wider consequences.

Initially, many believed that the 1996 campaign would mark a giant step forward in Asian Americans' political engagement. Many Asian American community organizations had joined together for a massive voter registration drive, which "eventually registered over 75,000 new voters" (Lien 2001, 73). Growing numbers of Asian Americans were running for office and playing other important roles. But, within a year, allegations of campaign finance violations triggered a backlash that left many disillusioned, and their dream of a new era for Asian American politics was transformed into a nightmare of accusations and mistrust.

The controversy had its roots in the insatiable drive for money to fund American elections. Although campaign finance laws had attempted to limit these efforts, court decisions had overturned some key provisions, and enterprising political activists had discovered ways to raise large sums of money in

support of campaigns. Some legal limitations remained, including prohibitions against contributions from foreign nationals (this restriction does not
apply to "green card" holders – i.e. U.S. residents with permanent resident
alien status). Foreign corporations also could not make contributions,
although a U.S.-based subsidiary of a foreign corporation can set up a political
action committee, if it meets certain requirements. Campaign finance law also
prohibited corporations from contributing directly to a candidate's campaign,
but corporate donations could be funneled through political parties, known
as the "soft money" route.[4] However, with the parties competing to raise hundreds of millions of dollars, there was a strong motivation to push the rules as
far as possible.

Large contributors rarely give out of the goodness of their hearts, of course.
While many Americans give small donations simply because they support a
candidate or cause, large donors hope to wield more influence. Those who
make large contributions may gain access to important government officials,
or, at least, they may help elect candidates who share their viewpoints.

Fundraisers are critical intermediaries in this process. While prominent persons such as the president can attract many donations, most elected officials
have limited time to find contributors. Fundraisers connect potential donors
with those seeking donations. The most successful fundraisers also gain access
to important decision makers, which in turn increases their value to well-
funded interests who wish to influence the political process through financial
contributions.

John Huang was a fundraiser. Immigrating to the U.S. in 1969, Huang
became a naturalized citizen in 1976, and, by the late 1980s "became active in
Democratic politics," eventually working as a party fundraiser credited with
raising $3.4 million for the Democrats in 1996 ("Campaign Finance Key Player"
1998). However, by the fall of that year, newspapers were beginning to report
that some of the donations solicited by Huang might have come from foreign
nationals.

Over the next several months, Huang, Johnny Chung, Maria Hsia, Pauline
Kanchanalak, Yah Lin "Charlie" Trie, and other Asian American fundraisers
found themselves facing a growing wave of allegations that they had accepted
money from sources prohibited from making political donations. More sensational were claims that the Chinese government had sought to buy influence
through campaign contributions (Harris 1997).

Eventually, the government obtained several convictions. Democratic
fundraiser Maria Hsia was convicted of filing false information to the Federal
Elections Commission (FEC), concealing that donations had come from
sources such as a religious organization (forbidden from making contributions, because of its tax status) or foreign contributors (Jackson 2000; Lewis
2000a; Lewis 2000b). Huang pleaded guilty to conspiracy to defraud the FEC by
concealing illegal contributions, many of which had come from foreign
nationals ("Campaign Finance Key Player" 1998; Edsall and Walsh 2002).

Kanchanalak and Trie pled guilty to making false statements, and Chung pled guilty to using "straw donors" to conceal the true source of donations (Johnston 1999; Rosenzweig 1998; Seper 2000). All three agreed to cooperate with the government in exchange for leniency.

While there was evidence that several fundraisers had indeed broken campaign finance laws, the consequences would be felt by many Asian Americans who had nothing to do with such wrongful activity. The forever foreigner stereotype helped to blur the distinction between actual foreign Asians and Asian Americans, making the latter vulnerable to charges which could only apply to the former. Frank Wu and May Nicholson analyzed media coverage of the campaign finance controversy. They found frequent references to "Asians" and "Asian Americans," with little distinction made between the two very different categories (Wu and Nicholson 1997). The legal difference, however, was critical, because Asian Americans had a right to make political contributions, while Asians did not, because they were foreign nationals.

The failure to make this critical distinction was not limited to the media. As the controversy and legal charges grew, the Democratic National Committee (DNC) began calling Asian American donors, asking if they were citizens and seeking information about their finances (Nash and Wu 1997; Zia 2000). What made them targets were their names and the perception that all Asian Americans are foreigners. Had a similar scandal involved individuals named "Thompson" or "Nelson" it is highly doubtful that officials would have tried to investigate any donors that had English or Scandinavian-sounding names.

Asian Americans did not accept all this passively. Dismayed by the racially charged language used by members of Congress and others, the stereotyped and racially charged images in the media, and the treatment by the political parties, over a dozen Asian American organizations joined together to protest this treatment and to petition the U.S. Civil Rights Commission to investigate (Lien 2001, 75).

Challenging Asian American Invisibility

Stereotypes are harmful, but invisibility may be just as bad. In addition to fighting stereotypes, Asian Americans have taken on the related challenge of ending their invisibility in popular culture. This has two aspects: working to increase the presence of Asian Americans where there has been none at all, and working to replace ersatz Asian characters with real ones (other ethnoracial minorities have engaged in similar efforts).

Increasing the Presence of Asian Americans

Asian Americans have usually been missing from the stage of popular culture. Several Asian American groups have joined together to work to reverse this, forming the Asian Pacific American Media Coalition (APAMC).[5] APAMC monitors and evaluates media efforts to increase diversity in front of and behind the camera in television productions, and releases an annual report where they describe and evaluate television network efforts to increase ethnoracial diversity in their programs and the staff who produce the programs. The APAMC has also worked with the National Latino Media Council and American Indians in Film and Television (AIFTV) to call attention to the presence of Latinos and American Indians in television.

Replacing Phony Asians with Real Ones

A second, and somewhat more controversial, problem is the predominance of phony, stereotypical Asian American characters in popular culture. For much of the twentieth century, so-called Asian American characters were played by non-Asian Americans. Asian American viewers knew the difference, but most audiences, who had little exposure to actual Asian Americans, were probably little aware of these "yellowface" portrayals.[6] One of the earliest examples was the offensive movie character Charlie Chan, who was always played by actors of European descent. Because Asian American heroes were nonexistent during the heyday of the Charlie Chan movies (the 1930s and 1940s), he won popularity with some Asian Americans, even though the character's dialogue reflected stereotypes that had no similarity to actual Asian Americans. The frequent use of European Americans to portray Asian Americans helped to make real Asian Americans invisible in the popular culture.

By the end of the twentieth century, however, many Asian Americans had had enough. In 1990 news came that British producer Cameron Mackintosh was bringing the play *Miss Saigon* to America, and the European actor Jonathan Pryce would continue in the key role of Engineer, which was supposed to be an Asian character. Asian Americans began to organize in opposition.[7]

Asian American actors were initially successful in winning support, and their union, Actors' Equity, voted to deny Jonathan Pryce's work visa application. Denial of the visa would have meant the Pryce could not play the role, but it was widely expected that Mackintosh would appeal and win, and Pryce would end up in the role. Mackintosh, however, went on the offensive, announcing the cancellation of the show, which was guaranteed to trigger a powerful backlash against Actors' Equity and Asian Americans, who were accused of reverse discrimination. In short order, the union rescinded its vote, and Mackintosh got his way. After Pryce left the production, however, the role of Engineer was played by Asian American actors.

The episode highlighted an important point: the need for genuine representation of Asian Americans. Many whites simply could not understand the Asian American concerns. This was understandable, since whites never had to worry about being unrepresented on stage and screen, and no whites had spent entire lifetimes seeing characters of European descent always played by

Chan is Missing

A brilliant blow against the Charlie Chan image is a film by Wayne Wang (who went on to make major Hollywood pictures such as *The Joy Luck Club*, *Because of Winn-Dixie*, and *Chan is Missing*. Real Asian Americans were depicted in such convincing fashion that one could mistake it for a documentary. The stereotypical figure of Charlie Chan is missing, but not missed. At the same time, the movie spoofs Charlie Chan films, with the lead characters – Jo and Steve – parodying Charlie Chan and his number one son. In addition, the title refers to the fading away of the immigrant generation. The title character, Chan Hung, is missing, and as Jo and Steve search for him, they learn of Chan's struggle's to adapt to America. (The film also includes one of the most hilarious spoofs of a scholarly view of cultural adaptation.)

Jo and Steve learn about struggles linking the old country and the new – what today is often called transnationalism – and how Chan may have been caught in the middle. At the same time, Jo and Steve spar over the significance of Chan's struggles compared to those of the American-born Chinese – the ABCs, which include both Jo and Steve. They meet Asian Americans who are striving to help others succeed, and who themselves have become very successful, but they find some who have given up hope that they will ever find full acceptance in America.

Chan is Missing is filmed in San Francisco's Chinatown, done in black and white, and with touches that suggest one of the greatest films ever made, *Citizen Kane* – which was also filmed in black and white. Like the reporter in *Citizen Kane*, Jo and Steve struggle to understand Chan as they talk to many people who knew him. As with John Foster Kane, Jo and Steve find that each person has a very different view of Chan, and, perhaps, each person's view reveals as much of that person as it does of Chan.

The conclusion is poignant, sad, and inspiring. The challenge of cultural blending is portrayed in all its glory and confusion, with the resilience and energy of the new generations contrasted respectfully against the fading memory of the old. One of the most powerful and honest depictions of Asian Americans on film, it is a wonderful antidote to the many stereotyped images that long dominated movies and television.

actors of non-European descent. If Asian Americans had not contested the casting in *Miss Saigon*, no one else was likely to have raised strong objections. When Asian Americans remain silent, misrepresentation is likely to continue, and harmful stereotypes like the forever foreigner can persist unchallenged.

Representations of Asian American Women

Another important sphere of (mis)representation in popular culture relates to images of Asian American women. These images draw on stereotypes of the entire Asian American subpopulation, but the particular forms are different for men and women. Yen Le Espiritu observes that "Asian women have been reduced to one-dimensional caricatures in Western representation," resulting in a gross simplification which "obscures the social injustice of racial, class, and gender oppression" (Espiritu 1997, 93).

The most memorable images have grown out of descriptions of Asians, not Asian Americans. The Empress Tsu-hsi, who "ruled China from 1898 to 1908 from the Dragon Throne," was described by the *New York Times* as "'the wicked witch of the East, a reptilian dragon lady," creating an image that has emerged in many other portrayals of Asian women (Shah 1997). Although the popular culture depictions of the Dragon Lady have usually applied to Asians, not Asian Americans, the forever foreigner perception makes it easy for many Americans to apply this characterization to Asian American women, even those whose families have been in the U.S. for multiple generations. "At the opposite end of the spectrum" from the Dragon Lady "is the Lotus Blossom stereotype . . . [d]emure, diminutive, and deferential" (Espiritu 1997, 94). Renee Tajima notes that "this view of Asian women has spawned an entire marriage industry. Today the Filipino wife is particularly in vogue for American men who order Asian brides from picture catalogues" (Tajima 1989, 309).

Images of Asian Americans and the Politics of Identity

Stereotypes of Asian Americans are part of what we have called the politics of identity. The struggle over stereotypes is a struggle to control one's identity, and, as we have seen, control over one's identity is an important prerequisite for political inclusion and opportunity. Stereotypes have deep roots, and are not likely to be eradicated quickly, but the struggle to eliminate them is an important part of the Asian American battle for equality and acceptance.

Respect and Recognition

Part of what is at stake is what philosopher Charles Taylor calls the "politics of recognition" (C. Taylor 1992). Respect is seen today as a basic right, and adequate respect requires that one be recognized as one wishes to be recognized. Defining yourself establishes you as a human being equal to others; letting others define you implies a lesser status. Parents do this for small children – answering questions for them, filling out forms – but as children become adults, they do these things for themselves. Self-definition is a privilege of adulthood. For a long time, those defined as nonwhite were denied the opportunity to define themselves. In a sense, they were treated as perpetual children prevented from enjoying the rights and opportunities that were supposed to be available to all adults.

The struggles of ethnonoracial minorities to assert control over their own identities can be seen in the campaigns many groups have undertaken to change the labels others use to name them. Many people are familiar with efforts of African-ancestry activists since the 1960s to replace the term "Negro" with "Black" or "Afro-American," and later to replace those terms with "African American." Similarly, Asian-ancestry activists have called for "Oriental" to be replaced with "Asian American."[8]

Control over one's name is not a trivial matter, but neither is it sufficient for respect, because negative stereotypes can persist under any name. Battling these stereotypes is an ongoing challenge.

Challenging Stereotypes

As we will explain in chapter 8, challenging stereotypes is not simply a matter of preventing feelings from being hurt, or promoting "political correctness." Stereotypes can harm more than feelings; they can cause considerable injustices. Battling racial stereotypes is part of the effort to end those injustices. Because these stereotypes are perpetuated through everyday language and images, seemingly small offenses are worth challenging. The repeated, unchallenged use of racial stereotypes helps convey the impression that they are acceptable and accurate.

So, when Rosie O'Donnell (one of the hosts of a talk show called *The View*) joked that Chinese would discuss a recent event by saying "ching chong, ching chong," groups such as the Organization of Chinese Americans protested vigorously and called for an apology ("OCA Demands Apology" n.d.). Although O'Donnell was referring to residents of China, she was drawing on stereotypes that had long been used to mock Asian Americans. "Ching chong, ching chong" is one of the cruder embodiments of the forever foreigner stereotypes, used by bigots who want to emphasize the alien nature of Asian Americans. Today, however, Asian American activists refuse to accept the use of that language by prominent individuals, and they are quick to respond to offensive remarks.

Stereotyped and derogatory images of Asian Americans have long been used to define them as alien and dangerous. The Fu Manchu novels of the early and mid-twentieth century portrayed a villainous Asian whose evil minions could be found gathered in Chinatown, seeking to subvert American society (R. Lee 1999, 114–15). While the more blatant racial slurs have disappeared, the underlying message retains a strong hold in popular culture, as illustrated by Michael Crichton's novel *Rising Sun*, where Crichton warns that Japan is using "trade like war, trade intended to wipe out the competition" (quoted in T.P. Fong 2002, 196).

Racial stereotypes – even trivial ones – are part of what Michael Omi and Howard Winant have called a racial project. Omi and Winant argue that it is through the interaction of different racial projects that racial categories are challenged and ultimately changed (Omi and Winant 1994, 55). Resisting stereotypes is one way to contribute to an alternative racial project, one that can challenge the inequities of racialization. Thus battles against stereotypes are not an overreaction to personal slights, but rather are an integral part of a larger effort to gain acceptance and equal treatment in American society.

CHAPTER EIGHT

Asian Americans, Public Policy, and Intersectionality

In this chapter we turn to an examination of public policies important to Asian Americans. We have briefly discussed some policies in chapter 3, as a way of illustrating some of the activities of interest groups, but here we look at the way that Asian Americans are affected by some selected policies.

This chapter builds directly on our discussion (in chapter 7) of images of Asian Americans. As we explain in the next section, the model minority image has obscured the struggles of some Asian American subgroups. Overcoming that misconception has required dissemination of more accurate perceptions of Asian Americans. In part, this effort has been promoted by the development of Asian American studies programs, which have also been fueled by the emergence of a panethnic identity, and the efforts of determined young activists who pushed colleges to expand their curriculum. Another area of great importance to Asian Americans has been immigration policy, which we also discuss here.

Issues of race are often closely bound to other concerns. Individuals are always perceived to fit into more than one socially constructed category, and those multiple placements can sometimes strengthen inequality. African American women, for instance, may be disadvantaged by both race and gender, making it particularly hard to overcome difficult circumstances. Such situations are sometimes referred to as "intersectionality." In the latter part of this chapter, we explain how many public policy efforts illustrate the relevance of intersectionality. In this chapter, you will learn:

1 How racial concerns overlap with important aspects of an individual's life (i.e. the importance of intersectionality).
2 Why the model minority image is not an accurate reflection of the educational attainment of all Asian Americans.
3 How college admissions policies have sometimes penalized Asian Americans, and how controversy over these policies can lead to conflicts between some Asian Americans and other ethnoracial minorities.
4 Why immigration policy is important for Asian Americans today.
5 How experiences in and connections to their native countries continue to shape the Asian American experience in the U.S.
6 What has been done to redress wrongs against Japanese American and Japanese Latino internees, and to secure equal treatment for Filipino veterans, and how these redress movements differ.

Education

Education is important to everyone. Educational attainment has a powerful influence on an individual's economic prospects and, for immigrants, it can serve as an important vehicle for socialization, particularly English language acquisition.

Education is important not only for individuals, but also for categories of people. In the past, marginalized subpopulations in the U.S. have found that one way to combat invisibility and lack of control over their identity has been to insist on more prominent and accurate representation in educational settings – to work for changes in the organization and staffing of disciplines in higher education and for changes in the subjects that are researched and taught. The development of Asian American studies programs in colleges and universities across the United States has been an important political development in this regard.

Education can also help groups overcome the disadvantages of racialization, through policies of affirmative action or targeted financial aid. The model minority image might suggest – inaccurately – that Asian Americans are not in need of such government assistance. For example, a *Newsweek-on-Campus* issue titled "A Drive to Excel" emphasized the educational achievements of Asian immigrant youth ("A Drive to Excel" 1984), while a *New York Times Magazine* article focused on possible explanations for what it called the "extraordinary record" of Asian Americans (Butterfield 1986). A closer examination reveals the inaccuracies in the stereotypical image.

As we will see below, that rosy picture presented by such media reports masks the fact that many Asian American families are wrestling with poverty and lack of education.

The Model Minority in Education: Image and Reality

Data on income and education – often known collectively as "socioeconomic status," or SES – can be misleading. When a single figure is given for an entire group, it implies a *normal distribution* where the largest portion of the population would have scores that place them in the middle of a distribution chart. If we were to draw this as a graph, it would resemble the classic "bell curve," with a single large hump in the middle. Figure 8.1 shows what this would look like, if we presented it as a bar graph.

However, Asian American educational attainment is actually *bimodal*. Asian Americans cluster in two different groups, with large numbers of high performers at one end and large numbers of relatively low performers at the other. This uneven distribution can be seen most clearly when the Asian American category is broken out by ethnic subgroup, as figure 8.2 does. While East and South Asian Americans tend to have high educational attainment, with 40 per cent or more having at least a bachelor's degree, Southeast Asian Americans tend to fall at the other end of the spectrum, with 40 to 60 per cent

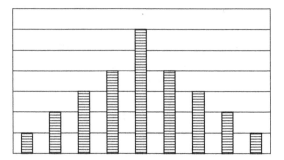

Figure 8.1 *Sample bell curve in bar graph form.*

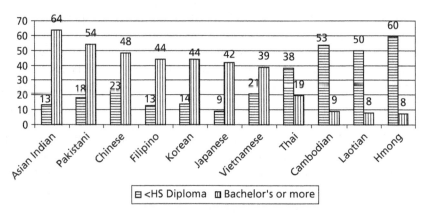

Source: Terrance J. Reeves and Claudette E. Bennett, "We the People: Asians in the United States," *Census 2000 Special Reports* (Dec. 2004), Census 2000 special tabulation.

Figure 8.2 *Educational attainment by detailed Asian American group (figures are percentages for individuals 25 or older).*

not completing high school. The low level of education for Vietnamese, Cambodians, Hmong, and Laotians mainly reflects their entry to the country as refugees, and, in the case of the Hmong, their very different cultural experiences when living in Asia.

As always, we should avoid generalizing too much. Although it is true that large numbers of Southeast Asian Americans have lower education attainment, many do have college degrees. Similarly, we should not assume that all East and South Asian Americans are highly educated. Among South Asian (Asian Indians and Pakistanis), a majority of whom have a bachelor's degree or higher, more than 10 per cent have attained less than high-school diplomas. However, research continues to show this bimodal pattern, with Southeast Asian Americans – and also Native Hawaiians and other Pacific Islanders – facing the greatest obstacles to their educational attainment, with South and East Asian Americans in much better circumstances ("Information Sharing Could Help Institutions" 2007).

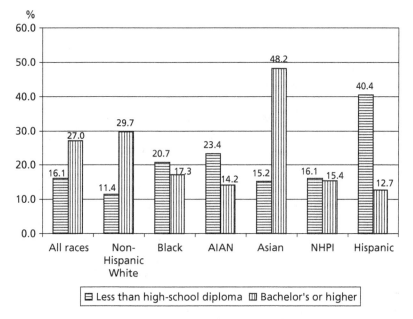

Source: U.S. Census Bureau, 2004 American Community Survey, tables B15002B–B15002E, B15002H, B15002I.

Figure 8.3 *Educational attainment by ethnoracial group (figures are percentages for individuals 25 or older).*

So why does the model minority image persist? Because Asian American educational data is rarely broken down as it is in figure 8.2. Instead, all Asian Americans are lumped together (suggesting a normal distribution). Figure 8.3 shows this typical way of presenting educational attainment data, for individuals 25 years and older. Looking at this distribution by itself, you might find it easy to accept the stereotype of Asian Americans as academic overachievers. Among Asian Americans 44 per cent have earned a bachelor's degree or higher, compared to a little under 25 per cent of the overall population. Indeed, one census report comparing educational attainment by racial groups has a section headlined: "The 'Asian alone' race group led in attaining bachelor's and advanced degrees" (Bauman and Graf 2003, 5). Even with this graph, however, some hint of the bimodal distribution can be seen. While Asian Americans exceed the general population in the percentage with high levels of education, they also have a high percentage with low levels of education (less than a high-school diploma).

These misimpressions have consequences. Policymakers use them to make decisions about who should be eligible for assistance. For instance, Asian Americans are not eligible for National Science Foundation (NSF) programs designed to help under-represented groups, because the NSF does not consider Asian Americans to be under-represented in the sciences. Also, in recent years,

Asian Americans have increasingly been assumed to be ineligible for various affirmative action programs. Because affirmative action appears to be undergoing substantial changes (see text box 'Affirmative Action'), it is difficult to say how much this will matter in the future, but in the past few decades, the image of Asian Americans as highly successful has helped to limit their eligibility.

This is not always unfair. Many Asian Americans are indeed prospering, and should not be considered socioeconomically disadvantaged. However, the considerable disadvantages of subgroups such as Southeast Asian Americans can be missed when all Asian Americans are lumped together.

This illustrates yet again the complications of what we have called the politics of identity. In most cases, small Asian American subgroups benefit from joining together, but a common identity may not be beneficial when it comes to educational issues. The more that Southeast Asian and other disadvantaged Asian American groups can distinguish themselves from the larger panethnic group, the better the chances that their distinctive characteristics – and distinctive educational needs – will be recognized. Practically speaking, smaller groups such as Southeast Asian Americans benefit from belonging to larger, panethnic coalitions when it comes to political engagement, but they also benefit from educating others about the specific challenges that they face.

Although there is no simple solution to the problem of educational opportunity, better data on Asian American subgroups would help policymakers to do what's right. Given the very small numbers of Asian Americans in various subgroups in many regions, it is unlikely that governments and organizations would want to undergo the expense of collecting more detailed data about them. However, in California, Asian Americans are sufficiently numerous to make this more feasible, and students at University of California campuses have launched a campaign to collect better information. Dubbed "Count Me In!," the campaign calls for data to be collected on ten more subgroups, such as Bangladeshi and Hmong, and also for a separate Pacific Islander racial category (Lin 2007), which would reflect the most recent approach used by the U.S. Census.

College Admissions

Some suspect Asian American's perceived high levels of educational success have prompted elite college to impose quotas on the number of Asian Americans they admit. The existence of quotas is hard to prove, because many of these elite schools, being private, are able to limit access to their admissions data, but there is evidence that some of the most prestigious universities have expressed concern over the high percentage of Asian American students being admitted. Several studies have also found evidence that racial preferences in college admissions work against Asian Americans (Espenshade

Affirmative Action

Affirmative action is a complex issue which has become even more complicated because of important recent political and legal changes. Because of its complexity, there are widespread misunderstandings.

Before the notion of affirmative action emerged, there was a crusade for antidiscrimination measures. In the 1950s, efforts of African American activists blossomed, although not without great struggle. Lives were lost and bodies were shattered, but determined citizens eventually won landmark court and legislative victories. By the passage of the Voting Rights Act of 1965, civil rights advocates had compiled an impressive record of triumphs which would make it much more difficult for governments to discriminate against citizens on the basis of race or national origin.

Even as they were succeeding, however, some began to realize that a continuing problem was unsolved. Preventing future discrimination was important, but it did not necessarily do anything for victims of past discrimination. To help those individuals, it might be necessary to go beyond antidiscrimination measures and to take positive action to provide for equality of opportunity.

President Lyndon Johnson crystallized this view in an important speech at Howard University in 1965. Johnson declared:

> You do not take a person who, for years, has been hobbled by chains and liberate him, bring him up to the starting line of a race and then say, "you are free to compete with all the others," and still justly believe that you have been completely fair. . . . it is not enough just to open the gates of opportunity. All our citizens must have the ability to walk through those gates. . . . This is the next and the more profound stage of the battle for civil rights. We seek not just freedom but opportunity. We seek not just legal equity but human ability, not just equality as a right and a theory but equality as a fact and equality as a result. (*Public Papers of the Presidents of the United States* 1966)

While few denied that past discrimination could hurt one's future chances, there was sharp disagreement over how to remedy those wrongs. By the early 1970s, one proposal that gained support was to give some sort of extra recognition to those who had faced substantial disadvantages. For instance, in colleges, a student who was part of a racial minority might be able to be admitted with test scores that were lower than nonminority students who were not admitted. This has led some to be very critical of affirmative action.

By the early twenty-first century, critics had succeeded in getting the U.S. Supreme Court to curtail affirmative action sharply. Some states have also passed laws forbidding the use of race in admissions decisions in public universities. Supporters of affirmative action fear that this will cause racial inequality to increase.

This already complex issue becomes even more vexing when Asian Americans and Latinos are considered. In the 1960s and 1970s discussions of affirmative action usually focused on African Americans, but the growing presence of other ethnoracial minorities adds yet another dimension to this already-challenging issue.

et al. 2004; Espenshade and Chung 2005). To put it simply, these studies have found that, if race were not taken into account in admissions at elite universities, the percentage of Asian Americans admitted would likely increase significantly.

This is a complex, sensitive, and potentially divisive issue. The most prominent Asian American interest groups strongly support the continuation of affirmative action, as do many individual Asian Americans. Others, however, have opposed affirmative action policies, and, not surprisingly, opposition appears to be strongest when Asian Americans believe that their interests are at stake.

Differences over affirmative action are part of the politics of identity. Like so many issues, this one leads back to the question: who are the Asian Americans, and where do they fit along the color line? As we noted earlier in the book, Gary Okihiro captured the question nicely in an essay titled "Is Yellow Black or White?" Okihiro argues that "Yellow is emphatically neither white nor black; but insofar as Asians and Africans share a subordinate position to the master class, yellow is a shade of black, and black a shade of yellow" (Okihiro 1994, 34). From this point of view – shared by many Asian Americans on the political left – support for affirmative action is justified even if it does not always directly benefit Asian Americans. Some agree with Paul Ong, who has written that "it is also important to acknowledge that prejudices against APAs are more benign than those for other minority groups" (Ong 2000, 18).

Not everyone agrees with Okihiro's placement of Asian Americans along the color line, though. Some believe that differences with whites have been exaggerated. Eric Liu, for instance, has suggested that "Asian American identity as we know it may not last another generation" (Liu 1998, 82). Richard Alba and Victor Nee have argued that both the mainstream and newcomers adapt to each other, and they believe that intermarriage and other data strongly suggest a substantial degree of assimilation, although they do not believe that Asian Americans will soon be seen as "white" (Alba and Nee 2003).

More conservative commentators, such as Dinesh D'Souza, do see considerable differences between ethnoracial groups, but do not see such differences as justification for affirmative action. D'Souza does not deny that ending affirmative action would result in negative consequences for some groups, declaring that we should have "the courage to say that we are willing to live with these outcomes until blacks are able to raise their own standards to compete at the highest levels" (D'Souza 1995). If affirmative action programs survive, and if increasing numbers of Asian Americans are ineligible, it is possible that some may come to share D'Souza's position and see their interests as closer to whites' than to blacks'. However, as we explain in chapter 6, it is far from certain that this will happen.

What is clear, however, is that the image of Asian Americans as model minorities that have achieved high levels of educational success on their own, without extra governmental assistance, is a valuable weapon for conservatives in their attack against affirmative action (e.g. Rohrabacher 1989). It is possible that Asian Americans are merely pawns in the conservatives' attacks on affirmative action, which they would probably oppose in any case. But there is little question that some Asian Americans have joined in the assault, challenging affirmative action programs on the grounds that they harm Asian Americans, and calling for racial preferences to be replaced by programs which admit students based on merit alone. Of course, the definition of merit can vary widely from person to person.

In San Francisco, a group of Chinese American parents sued to change the admissions policy at prestigious Lowell High School. The San Francisco Unified School District (SFUSD) policy had been to limit each racial group to no more than 40 per cent of a school's population, but the city's growing numbers of Chinese Americans and declining numbers of African Americans meant increasing pressure on those numbers. A coalition of Latinos and Chinese Americans tried to negotiate more flexible caps, but the NAACP (a group founded to advance the rights of African Americans) opposed that, and the effort failed. Then, in the mid-1990s, a different group of Chinese American parents went to court and succeeded in ending the use of race in admissions considerations at Lowell. The number of African American and Latino students admitted then plummeted, while Asian American admissions increased (Hing 2001).

Some conservatives used the Lowell case to attack affirmative action, and drew the support of some of the parents (the plaintiffs) that had sued the SFUSD. However, other plaintiffs in the suit defended affirmative action, saying that they were only objecting to discrimination against Chinese Americans. A 1998 poll by the Chinese American Voter Education Committee (CAVEC) found similar divisions among Chinese American voters in San Francisco: while 45 per cent said the admissions quotas were a "bad idea," 32 per cent considered them to be a "good idea" (Ong 2000, 339).

More recently, Jian Li filed a complaint against Princeton University, in fall 2006. Li, a first-year student at Yale, had been rejected by Princeton, despite a perfect 2400 on his SAT, and 2390 (10 points below the top possible score) on his SAT II test. Li believed that his race had made it more difficult for him to be accepted at Princeton (Golden 2006).

More challenges from Asian Americans seem likely, if race continues to be a factor in admissions decisions. And, if challenges succeed in placing greater emphasis on academic factors (such as test scores and grades), it is likely that Asian American admissions will increase and those of other ethnoracial minorities will decline.

Not all opponents of existing admissions programs welcome this. Although some Asian Americans joined with conservatives in attacking the goal of diversity, those on the political left defended affirmative action and other policies that promoted ethnoracial diversity (Takagi 1998/1992). However, given the increasingly tenuous status of affirmative action programs (see text box), there was some uncertainty about the best way to defend it.

Two major alternatives have developed in recent years: class-based affirmative action, and school-based admissions. Class-based affirmative action focuses on providing assistance to individuals from economically disadvantaged circumstances. Under this approach, special considerations might be given for an individual who grew up in an impoverished household. This provides no guarantee that ethnoracial minorities will be the primary beneficiaries, but some supporters of affirmative action see this as a way of preserving some targeted programs in the face of an increasingly hostile political environment. Asian American subgroups such as Southeast Asians are likely to benefit, given high poverty levels and fairly low levels of educational attainment. However, more advantaged subgroups could perceive themselves as losers, if they believe that this makes it harder for them to gain admission to prestigious universities.

"Percentage admissions plans" have been adopted in some states. These programs guarantee admission to the top students at public high schools. Although this appears to be a merit-based program, it serves as a quasi-affirmative action plan because of the composition of high schools in America today. Tremendous disparities exist between high schools, with some filled with students from prosperous families while other schools have high percentages of students from poor families. Because of this, percentage admissions plans are likely to lead to guaranteed admissions for some hard-working students in high poverty areas. In a sense, this makes this program similar to class-based approaches. Also similar is the fact that this plan also provides no guarantee that ethnoracial minorities will be the primary beneficiaries, although some undoubtedly will benefit.

Because affirmative action continues to evolve – or, some would say, erode away – it is difficult to be confident about Asian Americans' perceptions. Over the past decade or so, however, polls have indicated that pluralities or majorities of Asian Americans support affirmative action, although their support is not as strong as that of African Americans or Latinos (Lien 2001, ch. 4). It is unclear if that support would weaken if large numbers of Asian Americans come to believe that they do not benefit from affirmative action.

English Language Learners

Another important educational policy area has addressed the issue of what kind of assistance is appropriate for students designated as English language learners (ELL).[1] Although views differ over the best approach, there is little question that school can be very difficult for new arrivals who know little or no English. Although there has not always been sympathy for helping these students, a landmark U.S. Supreme Court decision, *Lau* v. *Nichols* (1974), found "that unlawful discrimination has occurred . . . when public schools try to teach students only in a language that they cannot understand" (Schmidt, 2000, 2).

The stakes have risen with the increased testing in schools in recent years. States have increasingly required students to pass tests to graduate from high school, which can be very challenging for immigrant students, if they are required to take the tests in what is for them a foreign language. Even before the most recent federal testing requirements, a report by the U.S. Commission on Civil Rights found that Asian American students with limited English proficiency were not receiving the assistance needed for an equal educational opportunity (Kiang and Lee 1993). The expansion of high-stakes testing will make the issue of adequate language services even more important.

Asian American Studies Programs

One other very important educational policy area has been the development of Asian American Studies programs. These have played an important role in challenging stereotypical images of Asian Americans and in a variety of political efforts. While not all Asian American studies programs take the same approach, many have members who have been active in local communities, helping to provide the expertise and information that is valuable whenever a group is working for change. Despite the value of these programs, however, they have not always found it easy to become established.

Asian American Studies programs emerged out of the political and social ferment of the 1960s, with "the first programs . . . outcomes of the Third World Strikes at San Francisco State and the University of California, Berkeley in 1968–1969" (Endo and Wei 1988, 6). Many Asian American students found much in common with other students of color, and African American student activists encouraged them to join the movement, building a coalition which included groups such as the Asian American Political Alliance and the Third World Liberation Front (TWLF). The TWLF helped to lead a five-month-long student strike at San Francisco State, eventually producing a settlement which established the first ethnic studies school in the U.S. (Umemoto 1989).

Advocates of Asian American studies sought far more than simple additions to the curriculum. As with other ethnic studies programs, they worked to build the ethnic consciousness of Asian American students, engage those students in community activism, develop new scholarship and perspectives on Asian Americans, and generate resources that could help support the teaching of Asian American studies (Endo and Wei 1988, 7). As with other peoples of color, Asian Americans were largely absent from textbooks and lesson plans, and the establishment of formal programs helped to generate research and support scholars who would work to end that absence. Their analyses would examine history and contemporary society from the perspective of those who had been excluded (e.g. Takaki 1998), helping to correct the incomplete histories and analyses that schoolchildren had long been taught. In addition, they worked to move the analysis of race relations beyond the black–white paradigm that long dominated scholarly thought (Hune 1995; Aoki and Nakanishi 2001).

While existing programs have faced budget cuts and political attacks, Asian American studies programs have expanded in recent years. In the 1990s, students "east of California" fueled the "second wave" of the Asian American studies movement (Takeda 2001), leading to the establishment of Asian American Studies classes and programs at schools such as the University of Pennsylvania, Princeton, and Northwestern. The expansion of these programs is also aided by the increasing number of experts in Asian American studies, which can be seen in part in the bibliographies of books such as this one. ₁

Immigration Policy

Immigration policy has long been of great importance to Asian America. Bill Ong Hing has observed that immigration policy has been a key factor in determining the composition of the population (Hing 1993). For example, the Gentlemen's Agreement in the early twentieth century (which we describe in chapter 1) allowed Japanese immigrants to bring spouses, making it much easier for the Japanese to form families. At the same time, tougher restrictions on Chinese immigrants led to much slower growth of that population.

In chapter 1 we discussed how major immigration policies affected Asian Americans from about 1870 to 1965. Here we focus on developments in recent decades.

As we explained in chapter 1, the Immigration Act of 1965 (Hart–Celler Act) was a watershed for the U.S. With the end of the national origins quotas, and the introduction of a process which gave strong preference to family reunification, the 1965 act opened the door to massive new immigration from Asia and Latin America, and, in the last few decades, growing immigration from Africa. At first, small numbers of immigrants began to flow from countries where immigration had effectively been banned for many years. Then, as these migrants began to become established, they applied for immigration visas for their family members. Those family members, in turn, could apply for immigration visas for other family members, creating ever-growing numbers of applicants. In addition, the U.S. involvement in war in Southeast Asia led eventually to significant numbers of Southeast Asians begin admitted as refugees, putting them in position to one day apply for visas for their relatives to immigrate. Finally, economic and political upheaval helped fuel illegal immigration, much of it from Mexico, where the long unguarded border made it easier to enter undetected.

By the early twenty-first century, one of the consequences of the 1965 reform was that a majority of Asian Americans were foreign-born. This has in turn raised the importance of immigration for Asian Americans, many of whom have relatives overseas who would like to immigrate to the U.S.

Another consequence was that there was a growing backlash against immigration. Organized interests claimed that it was only unauthorized immigration that they opposed, but many Americans appeared to hold negative feelings toward immigration and immigrants more broadly. By the end of the first decade of the twenty-first century immigration policy had become a highly contested issue.

Reflecting the deep divisions, Congress struggled unsuccessfully to pass an immigration reform bill. Although there were strong disagreements, one point had widespread support: the current system was not working. Exactly *what* was not working was also the source of deep disagreement, however, which made it very difficult to craft an agreement that could satisfy different viewpoints.

A good example was a bill that emerged in the U.S. Senate in 2007. The bill, titled The Comprehensive Immigration Reform Act of 2007 (S. 1639), was the product of difficult negotiations between conservatives and liberals, requiring considerable compromise on both sides. One of the most important provisions of the proposal law would offer amnesty to those who were here illegally, through the creation of a new "Z" visa. Many conservatives have been bitterly opposed to this. On the other hand, the bill proposed a dramatic change in immigration preferences. The old family preference system (see figure 8.4) would be largely swept aside, to be replaced by a new point system that greatly favored those with greater skills, education, and knowledge of English (see figure 8.5). Many immigrant groups insisted on changes in the point system. In addition, the new law would make it difficult for newly legalized immigrants to become citizens. The proposal required them to pay fines that could reach four or five thousand dollars, and heads of households would have to return to their native country to apply. This too was opposed by many immigrants.

The amnesty provision was most important to Mexican Americans, but it still would have affected about a million Asian Americans. The best evidence suggested that Mexican migrants make up close to 60 per cent, and Latin Americans as a whole approximately 85 per cent of unauthorized migrants, while Asians make up only about 10 per cent (Passel 2005).

The changes in immigration preferences were of somewhat greater concern for Asian Americans than the amnesty provisions, since a higher percentage of Asian immigrants come through that route. The new system would have essentially abolished the family preference categories, replacing it with a small number of points given for family ties. In addition, the "cut-off date" – the date for the transition – would have been in 2005, which meant that hundreds of thousands of Asians who had applied after then would fall under the new system rather than the old, and would presumably no longer be eligible for immigration visas.

Not surprisingly, Asian American groups strongly opposed the provisions that would dramatically reduce the number of visas granted for family reunification, while supporting the provision providing a path for legalization of unauthorized migrants. At the same time, they criticized the provisions that made it difficult and expensive for the unauthorized to naturalize (e.g. "Organizations Call for Historic National APA Mobilization" 2007).

Ultimately, views on immigration were so deeply divided that the bill might never have had much of a chance. Some features were bitterly opposed by immigration opponents, and other features were heavily criticized by

Current immigration quota categories

Family preference categories	minimum of 226,000
Employment-based	minimum of 140,000

In addition, there are 55,000 "diversity lottery" visas, plus visas for those seeking asylum, refugees, and other categories. For those who wish to do temporary work or to travel in the U.S., non-immigrant visas are issued. Non-immigrant visas are also used by foreign students who will be studying in America.

Family preference categories*

Category	Category includes	Quota
Immediate relatives	Spouses of U.S. citizens; unmarried minor children (under 21) of a U.S. citizen; parents of adult U.S. citizens (21 or older)	No quota
Family preference (1)	Adult (21 or older) unmarried sons and unmarried daughters of U.S. citizens	23,400 plus unused 4th preference visas
Family preference (2)	2A: Spouses of green card holders; unmarried minor children (under 21) of green card holders 2B: Adult (21 or older) unmarried sons and unmarried daughters of green card holders	114,200 plus unused 1st preference visas; at least 77% must go to individuals in category 2A
Family preference (3)	Married children of U.S. citizens	23,400 plus unused 1st and 2nd preference visas
Family preference (4)	Siblings of adult (21 or older) U.S. citizens	65,000 plus unused 1st, 2nd, and 3rd preference visas

*This is a partial list. There are many special categories not listed.

Source: U.S. Citizenship and Immigration Services, 8 U.S.C. 1151 and 8 U.S.C. 1153; available at www.uscis.gov.

Figure 8.4 *Immigration categories and quotas.*

immigration supporters. The bill died, but immigration reform remains a priority for many Asian Americans.

Language Policy

With such a high percentage of immigrants, Asian Americans are strongly affected by language policies. Concerns here go well beyond issues of convenience or comfort. The ability to converse in a language you understand can have a critical influence on your health and welfare. Access to a language you understand can also make participation in politics much easier. Because this issue has become so emotionally charged, it is useful first to review some important points we have discussed earlier, before looking in more detail at language policy and Asian Americans.

Most importantly, the dominance of English does not appear to be in question. As we observed in chapter 7, the evidence strongly suggests that immigrants have an overwhelming desire to have their children learn English, and to learn English themselves, if they are able. Furthermore, there is much evidence suggesting that it is not English but other languages that are in danger, as the children of immigrants often prefer to speak English, and the third generation (the grandchildren of immigrants) often speaks only English. While the huge pool of Spanish speakers might make it more possible for the

Employment points

20	Specialty occupation
16	High-demand occupation
8	STEM (science, technology, engineering, mathematics) or health occupation
6	Job offer or recommendation from a U.S. employer
2	For each year of work for a U.S. company (10 points maximum)
3	Worker's age from 25 to 39 years

Education points

20	MD, MBA, or other graduate degree
16	Bachelor's degree
10	Associate's degree
6	High school diploma or GED
8	Degree in STEM or health occupation
8	Completed apprenticeship program
5	Completed Perkins vocational education program

English and civics points

15	Native English speaker or has a score of 75 or higher in TOEFL (English proficiency test)
10	Has a score of 60-74 in TOEFL
6	Pass citizenship tests for English and civics

Can be applied if applicant has 55 points from categories above:

Extended family Points

8	Adult children of a U.S. citizen
6	Adult child of a U.S. permanent resident
4	Sibling of a U.S. citizen or permanent resident

> *Note:* This bill, which died in the Senate in the summer of 2007, would have dramatically changed the U.S. immigration policy so that the greatest preference would be given to applicants with needed skills, rather than giving most visas to applicants with relatives in the U.S. Under the Senate bill, those with the highest point totals (maximum of 100) would get permanent-residence visas.
>
> *Source: New York Times* graphic, June 5, 2007.
>
> **Figure 8.5** *Immigration point system proposed in S.1639 (Senate Immigration Reform Bill).*

second and third generation to continue to speak it, this is not the case for Asian Americans. Asian immigrants speak many different languages, and none is nearly as widely used as Spanish. Fluency in Asian languages is not likely to survive to the third generation.

Nevertheless, language issues are important to immigrants, and often to their children. Although the children of immigrants have long been called upon to serve as translators for their parents, there are many cases where this is undesirable – for example, doctor's appointments, where even adults would be challenged to find the proper translation for specialized medical terms. In addition, there are times when it is inappropriate for a child to be the first to learn of a parent's medical condition. School conferences are another situation where it may be very undesirable to rely on a child to translate what a teacher is telling a parent (although some students might wish that they could).

Asian Americans have tried to influence language policy in two ways: expanding access to translation services, and protecting the right to use one's preferred language. The first is often of more practical importance, but the second can sometimes have concrete consequences as well.

For example, the organization Asian Americans for Civil Rights and Equality has pushed for the California legislature to pass bills that would require translation for some loans, permit pharmacies to translate labels on prescriptions, and allow English language learners to "take standards-based achievement tests in their primary language" ("AACRE 2007 Legislative Agenda" n.d.). These examples illustrate the practical importance of language issues. Translation of prescription labels, for instance, can be enormously important, since mistakes with medication can have serious, sometimes fatal, health consequences. For students, appropriate language instruction can be essential, as we have noted above.

Several Asian American advocacy groups have joined with others to work for language access at the ballot box, especially through the reauthorization of the Voting Rights Act (VRA). The Asian American Legal Defense and Education Fund (AALDEF) compiled a report documenting the benefits from a provision of the Voting Rights Act (known as "Section 203") that required translators when certain conditions exist.[2] The AALDEF report also described continuing problems faced by non-English speakers attempting to vote, and how the use of federal monitors, as authorized by the VRA, has helped to reduce these problems ("Asian Americans and the Voting Rights Act" 2006).

One of the most controversial areas of language policy is "English only" laws. There are a wide range of these laws and proposals, from "the purely symbolic" which simply state that English is the official language, to those which try to prevent state agencies from using any language other than English (Schmidt 2000, 28–30). The symbolic statutes are not a major concern, but ones that would restrict the use of languages other than English could have serious consequences for many Asian Americans and others who struggle in English. Not surprisingly, Asian American groups have been among those actively opposing these more restrictive measures. The Asian American Justice Center, for example, has collected a variety of materials to help community groups battle proposals for English-only laws ("Language Access Publications and Materials" n.d.).

Social Welfare

As we have explained, the model minority image obscures the fact that many Asian Americans are struggling. As we noted above, many refugees in particular continue long after their arrival to cope with the consequences of warfare or other traumatic incidents that caused them to flee to America. Because of that, many Asian American groups work on programs that aid disadvantaged Americans.

Programs to aid low-income Asian Americans have vocal critics. In recent years, this criticism has sometimes overlapped with criticism of immigration, leading to legislation which has had a big impact on some Asian Americans.

Many Americans are critical of government assistance for immigrants, believing that those coming to the U.S. should not expect a handout. In 1996, acting on this sentiment, Congress passed two bills that dramatically limited and changed the benefits that newcomers could receive: the Personal

Responsibility and Work Opportunity Reconciliation Act (PRWORA), and the Illegal Immigration Reform and Immigrant Responsibility Act (Fragomen 1996). We do not have the space to cover all of the PRWORA's sweeping changes in government assistance programs, so we will focus on provisions that were particularly important to Asian Americans.

One of the most drastic changes in the PRWORA would have cut off most benefits for non-citizens, with the exception of refugees and asylees (Fujiwara 1998). Elderly recipients who had been receiving Supplemental Security Income (SSI) would have seen their benefits slashed, if they were not citizens. Given that they were already living in poverty, and had few prospects of find-ing work, elimination of their SSI would likely have been devastating.

Asian American groups joined a broad coalition of religious, civil rights, and other organizations to oppose the PRWORA. Although they were unsuccessful, they found considerable support for easing the most severe provisions, and in 1997 Congress restored SSI for non-citizens who had been receiving it prior to the passage of the PRWORA (Fremstad 2002; Fujiwara 1998).

However, for those arriving after August 22, 1996, sweeping limits remained. Most "qualified aliens" (essentially, those who were in the country legally) were barred from receiving most federal aid for five years (Horn 2006), while SSI and food stamps were prohibited until they became citizens (Fix and Haskins 2002). Exceptions were made for refugees, Amerasians, asylees, Cuban and Haitian entrants, veterans, and a few other groups, who were allowed to receive SSI and food stamps for seven years (Fremstad 2004; USDA n.d.), at which point they would presumably be eligible for naturalization.

Although the principles of the PRWORA sounded reasonable – require recipients to work so that assistance would be temporary, not lifelong – they ran into the complexities of real life. For some Asian Americans, an inter-related set of obstacles make it very difficult to become self-supporting. For example, a study of the Wisconsin Works (W-2) program found that

> More than 90 per cent of Hmong respondents read little or no English and over 70 per cent have little or no literacy in Hmong. More than 60 per cent have no formal education and an additional 30 per cent have attended only adult education classes including English as a Second Language. . . .
>
> Nearly 95 per cent do not have job skills in any of the employment areas for which W-2 can provide training . . .
>
> Most Hmong aid recipients cannot communicate directly with their W-2 caseworker and fully 67 per cent cannot reach their caseworker by phone. Furthermore, 87 per cent of respondents have difficulty understanding the written materials they receive from W-2 agencies. (Moore and Selkowe 1999, ii)

Although some have argued that Americans should not be obligated to respond to the problems immigrants bring with them, it should be noted that the Hmong are here as a result of U.S. actions. Recruited during the Vietnam War because they were valued fighters, they had to flee for their lives when the U.S. pulled out of Southeast Asia. Because they had been allies of the

U.S., rescuing American airmen and fighting communist forces, many Hmong found themselves at great risk if they stayed in Laos, so they made their way to America, where they struggled to adapt to a profoundly different way of life.

Little wonder then that many Asian American organizations have been working to moderate the effects of the PWRORA. For example, groups such as the Southeast Asian Resource Action Center (SEARAC) have been supporting efforts to extend the 7-year limit on SSI benefits for aliens. The unique history of the Hmong and U.S. forces has generated more support than other groups are likely to garner. For example, in 2000, bipartisan support in Congress led to the passage of the Hmong Veterans' Naturalization Act (HVNA), which eased naturalization for Hmong veterans and their spouses by waiving the English language requirement and easing the civics test requirement ("Changes to the Hmong Veterans' Naturalization Act of 2000" 2001). However, many Hmong Americans are not covered by the HVNA, nor are other Southeast Asian Americans who are likely to struggle with citizenship requirements.

Race, Public Policy, and Intersectionality

Many public policies highlight the relevance of intersectionality, that is, the interaction of other kinds of social categories with race and ethnicity. Asian Americans who fit into other socially constructed groups that suffer discrimination may find themselves doubly disadvantaged. Sexual orientation and gender are two of the most prominent categories that can interact with race to result in greater inequality.

Gay, Lesbian, Bisexual, and Transgendered (GLBT) Issues

Intersectionality is clearly evident in the political concerns of the GLBT community. For example, while all Asian Americans are likely to encounter issues of race, gay or lesbian Asian Americans may also have to deal with the fact that some Asian Americans hold derogatory views of gays and lesbians. At the same time, some white gays and lesbians can harbor prejudices toward Asian Americans. Asian Americans who are gay, lesbian, bisexual, or transgendered can suffer a double discrimination, based on both race and sexual orientation.

The same-sex marriage debate illustrates this well. Some Asian Americans strongly oppose same-sex marriage (Shore 2004) – and some of them have reported that they in turn have been the targets for racially based attacks from those who favor same-sex marriage (Soo 2004). On the other hand, other Asian Americans have encouraged their communities to be more accepting (e.g. Rhee 2006), and a wide range of Asian American groups have filed legal briefs in support of same-sex marriage (Villaroman 2007).

The intersection of race and sexual orientation is complex. GLBT Asian Americans will not always find that their different communities are in agreement, or they may have to choose between competing priorities. For example, Glenn Magpantay, a co-chair of the Gay Asian and Pacific Islander Men of New York (GAPIMNY) and staff attorney for the Asian American Legal Defense and Education Fund, has argued the racial concerns should take precedence: "While gay APA families need the protection that same-sex marriage would offer, such rights are elusive and more urgent issues face the community, such as immigrants' rights, racism, media defamation, and visibility" (Magpantay 2006). Magpantay is not arguing for support of Asian American groups that oppose same-sex marriage, of course, but rather conceding that issues of race are more pressing than some issues of concern to GLBT Asian Americans. Others, however, would navigate that particular intersection of race and sexual orientation differently.

Gender, Immigration, Labor, Social Class

Other examples of intersectionality can also be found in issues dealing with women and the workplace. Some of the most powerless individuals are those who face the cumulative effects of disadvantages stemming from gender, immigration status, workforce position, and income level. Asian American activists have been increasingly engaged with these issues, often with the institutional support of the scholarly community.

For example, UCLA houses the Center for Labor Research and Education, where students gathered information for a book on Asian Americans in the garment industry (*Sweatshop Slaves* 2006). In 2002, they opened the Downtown Labor Center in Los Angeles, in part "to provide more access to unions and working people to the resources of the Labor Center" (Cervantes 2007, 11). Many of the working people served are immigrants.

Asian American women have been active in international efforts to improve conditions for working women around the world, many of whom are desperately poor. With economic globalization, corporations increasingly shift manufacturing facilities to areas where labor costs are lowest, and women often make up a substantial part of the workforce. Often, these women are also migrants, crossing national borders in search of work (Louie 1997). The Asian Immigrant Women Advocates (AIWA) is one of the most notable groups that has worked to organize immigrant women, providing leadership training and educational services intended to help workers advocate effectively for themselves (Wong and Hayash 1989; Louie 1997). Based in Oakland, California, the AIWA helped lead the four-year boycott of designer Jessica McClintock, which succeeded in winning agreements where designers pledged to provide stronger protections for workers (Lien 2001, 215).

Coalition-building is an important part of this effort (Kim 1993). Actually forging alliances can be daunting, however, as the reality of diversity creates many challenges. Women in different socioeconomic positions can have very different policy concerns:

[W]hile sexual orientation, sexual harassment, redistribution of household labor, and reproductive choice are important issues to all Asian American women, limited English-speaking immigrant women in low-wage, unskilled and semi-skilled employment . . . are typically more concerned about wages, benefits, and working conditions than about the issues highest on the agenda for middle-class Asian and other women. (Kim 1993, 255).

This intersection of gender, labor, and race raises complex issues that make coalition-building a sensitive challenge.

Comparing Policy Outcomes

What makes some policy efforts more successful than others? While we do not have space to give an extensive answer, we use three similar cases to suggest some reasons. In all three examples, groups have tried to rectify wrongs committed during World War II, but their degree of success has varied widely.

Righting a Wrong. Asian Americans and the Movement for Redress

Perhaps the most politically important Asian American social movement has been the effort to win reparations – usually known as "redress"[3] – for the World War II internment of Japanese Americans.[4] The redress effort was part of a larger movement to rectify a number of wartime injustices. For instance, over twenty-five years after the end of the war, Executive Order 9066 (which provided the legal authorization for the removal of Japanese Americans) was still legally in force. In addition, key Supreme Court decisions had upheld the internment, and they too had never been overturned.

The civil rights movement of the 1960s helped to inspire the redress effort, and it was the third-generation Japanese Americans (known as Sansei) who provided the momentum for this movement.[5] Although many Nisei still seethed with anger at the injustice that had been done to them, there was often a feeling that it might be better to let the bad memories fade away.

The lead group in the redress movement was the Japanese American Citizens League (JACL), but the movement extended well beyond that. In addition to numerous groups formed to work specifically on redress, there was ferment on college campuses and high schools, as Sansei researched the history of the camps and began to educate their classmates about the imprisonment. Former camp residents started to publish books on their experiences, and scholarly works appeared, exposing the government deliberations that led to the relocation orders.

By the mid-1970s, the movement began to swell. A milestone in the redress movement occurred in 1976, when the JACL national convention "unanimously adopted a resolution calling for monetary reparations" (Maki et al. 1999, 75). Another important development was the decision to support a commission. Redress was not an issue that could wait, as many internees were elderly, and a commission meant delays in the effort to enact legislation. Many

Creating a Wrong: The Imprisonment of Japanese Americans

Japan's surprise attack on Pearl Harbor on December 7, 1941, helped fuel bitter prejudice against Japanese Americans. First a curfew was placed on Japanese Americans, and
then they were ordered to "relocation centers," prison camps ringed by barbed wire
and armed guards.

However, although federal agents had arrested over 2,000 Japanese American community leaders by February 1942 (Hatamiya 1993, 11), FBI director J. Edgar Hoover saw
no need for mass arrests of Japanese Americans. Furthermore, Army Intelligence
had sent a memo to Secretary of War Henry Stimson declaring that "widespread sabo-
tage by Japanese is not expected" (Daniels 1981, 28). Most notably, General Delos
C. Emmons, the military governor in Hawai'i, saw little need for mass evacuation of
Japanese Americans, seeing them as no threat to the critical military bases there
(Melendy 1984, 158; Daniels 1981, 73; Chuman 1976, 146).

The "leading naval intelligence specialist on the Japanese Americans," Lt.
Commander Kenneth D. Ringle, also doubted that they posed a risk. Early in 1941, he
had overseen a break-in at the Japanese consulate in Los Angeles, where they discovered evidence that Japanese officials considered Japanese Americans – both immigrants
and the children of the immigrants – to be "'cultural traitors' who were not to be relied
on for anything important" (Daniels 1988, 210–12).

In the press and the general public, however, the reaction was hysterical. A *Los
Angeles Times* editorial screamed "A viper is nonetheless a viper wherever the egg is
hatched – so a Japanese American, born of Japanese parents – grows up to be a
Japanese, not an American." The *San Diego Union* claimed that "In Hawaii . . . treach-
ery by residents . . . has played an important part in the success of Japanese attacks"
(quoted in Takaki 1998, 388). Walter Lippman, perhaps the most influential columnist
at that time, "called for the mass removal of Japanese Americans" from the West Coast,
and the American Legion called for Japanese Americans to be placed in concentration
camps (Takaki 1998, 388; Chuman 1976, 148).

Although initially reluctant, Secretary of War Henry L. Stimson and Assistant Secretary
of War John J. McCloy became key supporters of mass evacuation, outweighing the
opposition of civil libertarians such as United States Attorney General Francis Biddle.
Even people such as future U.S. Supreme Court Chief Justice Earl Warren, who was
later seen as a champion of civil liberties, came to support the evacuation (Daniels 1981,
50–1; Petersen 1971, 79–81).

Some Japanese Americans resisted. In Portland, Oregon, Minoru Yasui defied the
curfew order, believing it to be unconstitutional. "On 28 March 1942, the first day the
curfew was in force, Yasui walked around the streets of Portland for hours trying to get
himself arrested," but finally had to go to a police station, where he "insisted that he
be detained" (S. Chan 1991, 136). Gordon Hirabayashi, a University of Washington student, refused to obey the evacuation order and went to the local FBI office to be
arrested. Fred Korematsu was arrested as he was staying with his fiancée in the evacuated area in San Leandro, California.

Yasui, Hirabayashi, and Korematsu all challenged legality of the evacuation orders
(Maki et al. 1999, 46; Yamamoto et al. 2001, 174–5). Their cases made it to the U.S.
Supreme Court (see table 8.1), which ruled against Hirabayashi and Yasui on the same
day in 1943. The Court ruled against Korematsu in December 1944, on a sharply divided
6–3 vote, in which minority opinions strongly condemned the internment as racist in
nature. To help the government's case, Justice Department officials concealed critical
facts which would have severely undermined their claim that evacuation was justified
by military necessity (H. Kim 1994, 134–6). It would be almost forty years before the
truth was revealed.

TABLE 8.1 Four landmark internment cases

Minoru "Min" Yasui	March 28, 1942 Went to police station in Portland, Oregon, to demand his arrest to challenge curfew order.	Jan. 1983 Filed *coram nobis* petition with District Court in Portland.
	Nov. 16, 1942 District Court judge ruled the curfew order was unconstitutional as applied to US citizens but that Yasui renounced US citizenship by having worked for Japanese Consulate.	Jan. 26, 1984 District Court judge vacated (that is, nullified) Yasui's conviction but dismissed his *coram nobis* petition. Because this ruling did not acknowledge government's wartime suppression of evidence, Yasui appealed to the Ninth Court of Appeals.
	June 21, 1943 Citing Hirabayashi case issued on the same day, U.S. Supreme Court held the curfew order constitutional (320 U.S. 115). It also returned the case to District Court for resentencing on citizenship issue. Yasui eventually served nine months in prison.	Nov. 1986 Before the Court of Appeals ruled, Yasui died, ending the legal cause of this lawsuit.
Gordon Hirabayashi	May 16, 1942 Appeared at FBI office in Seattle to challenge exclusion order.	Jan. 1983 Filed *coram nobis* petition with District Court in Seattle.
	Oct. 20, 1942 Judge ordered the jury to convict Hirabayashi on failure to register for exclusion and curfew violation.	Feb. 10, 1986 District Court judge granted a writ of *coram nobis* on exclusion conviction but not on curfew violation conviction (627 F. Supp. 1445 (W. D. Wash. 1986)).
	June 21, 1943 U.S. Supreme Court unanimously held the curfew order constitutional (but did not rule on exclusion order) (320 U.S. 81).	Sep. 24, 1987 Ninth Court of Appeals reversed District Court's decision on curfew violation and remanded (that is, returned) the case to the District Court (828 F. 2d. 591 (9th Cir. 1987)). Jan. 12, 1988 District Court vacated Hirabayashi's curfew violation conviction.
Fred Korematsu	May 30, 1942 Arrested in San Leandro, California, for remaining in the designated evacuated area (to stay with Italian American fiancée). Korematsu then decided to fight.	Jan. 19, 1983 In the first of the trio *coram nobis* cases, filed petition with District Court in San Francisco.
	Sep. 8, 1942 District Court judge convicted him for violation of	Nov. 10, 1983 In the first of the three cases, District Court

TABLE 8.1 *continued*

	exclusion order and sentenced him to five years' probation. Dec. 18, 1944 U.S. Supreme Court, in a 6–3 decision, upheld the exclusion order (323 U.S. 214).	Judge granted a writ of error *coram nobis*. Korematsu's conviction was now vacated. This opinion of the court was issued in a written opinion later on April 19, 1984 (584 F. Supp. 1406 (N.D. Cal. 1984)).
Mitsue Endo	July 12, 1942 Filed a habeas corpus petition in San Francisco District Court from an assembly center through a lawyer who picked her as an ideal plaintiff to challenge internment. July 3, 1943 District Court dismissed Endo's petition. Dec. 17, 1944 War Department announced that Japanese internees may go back to restriction areas on the West Coast (the process began on January 2, 1945). Dec. 18, 1944 US Supreme Court unanimously ruled that War Relocation Authority had no authority to detain Endo and she should be released (but did not judge on constitutionality of Congress and president's involvement in conducting internment) (323 U.S. 283).	Since the 1944 Endo case was decided in her favor, even though superficially, no *coram nobis* petition was filed.

Sources: Complied by authors from Daniels (1988), Irons (1989b), Maki et al. (1999), Niiya (2001), Yamamoto et al. (2001).

experienced activists and officials saw a commission as important, however, because it could help educate the public about the imprisonment and its effects. Perhaps most importantly, Senator Daniel Inouye (D-Hawai'i), a member of the powerful Senate Appropriations Committee, felt that a commission was needed. Inouye's support was necessary if a redress bill was to have a chance of passage, and those pushing for redress felt they had little choice but to accept his suggestion.

Once again, the politics of identity was important. Members of Congress would likely be unwilling to support any redress bill that did not have strong support from Japanese American Representatives and Senators. For the Japanese American members of Congress, however, a redress bill presented a difficult dilemma. Like all Asian Americans, they had worked hard to be viewed as fully "American," but this bill could give the impression that they were working only for the interests of their ethnoracial group. On the mainland, representatives Norman Mineta and Robert Matsui (both Democrats from California) had to be able to appeal to large numbers of non-Asians in order to get elected, because no mainland district came close to being majority Asian Americans, and Japanese Americans made up an even smaller percentage of Mineta's and Matsui's constituents. For them, a commission was particularly valuable. If an independent commission reported that redress was justified, Mineta and Matsui could point to the report as evidence that redress had broad-based support, rather than being a special benefit being pushed only by their own ethnoracial group (Maki et al. 1999, 86–7).

In the summer of 1980, a bill was passed creating the Commission on Wartime Relocation and Internment of Civilians (CWRIC). Senator Inouye insisted that there be only one Japanese American on the committee, because if the committee's work was to win widespread support, it would have to be seen as reflecting a broad range of views, not just those of Japanese Americans (Maki et al. 1999, 96). In the second half of 1981, the commission traveled around the country, hearing testimony from former internees, and generating news coverage that helped to publicize the injustice of the internment. In addition, "the CWRIC documented the extensive economic and intangible losses of income and property incurred by Japanese Americans" (Maki et al. 1999, 111). In February 1983, the CWRIC unanimously agreed that the incarceration of Japanese Americans had been unjustified, and in June 1983 it recommended that Congress pass a resolution apologizing for the imprisonment, and that survivors receive $20,000 in compensation (Maki et al. 1999, 112).

In the next few years, challenges to the internment grew more focused. A challenge to the three critical Supreme Court cases, *Korematsu*, *Hirabayashi*, and *Yasui*, was fueled by a fortuitous discovery by researcher Peter Irons, who uncovered conclusive proof of government misconduct. Irons's research produced a memo written by Justice Department attorneys Edward Ennis and John L. Burling in 1943, in which Ennis and Burling urged solicitor general Charles Fahey to tell the Supreme Court of government intelligence that concluded that Japanese Americans posed no threat. Instead, Fahey told the court that he fully agreed with claims that the Japanese Americans were a danger to American security (Irons 1983, 1989a). Because the government's representative had knowingly misled the court, it raised the possibility of a rare legal appeal, known as a writ of error *coram nobis*. *Coram nobis* (meaning "before us") petitions request that criminal convictions based on government errors be overturned. The three appeals were heard by three different judges, two of whom were seen as sympathetic to civil rights concerns, while the third was not. In the first two courts, the *coram nobis* petitions were granted, and Fred Korematsu's and Gordon Hiabayashi's convictions were vacated (Irons 1989b). In the third, the judge ruled against Minori Yasui. Yasui appealed, but died before the appeal could be heard (Irons 1989a).

By the mid-1980s, prospects for redress were improving. Backers worked to build a broad coalition, enlisting the American Civil Liberties Union, the American Bar Association, the Anti-Defamation League of B'nai B'rith (ADL), and the National Association for the Advancement of Colored People (NAACP). A wide range of governmental, labor, political, professional, religious, and veterans organizations also endorsed redress proposals, including the National Education Association, the AFL-CIO, the American Legion, and the United Methodist Church (Hatamiya 1993, ch. 10, 199–203).

Although redress was gaining ground in Congress, it faced strong opposition in the White House, and President Ronald Reagan was being advised to veto the bill.[6] Redress supporters launched a campaign to convince Reagan to sign the bill, enlisting individuals who were able to speak with Reagan directly – such as New Jersey Governor Thomas Kean – and also convinced some influential conservatives to support the bill. By the spring of 1988, Reagan decided to support redress, and Congress passed the bill in early August of that year. On August 10, 1988, President Reagan signed the bill into law (Maki et al. 1999, 195).

A number of questions still remained about eligibility and funding for redress. Passage of the bill did not guarantee funds, which had to be approved in a separate bill, known as an appropriations bill. In 1989, when the appropriations bill came before Congress, Japanese American members of Congress played a key role. Senators Daniel Inouye and Masayuki "Spark" Matsunaga, both Democrats from Hawai'i, helped influence uncertain Senators. Inouye had been reluctant to play a prominent role, fearing that it could be seen as no more than an effort to help co-ethnics, but now he made emotional appeals for the funding of the redress bill. Inouye, a member of the all-Japanese American 442 Regimental Combat Team, was a decorated veteran who had been critically wounded in World War II. He told Senators about his experience fighting alongside other 442 members who had volunteered even as they and their families were imprisoned behind barbed wire, and of those who had never returned from the war. The Senate voted overwhelmingly to approve funding. Funding for redress was approved by both houses of Congress and signed into law by President George H. W. Bush on November 21, 1989 (Maki et al. 1999, 206–10). An effort over two decades in the making had finally come to fruition.

Japanese Latin American Redress

A lesser-known effort was for redress for Japanese Latin Americans. During World War II, 2,264 Japanese families living in thirteen Latin American countries (80 per cent of them from Peru) were moved to the United States under the claim of military necessity. The government interned Japanese Latin Americans in Department of Justice camps, most notably in Crystal City, Texas. Approximately 865 of them were sent to Japan in 1942 and 1943 in exchange ships that were arranged to return Japanese diplomats and citizens from the allied countries. In fact, one of the motivations of the U.S. government to bring Japanese Latin Americans to America was to facilitate the exchange arrangement and bring back Americans stranded in Japan and China by the war.

When the war ended, the U.S. government deported more than 900 interned Japanese Latin Americans to Japan on the grounds that they had entered the United States illegally. This was an outlandish rationale, since the U.S. government had brought them to the U.S. against their will, and their passports had been confiscated prior to their landing. Of the 365 Japanese Peruvians who fought deportation, many succeeded, but only about 100 were able to return to their original countries in Latin America (Campaign for Justice n.d.; CWRIC 1983 [1997], 305–14; Niiya 2001, 229–30).

Although the internment of Japanese Latin Americans was noted in the 1983 report of the Commission on Wartime Relocation and Internment of Civilians (CWRIC), the redress bill made Japanese Latin Americans ineligible for compensation. Eligibility was limited to Japanese Americans who were citizens or permanent residents at the time of internment. As it became clear to Japanese Latin Americans that most were not covered by the 1988 act, they formed a group called Campaign for Justice, and filed a class action lawsuit in 1996 (*Mochizuki et al. v. United States*). The lawsuit ended with a 1998 settlement that called for a government apology and $5,000 compensation. However, only 145 individuals were paid before the redress fund ran out. Some Japanese Peruvians were not satisfied and filed individual lawsuits against the U.S. government. In order to seek full compensation and acknowledgement of wartime violation of domestic and international law by the U.S. government, Campaign for Justice then pushed legislation to establish a federal commission similar to CWRIC (Campaign for Justice, n.d.; Maki et al. 1999, 222; Yamamoto et al. 2001, 428–30). A bill to do so was again introduced in Congress in February 2007, but, as of this writing, has not passed.

Filipino Veterans

Another policy effort tied to wartime actions was the Filipino veterans' quest for equity in recognition and benefits. During World War II, two to three hundred thousand Filipinos fought for the U.S. against Japan in the Pacific theater, but did so under a confusing legal status that generated problems that persist to this day. In 1898, when the Philippines became a part of the United States, Filipinos had been deemed U.S. nationals but not citizens. This meant that Filipinos had to pledge allegiance to the United States even though they were not given full citizenship rights (such as sending voting members to the U.S. Congress). Because of their status as U.S. nationals, President Franklin Roosevelt inducted the Philippines Commonwealth Army into the U.S. Armed Services n July 1941 (Vergara 1997; Nakano 2000).

Japan invaded the Philippines immediately after its attack on Pearl Harbor in December 1941. Filipino soldiers served alongside Americans, and were part of the infamous Bataan "death march" in April 1942. Many other Filipinos joined the guerrilla war against Japan. After the surrender of Japan in August 1945, the Philippines became an independent country in July 1946.

Filipino soldiers believed that their military service and their loss of thousands of lives to the war would be recognized with honors equal to those given to U.S. soldiers. In fact, one U.S. veteran testified in Congress that he remembered President Roosevelt boosting the morale of Filipino soldiers by promising to recognize them as members of the U.S. armed forces (Vergara 1997, 163). The U.S. Congress, however, broke that promise in 1946, with the Rescission Acts.[7] As a result, the sacrifices of Filipino veterans were not defined as active service, and their veteran benefits were set at the rate of half those of U.S. veterans.

Why Congress passed such a measure is a question that still needs to be investigated. Perhaps members of Congress at that time were ignorant of the contribution of Filipino soldiers in pushing back the Japanese military in the Pacific theater (Vergara 1997, 166), or perhaps the U.S. government was unwilling to send funds off to the Philippines, which was about to become an independent country (Nakano 2000).

What seems likely is that Congress's discrimination against Filipino veterans was influenced by racial thinking. Non-US citizens in European countries who fought in World War II as members of the U.S. armed forces were eligible for full benefits at the same level as U.S. veterans (Vergara 1997, 171–2). Filipino veterans living in the Philippines had protested this unfair treatment since the enactment of the Rescission Acts, But, starting in 1990, they were able to exert some pressure from within the United States, thanks to a special provision included in the 1990 immigration law that made Filipino veterans eligible to naturalize as Americans without having lived in the United States. Taking advantage of this provision, approximately 24,000 Filipino veterans immigrated to the United States – most of them more than seventy years old and with few sources of income (Nakano 2000; American Coalition for Filipino Veterans n.d.).

Like many other movements for civil rights and racial justice, these Filipino veterans and their advocates have engaged in various forms of action: opening websites, holding rallies, writing to the media, and contacting public officials. They formed the American Coalition for Filipino Veterans (ACFV) to press their cause, and they lobbied members of Congress for a repeal of the discriminatory benefit provisions. Their movement has had some successes: in 2000 they gained full war-related compensations as part of the Department of Veterans Affairs (VA) Appropriations Act (Title V of Public Law 106–377), and they won the right to receive health care in VA hospitals and nursing homes if they lived in the United States (Section 103 of Public Law 108–170) – but not if they went back to the Philippines. However, at the time of writing of this book, Filipino veterans are not entitled to non-service-related disability compensation, and, more importantly, to pension benefits (American Coalition for Filipino

Veterans n.d.). Access to pension benefits is critical for the Filipino veterans, many of whom immigrated without financial resources and are living in poverty. But the U.S. government, for which they fought, continues to fail to give equal recognition to the wartime service of the Filipino veterans, denying them benefits equal to that of other vets.

Several members of Congress have supported the cause of Filipino veterans. Bob Filner (D-CA), whose district includes parts of the San Diego area with large navy-related and Filipino populations, has repeatedly introduced so-called Filipino veteran equity bills. Other members of the House, including several Asian American members, co-sponsored the legislation. On the Senate side, Daniel Inouye (D-HI), himself a decorated World War II veteran, has been active on this issue, along with Daniel Akaka (D-HI). Both Senators represent the state of Hawai'i, which has a significant Filipino population. To some extent, these advocates represent a panethnic coalition – non-Filipino Asian officials working with and for Filipino Americans, but they have not yet obtained the level of success achieved by the Japanese American redress legislation.

Explaining Differential Success

Why were Japanese Americans able to achieve redress of the wartime internment, while Japanese Latin Americans and Filipino veterans have met only partial success in their campaigns? All these cases grew out of discrimination in the World War II era, and each seems to have strong arguments in favor of it. However, there are significant differences between the Japanese redress movement and the other campaigns, including the complexity of the arguments, size of the constituencies involved, the status of activists, and the level of personal involvement of government representatives. It is instructive to examine these differences, to understand the factors that help ethnic activists successfully to influence policy decisions.

The Japanese American case was simpler, easier to frame as a clear violation of American principles. Helping to simplify the case was the fact that Japanese American internment occurred entirely on American soil. Campaigners for the redress, therefore, were able to frame the issue "as a constitutional issue, not a racial issue" (Hatamiya 1993, 152). In contrast, the Filipino veteran and Japanese Latin American cases were more difficult to understand, and they unfolded at least partly in other countries. Superficially, at least, they might appear to many Americans to be a matter of foreign affairs, and not obviously issues involving civil rights. So one significant factor that helped these activists achieve success seems to have been their ability to frame the case for redress as a case of making amends for injustice done by Americans to other Americans.

The size of the groups involved also played a role in how successful the campaigns were. In the 1980s, over 80,000 former Japanese American internees were still alive and living in the United States, while relatively few Filipino vets or Peruvian Japanese internees were in the U.S. then. Although Filipino Americans overall greatly outnumbered Japanese Americans, most were not closely related to the World War II veterans. In contrast, most Japanese Americans who are not recent immigrants are related to someone who was interned. The World War II experience was a defining moment, imprinting itself deeply not only on those who experienced it, but on the next generation, even though they had no direct involvement (Takezawa 1995).[8] So, although there were fewer Japanese Americans than Filipino Americans, reparations for Japanese Americans matter deeply to a much higher percentage of the latter.

The groups of activists also differed in some significant ways. Many of Filipino vets were low-income, heavily dependnt on Supplemental Social Security (SSI) to survive (Lachica 1999). In contrast, Japanese American activists were overwhelmingly middle- or upper class, with the greater access to resources and networks that comes with a higher class status.

Another likely factor was the personal role of Japanese American members of Congress (MCs). Although the Japanese American MCs worked on behalf of all these causes, they were able to tell personal stories about the Japanese American experience. California House members Norman Mineta and Robert Matsui testified about being interned with their families (Hatamiya 1993, ch. 7). As we noted above, Senator Daniel Inouye delivered an emotional speech recounting his experience of fighting alongside soldiers whose families were imprisoned behind barbed wire. Such personal connections can often make an impact in Congress, but there were no Japanese Peruvians or Filipino veteran MCs to tell personal stories about those experiences.

Asian American Identity and Public Policy

Our discussion of public policy again highlights the complex ways that identity is important to Asian American politics. As we discussed in chapter 4, numbers matter in politics, and so groups can benefit from joining together to promote a common agenda. No Asian American subgroup makes up more than a small fraction of the population, making it even more important for them to form alliances. A strong panethnic identity would make it easier to form an alliance among Asian American subgroups. In some cases, such as English-only laws, it is relatively easy for Asian American subgroups to unite in opposition.

However, as we have also explained, there are drawbacks to too strong a panethnic identity. Differences among Asian American subgroups can be obscured if generalizations are made across the entire population. As the example of educational attainment showed, some subgroups face considerable challenges, but those challenges can be missed if statistical measures lump all Asian American subgroups together. Continued awareness of Asian American diversity is needed, but an excessive emphasis on diversity can make it more difficult to form broad panethnic alliances.

Not only is it important to consider the way that Asian Americans identify themselves, but it is also necessary to examine the way that others have identified them. For a number of reasons, many Americans continue to identify Asian Americans as foreigners, and sometimes as dangerous foreigners. This has been an evolving challenge for Asian Americans. In the early twenty-first century, some believe that Asian Americans can surmount this perception, but, even if they can, the path they choose can have profound consequences not only for them, but for the entire society. We turn to that topic in the concluding chapter of this book.

CHAPTER NINE

The Politics of Identity and the Future of American Politics

In this concluding chapter, we return the theme that has run throughout this book: the question of Asian American identity. Will Asian Americans ever win acceptance as Americans, or will they be forever perceived as foreigners? If Asian Americans gain greater acceptance, will they transform society, or only be absorbed by it?

The Politics of Identity

There is no question that Asian Americans have seen tremendous progress over the last century. Laws no longer define Asian immigrants as aliens forever forbidden to naturalize. Expressing anti-Asian bigotry is no longer always a reliable means for elected officials to build political support, although it still appears to beneficial at least in some cases.

What will it take to eradicate remaining discrimination? In a sense, the answer is easy: Asian Americans need to gain acceptance as "full" Americans. Today, elected representatives would be unlikely to get away with attacks on all Norwegian Americans or Polish Americans, or any other group seen as white. Anti-Asian remarks persist because Asian Americans are marginalized – often seen as foreign, or not fully American. Just as anti-Irish or anti-Italian slurs became increasingly intolerable as those groups won greater acceptance, anti-Asian attitudes will meet with less approval as Asian Americans win more acceptance.

Much more difficult, however, is explaining how this can come about. The forever foreigner stereotype feeds off perceptions that can be deep-seated and difficult to alter. Some attitudes can persist long after laws and rules have been changed.

In these cases, collective effort can be important. Although attitudes are difficult to change, behavior is more malleable. Asian American groups have moved to the front lines in the struggles against prejudicial language, racial slurs, and discriminatory behavior. The elimination of behaviors alone will not change attitudes, but when norms are established that define certain behaviors as unacceptable, over time, attitudes may follow. When groups work to challenge stereotypes or derogatory images, they are engaging in politics, as we define it. While attitudes do not change immediately, racist expressions become less acceptable, and, over time, greater numbers of people may cease to use them.

In terms we used earlier in the book, organized groups of Asian Americans and others are engaged in a racial project to redefine how Asian Americans are perceived. This is not likely to be a short-term effort, but it is an essential one if Asian Americans are to see a transformation of their place in American society.

Asian American Politics and Other Communities of Color

Asian Americans have many similarities to Hispanics. Most notably, both categories are relatively recent creations, and both are bolstered by official classifications used throughout government and much of the private sector.

There are also important differences, perhaps the most important of which is the vastly greater size of the Latino population, which gives this group attention and potential political clout that Asian Americans cannot hope to match. Although many Hispanics are not yet eligible to vote, at minimum, their American-born children will be citizens and therefore automatically eligible to vote once they turn eighteen. As we explained in chapter 5, Hispanics (and African Americans) are sufficiently numerous and geographically concentrated that a number of majority Latino or majority African American congressional districts have been created, something not possible for Asian Americans on the mainland. For Asian American candidates, appealing to a wider ethnoracial base is essential, so more coalitions must be built.

This is not always a disadvantage. Joining with larger coalitions can give Asian Americans more influence, although taking this approach may make it harder to get more Asian Americans elected to high office.

What Asian Americans clearly share with other communities of color is the experience of racialization. All have been defined as fundamentally different, putting them at a disadvantage in numerous and substantial ways.

On the other hand, as we noted in chapter 1, the racialization projects that marginalized each group have taken different forms for each group: American Indians were saddled with the "noble savage" image and faced devastating efforts to eradicate native cultures and to eliminate their reservations (Wilkins 2002, ch. 4); African Americans suffered an "American apartheid" (Massey and Denton 1993) that kept them highly segregated and often unable to access the opportunities available to most Americans; and, as we described in chapter 1, racialization for Asian Americans initially worked to prevent them from naturalizing and define them as inherently foreign. Because each group has endured a different kind of racialization, each group is likely to require different remedies to overcome the legacy of racialization. This does not mean that they cannot join together, but it does mean that measures that help one group may not be beneficial to another, and, as we noted in chapter 6, things that help one group might even be detrimental to another.

This reminds us of a point we raised in the first chapter: Asian American politics cannot be adequately understood if it is always lumped together with that of other ethnoracial minorities.

The Future of Asian American Politics

What do we foresee for Asian American politics? The future is always cloudy, but some important developments seem likely, given changing demographics. The Asian American population is very likely to become much more U.S.-born in the next few decades, as young immigrants reach adulthood and have children. The current high percentage of foreign-born reflects the small size of the Asian American population in the 1960s. Those long-established Asian Americans eventually came to be a minority as a huge influx of new immigrants changed the composition of the population. However, now that the Asian American population has surged, it is unlikely that future immigrants will make up such a large percentage of the total Asian American population. A similar process can be seen in the Latino population. While Hispanic immigration has been far greater than Asian immigration, the former started from a much larger base, and so immigrants continue to be a minority of the overall Latino population (a very large minority, to be sure).

When a greater percentage of Asian Americans are U.S.-born, more Asian Americans are likely to become involved in American politics, at a higher level of engagement. As we explained in chapter 3, participation is easier for natural-born citizens than for immigrants. U.S.-born Asian Americans do not need to overcome the hurdle of naturalization before they are eligible to vote, and they often find it easier to get information about political activities, because no language barrier exists for them.

Getting more Asian Americans into elected office is likely to continue to be difficult, for reasons we pointed out in chapter 5. However, if the percentage of Asian Americans in the general population continues to increase, it seems likely that a greater number will find their way into government as well. As we discussed in chapter 7, perceptions of Asian Americans will probably be a significant factor here. The "forever foreigner" image almost certainly makes it more difficult for Asian American candidates to gain support outside their panethnic community.

The most important question, though, may be the degree of Asian American political influence. While any answer must be speculative, we can draw on evidence we have presented elsewhere in this book. On the bright side, the size and distribution of the Asian American population may increase their influence, because it forces them to join and build coalitions. Since no group is large enough to change public policy on its own, alliances are always necessary. Asian American elected officials have something of a head start, since they must build coalitions with other ethnoracial groups in order just to be elected. On the other hand, as we have seen, Asian Americans can still quickly become political targets, reflecting their "forever foreigner" image. The 1996 campaign finance controversy is evidence that their political incorporation continues to be tentative.

Asian Americans, the Color Line, and the Promise of American Life

We conclude with an important idea we introduced in the opening chapter: the role of Asian Americans in defining America. We have explained how past laws and court decisions were drafted to exclude Asian Americans. America was defined as a nation of and for whites, and Asian immigration spurred an effort by white Americans to strengthen the color line that separated opportunity from oppression. Much has changed since those efforts in the late nineteenth century, but it remains to be seen if the changes will be sufficient to erase the color line.

One area of considerable change has been the repeal or overturning of discriminatory laws. Asian immigrants are no longer forbidden to buy land. Discriminatory taxes and fees are no longer allowed. The end to this discriminatory treatment has opened the door to many more opportunities today, and, as we have seen, many Asian Americans are prospering (although many are not). But the end to legal discrimination raises two related and very important question: what does this mean for Asian Americans, and what might this mean for all Americans?

Asian Americans and the Mainstream

As we have noted earlier in this chapter and elsewhere in the book, Asian Americans have seen their fortunes improve considerably over what they were in the late nineteenth and early twentieth centuries. Increasingly, Asian Americans are lumped with whites in discussions of education or income.

We have noted reasons to be concerned over this practice. First, there is tremendous diversity among Asian Americans, and viewing them as an undifferentiated mass of high achievers can blind us to the serious challenges facing some, especially refugee families. Second, this approach tends to obscure the continuing challenges facing all Asian Americans – challenges such as dealing with the consequences of the forever foreigner stereotype.

Nevertheless, there are undeniable benefits to achieving genuine parity with whites. The U.S. was built upon a political and social structure which powerfully favored some at the expense of others, and those deemed to be white – especially white men – have long had considerable advantages. It is easy to understand why those who have been on the outside would be eager to join the club and reap the benefits.

Although there are many spheres where Asian Americans are far short of equality – elective office being a good example – some believe that they are making substantial strides toward gaining an equal place in American society (see, for example, Alba and Nee 2003). We have examined substantial evidence that suggests parity is some way off, but, even if it is on the horizon, it can take different routes, with very different implications for America.

Asian Americans and the Color Line

Groups defined as nonwhite long found themselves on the margins of American society. We often use the term "defined as nonwhite" because, as we have explained, "white" and "nonwhite" are social creations. American society long operated under laws and rules that gave considerable advantages to those defined as white, so the fortunes of newcomers could be greatly influenced by whether they were able to convince others that they were "white." Some, such as Irish or Italians, eventually succeeded (e.g. Ignatiev 1995; Jacobson 1998), while others, including all Asian immigrant groups, failed.

However, the story of the color line in America has often been the story of only two groups. Although Asian Americans (and Latinos) have long been a part of the U.S., their ambiguous status with regard to the black/white color line usually attracted little attention because of their relatively small numbers and their concentration in a few parts of the U.S. Issues of race often were black and white. American Indians were here long before any other group, of course, but their small numbers and unique legal relationship have also caused them to have less prominence in many major controversies over race.

Waves of immigrants have complicated our racial order. With growing numbers of Asian and Latino immigrants, there is now much greater awareness of the variety of people who are often considered to be nonwhite. How might this change the color line?

Asian Americans and Latinos might soften the line. With the diversity they bring, there could be less stereotyping and, possibly, even greater awareness of the artificial nature of the white–nonwhite divide. If awareness of Asian American and Latino diversity grows, it might help build and complement greater awareness of African American diversity, which is an important step in undermining racialization.

At its best, Asian American politics holds the promise of making America a better place. Through their presence and through conscious effort, Asian Americans could contribute to a dramatic transformation of American life, helping to heal the deep wounds that racism has inflicted on this country.

The Promise – and Peril – of Asian American Politics

Over a hundred years ago, a prominent political analyst wrote a book titled *The Promise of American Life*. The writer, Herbert Croly, argued that the promise of American life was an ever-brighter future for the citizenry. Croly, like many writers up through that time, ignored the way this "promise" had been little more than a cruel joke for many, especially those defined as nonwhite.

The most optimistic possibility of Asian American – and Latino – politics is that it could redeem the promise that Croly saw. If the growing presence of Asians and Latinos helps to break down the color line and undermine racialization, American society can become more open to all. If racialization of African Americans, American Indians, Asian Americans, and Latinos declines, individuals may have more opportunity to define themselves, to choose or decline their "ethnic options" (Waters 1990). Some might choose to emphasize a panethnic identity, but many might not. Most importantly, stereotypes will be undermined and lose their power because racialization will no longer be perpetuating the notion that these vast groups of individuals are identical.

Ironically, the growth of a panethnic identity can help bring this about. As we have explained, larger coalitions are likely to form around a stronger panethnic identity. Larger coalitions tend to be more effective, and better enable Asian Americans to battle against discrimination and stereotypes. Activists have been doing this for over a hundred years, but only in recent decades have discriminatory laws been widely overcome. Large-scale immigration also can help fuel this process, if the newcomers are inclined to join panethnic alliances. As their numbers surge, they can be more able to undermine the foundations of racialization. Optimists hope that this tide is hastening the day when this country's scar of race begins to heal.

However, this optimistic scenario is not the only possibility. Asian American politics might not serve the common good. Groups can pull themselves up while leaving others behind. As we discussed in chapter 6, nineteenth-century Irish immigrants rejected calls to ally with blacks, instead working to "whiten" themselves at the expense of African Americans (Ignatiev 1995).

Asian Americans could also decide to pursue their own good without regard for others. The Lowell High School case we described in chapter 8 demonstrated how Asian Americans can benefit at the expense of blacks and Latinos. Given the success that Asian Americans have experienced so far, this is not an unrealistic possibility.

Will Asian Americans be able to pry open American society to accept those who have been deemed nonwhite? And, if they do, will they do so in a way to create an opening big enough for others to join them, or will they make a space only for themselves, thereby leaving intact racialization and its legacy? That chapter of Asian American politics remains to be written. The authors are likely to include many of you reading this book.

Defining and Counting Asian Americans

There are many complexities to consider when reading data collected by the United States Census Bureau. This appendix outlines some of the most important for the data used in this book.

Counting Asian Americans in the Census

"Asian" was one of five specified racial categories used in the 2000 census. The other four groups are "White," "Black or African American," "American Indian and Alaska Native," and "Native Hawaiian and Other Pacific Islander" ("Some Other Race" is a sixth category).[1] In the 1990 census, Pacific Islanders had been together with Asian Americans in a category known as "Asian or Pacific Islander (API)." In 2000, however, Pacific Islanders had a separate racial category, reflecting their argument that native peoples of Hawai'i and other Pacific islands have a very different history and face conditions different from the majority of the Asian American population. One notable difference was that Pacific Islanders – especially Hawaiians – were indigenous peoples whose land was occupied and controlled by others, while Asians came to the United States as immigrants. Nevertheless, most political and social organizations and activists continue to use some form of the combined term – e.g., Asian Pacific American (APA), or Asian American and Pacific Islander (AAPI) – in their group names. In Congress, for example, one can find the Congressional Asian Pacific American Caucus (CAPAC). Although this approach risks obscuring the unique history and issues of Pacific Islanders, it continues because of the view that political organizations need to be as inclusive as possible, and that Asian American groups should not exclude Pacific Islanders.[2] In this book, we focus primarily on Asian Americans, recognizing that Pacific Islanders often work in different political circumstances. At times, however, we include Pacific Islanders in our discussion.

People of Arab descent remain in a categorical limbo. Using geographers' definitions, countries such as Iraq or Syria would be considered to be Asian. On the other hand, many consider the Middle East to be a region distinct from Asia. In the U.S., Middle Easterners do not have their own racial category in the census. Groups such as the Arab American Institute (AAI) and the American-Arab Anti-Discrimination Committee (ADC) argued for the creation of a "Middle Eastern" or "Arab American" category, in view of their unique position in U.S. society and cases of discrimination against them (which were frequent even before September 11, 2001). Their proposal, however, was not included the 1997 OMB classification scheme. The Arab organizations therefore shifted their strategy and tried to maintain recognition as an "ancestry" group identifiable through a separate census question (Samhan 1999; Saliba 1999; Rodríguez 2000, 155–8).[3] This strategy succeeded, and, after the 2000 census, the Census Bureau produced its first report on the Arab American population (de la Cruz and Brittingham 2003).

Caveats in Reading Census Data

While census data provides the most extensive evidence for understanding demographic trends among Asians in America, it is certainly not the perfect tool. Before we turn to socioeconomic and geographic data, it is useful to note some cautions.

First, the ethnoracial groups listed on the census reflect a complex set of factors, and cannot be assumed to be a perfect mirror of society. Demographic change, policymakers' prejudices, and lobbying efforts of affected groups have shaped and reshaped census categories (Espiritu 1992). Chinese and Japanese appeared in the census form for the first time in 1870 and 1880 respectively, Filipinos in 1930, and Vietnamese in 1980. Koreans appeared first in the 1930 census, although they disappeared in the 1950 and 1960 censuses (Rodríguez 2000). The case of Asian Indians is particularly complicated. As discussed earlier in this appendix, the U.S. Supreme Court used a "common understanding" approach to classify race and declared a "Caucasian" immigrant from India a non white in 1923. We can see the unscientific nature of racial classification in the ever-changing approaches to categorizing Asian Indians. The 1930 and 1940 forms had a "Hindu" category, which disappeared in 1950 (Rodríguez 2000, 101), as Asian Indians were moved to the "white" category. In the 1980 census, however, the "Asian Indian" category was created, partly in response to petitions by groups such as the Association of Indians in America (AIA), and those with ancestral roots in India found themselves moved back into the larger "Asian" grouping. Even then, another problem emerged, as many native Americans, or *American* Indians, marked "Asian Indian" by mistake (Lai and Arguelles 2003, 51–6).

Like Arabs discussed earlier, some Asian groups have not been successful in placing their names on the census form. Taiwanese Americans, especially those whose families were already in Taiwan before 1949, have a strong identity as Taiwanese. Rejecting inclusion under the general "Chinese" category, they lobbied to create a separate "Taiwanese" category within the "Asian" classification. They did not succeed in changing the 2000 census, but many nonetheless asserted their identity by skipping the "Chinese" box, marking "Other Asian" category, and writing "Taiwanese" or "Taiwanese American." There were more than 118,000 individuals who chose that option (see table 2.2).

Second, racial classification in the census is based on self-description, and not on "objective" observation. Reading figure 2.1 carefully, we notice that the 2000 census worded the race question in the following way: "What is Person 1's race? Mark X one or more races to indicate *what this person considers him-self/herself to be*" (emphasis added). The census's reliance on self-description reflects gradual changes in American society in the last half-century. As society has become more race-conscious, the power to decide what race a person belongs to has shifted from government authorities (such as schoolteachers and census workers) to a person himself or herself. By 1980, the census switched completely to self-description for identifying a person's race (Rodríguez 2000, 85, 135).

Thus it is possible that people might identify themselves differently from the way that others see them. This discrepancy seems most likely for multira-cial persons, but it could happen to "single race" persons too. To begin with, outsiders often misunderstand a person's race. Moreover, a person may not want to disclose his or her entire racial composition on the census form, even though the census bureau promises confidentiality of personal information. Provided with an option to check multiple race boxes, a person may still not want to declare some parts of his or her racial identity because those races have been treated negatively in the neighborhood he or she lives in. Furthermore, a person himself or herself may not know the entire family his-tory. Few persons have "precise" information on racial compositions of all of their ancestors for three or four generations. The necessity of reliance on self-declaration for racial data shows part of the socially constructed nature of racial categories.

Third, minority groups, including Asians, tend to be undercounted in the census. The Census Bureau strives to count all persons living in the United States on a particular date (in the case of the 2000 census, April 1). Despite the efforts of the Census Bureau, however, it is known that some people, particu-larly immigrants, tend not to be fully counted. The reasons for undercount vary. Many undocumented immigrants fear that their illegal status may be detected and revealed to immigration authorities, even though the Census Bureau promises that it will use the information for statistical purposes only. When multiple families share one housing unit, only one family may provide information. Census workers are sent to seek households which have not returned questionaires, but in areas in which people have to live in crowded housing or unsafe neighborhoods, the workers may not reach all residents. Finally, language barriers and communication problems may aggravate these obstacles, despite efforts by community organizations to reduce them.

For the 1990 census, the Census Bureau estimated that the undercount rate (the proportion of the uncounted out of the estimated total population) was 0.9 per cent for whites, 4.4 per cent for blacks, 4.5 per cent for Native Americans, 2.3 per cent for Asian Americans and Pacific Islanders, and 5.0 per cent for Hispanics (U.S. Bureau of Census, n.d.). It therefore proposed to use "statistical sampling," or adjustment based on past undercount patterns, for the 2000 census. The plan was challenged in lawsuits by some members of Congress who, according to their opponents, did not like to see the rise of minority voting power. Those suing to block sampling argued that the Constitution required "actual enumeration" for congressional reapportionment (in Article 1, Section 2) and did not allow for statistical adjustment. The U.S. Supreme Court ruled in favor of the plaintiffs, citing a 1976 census act (in *Department of Commerce et al. v. United States House of Representatives*, 525 U.S. 316).

Although statistical sampling was not allowed in the 2000 census, there were many other ways to try to count hard-to-reach groups. The Census Bureau aired TV commercials in foreign languages in ethnic media beginning in 1999, promised not to share personal information with other government authorities – particularly law enforcement and immigration officials – and worked with community organizations to encourage participation. These organizations knew that undercounting could have negative consequences in areas such as housing assistance, education, and language rights, and appear to have been successful in encouraging more response to the 2000 census. Nevertheless, undercounting of ethnoracial minorities continues to be a concern when using census data, particularly for earlier censuses.

Fourth, census statistics of "Asian Americans" and other minority groups include non-citizens. The Census Bureau counts all individuals "with a usual residence" (Mills 2001, 6), regardless of legal status. Thus the "Asian American" population reported in the 2000 census included not only legal and illegal immigrants but also, for example, business persons transferred from Japan to a corporate branch in Manhattan, employees from India working for computer companies in Silicon Valley, and international students from China attending U.S. colleges. Only tourists and short-term visitors from abroad without an address in the U.S. were excluded. It may sound strange to include temporary residents in a national census, and it may sound even stranger to count them for the purpose of redistributing the number of seats for the U.S. House of Representatives among the states (called reapportionment), but that is what happens. Reapportionment figures also do not distinguish between voting-age and non-voting-age individuals (Mills 2001, 6). Constructing tallies by citizenship would be impossible, because reapportionment (which took place in time for the 2002 House election) is based on data from the "short form," which does not ask about citizenship status. Questions about citizenship are asked only on the census "long form," which provides a wealth of useful information.

Information from the long form shows that Asian populations in America have large proportions of non-citizens. About one-third (34.5 per cent) of "Asian Americans" were not U.S. citizens (Reeves and Bennett 2004, 9), so less than two-thirds of the Asian American population was eligible to participate in elections. As we saw in chapter 3, the voting power of Asian Americans is further reduced by other factors such as the low rate of voter registration. This is true of Hispanics as well. Although they numbered 35.2 million in 2000, 29.0 per cent of Latinos were not citizens (Ramirez 2004, 8). Immigrant groups cannot be assumed to have voting power equal to their numbers.

Terminology

OMB Statistical Directive 15 is fairly clear about how certain groups should be classified, but many Americans do not fully understand it. This raises questions about what terms should be used.

Most obvious is the problem of a single term to use when describing African Americans, American Indians and Alaskan Natives, Asian Americans, Latinos, and Native Hawaiians and Pacific Islanders. All of those subpopulations are classified as "races" in Directive 15, except for Latinos. While most Americans probably think of "Latino" or "Hispanic" as a racial group, most statistical tabulations follow Directive 15 and do not consider "Latino" to be a race. Nevertheless, there are many times when it makes sense to refer to all these groups together. What should we call them?

The most direct approach which does not contradict OMB and Census Bureau usage is to refer to them collectively as "ethnoracial groups." Among those who study these groups, it is common to refer to the Latino category as an "ethnic group," and the other categories as "racial groups," so the term "ethnoracial" is meant to include both.

It should be noted, however, that official government definitions do not identify "Hispanic" as an ethnic group, but rather refer to it as its own special grouping: "Hispanic origin." Nevertheless, the rationale for the Hispanic category draws on characteristics that are often used to described an ethnic group, as the key component is that a Hispanic individual is of a "Spanish culture."

A book such as this must address many other questions about terms. One of them is how to refer to individuals classified in the census as "Hispanic." Some prefer the term "Latino." We use both ("Hispanic" and Latino"), often using "Hispanic" when talking about census data.

We usually use the term "American Indian" to refer to the indigenous peoples of the lower 48 states in the U.S., because surveys and other tallies suggest that native peoples more often use that term. Some prefer "Native American," but there appears to be more acceptance of both terms today. Many American Indians prefer to use their tribal affiliation when identifying their heritage.

"Black" still appears to be the most commonly used term among Americans of African ancestry, but many prefer "African American." We use both terms in this book.

We use the term "Asian American" to refer to all Americans of Asian ancestry (which includes both citizens and permanent resident aliens). For Asian American subgroups, we usually use the appropriate "ethnic American" term (e.g. "Japanese American"), except when space considerations require us to shorten it (e.g. "Japanese" rather than "Japanese American").

Notes

1 Most of the respondents who checked the "Some Other Race" category (97.0 per cent) turned out to be Hispanic, suggesting that they saw Hispanic as a racial category, even though the census and the Office of Management and Budget (OMB) definitions treat Hispanic identity as something separate from race (so Hispanics can be of any race).

2 Whether Pacific Islanders welcome such inclusion is another story. The Association for Asian American Studies (AAAS) proposed a resolution to include "P" in its name at its 2002 meeting in Salt Lake City but eventually decided not to adopt the resolution. For delicate tensions between Asian Americans and Pacific Islanders, see Diaz (2004) and other articles in the same issue of the journal.

3 Census 2000 only asked the ancestry question on the long questionnaire (from five and a half to seven pages long), received by one out of every six housing units. The rest of the households, which received a short questionnaire (one page long), did not answer questions on ancestry and other items important to the study of immigrants – language spoken at home, place of birth, citizenship and year of entry to the U.S. Census data on these traits is therefore gathered by statistical sampling, the same technique used in public opinion polls by the media. Questions about racial identity and Hispanic origin, in contrast, were put to all respondents, in both the long and short forms,

Sources

Elizabeth M. Grieco and Rachel C. Cassidy, *Overview of Race and Hispanic Origin: 2000*, U.S. Census Bureau, Census 2000 Brief, March 2001.

Clyde Tucker, Brian Kojetin, and Roderick Harrison, "A Statistical Analysis of the CPS Supplement on Race and Ethnic Origin," Bureau of Labor Statistics, Bureau of the Census.

Notes

PREFACE

1 This should not be taken as a criticism of joint Asian American–NHOPI efforts, however. We believe that there are many situations where practical realities – especially numbers – make it very sensible for cooperation, as reflected in the many groups which seek to serve the interests of both populations.

CHAPTER 1

1 It has long been accepted among geneticists that populations that are geographically isolated for long periods of time will come to constitute a common gene pool. So, it is possible to find groups of people who have some common genetic characteristics. However, what we usually consider to be racial groups are far too big to correspond to any long geographically isolated group. Furthermore, geographic isolation is becoming increasingly rare, so that distinct gene pools will become less and less common.

2 In this chapter, we focus on an historical overview, so our discussion of racialization is descriptive. In chapter 2, we turn to a theoretical framework.

3 Around 1565, Filipino sailors pressed into service aboard Spanish galleons appear to have escaped when the ships stopped in the vicinity of the Yucatan Peninsula. Some of these sailors made their way northward, and their descendants were reported to be in the New Orleans area by the late eighteenth century (Espina 1988).

4 In this book, we use the spelling "Hawai'i" rather than "Hawaii," because that is the preference of many native Hawaiians. In some instances, we are quoting from other sources, in which case we use the spelling used in our source.

5 To blast away sections of granite along the sheer mountain walls, a worker would be lowered in a basket to chip a small hole, in which a charge would be placed. The worker would then light the fuse and hope that the others would lift him clear before the dynamite exploded (Tsai 1986, 17). Demolition mishaps were a minor concern, however, compared to the avalanches that could kill dozens at a time. See also Takaki (1998) and Melendy (1984).

6 This is not to say that there had been no efforts to regulate immigration before. Aristide Zolberg (2008) has argued that immigration policy played a central role in shaping the U.S. from the time of its founding. Zolberg explains that although political and constitutional constraints prevented the federal government from passing significant legislation prior to the Civil War, immigration was always a major concern of policymakers.

7 The Chinese population appears to have peaked in 1890, but Roger Daniels notes that the actual peak probably happened between the 1880 and 1890 censuses. Decennial censuses show a continued population decline through the 1920 census, suggesting a decline lasting 35 to 40 years. See Daniels (1988, 67–9).

8 There are three primary levels in the United States federal judicial system. Most cases are first heard at the district court level; appeals of district court decisions go to the appellate or circuit court level; and the U.S. Supreme Court is the highest court.

9 We examine this in further detail in chapter 4.

CHAPTER 2

1 The U.S. Citizenship and Immigration Services (USCIS, one of the agencies created after the U.S. Immigration and Naturalization Service was reorganized), considers "immigrants" to be only those permanent residents who have migrated here legally. We use the term more broadly, and consider anyone residing but not born in the U.S. to be an immigrant, unless they intend to be here only temporarily (e.g. tourists or students). Our definition of "immigrant" includes those who are here without legal authorization.

2 The famous movie trilogy *The Godfather* powerfully depicts the regional basis of Italian immigrant identity.

3 If we adhered to strict parallelism in terminology, the latter should be "panethnicization," a term which we find devilishly difficult to pronounce, and decline to inflict on the English language.

4 Michael Omi reports in his introduction to Williams-León and Nakashima (2001, xiii) that Tiger's father is "half-black, one-quarter Native American, and one-quarter Chinese" and Tiger's mother is "half-Thai, one-quarter Chinese, and one-quarter Dutch." Adding these heritages, Tiger is half Asian (a quarter Thai and a quarter Chinese), a quarter black, and one-eighth white (Dutch) and one-eighth Native American. Woods's multiracial background, which he himself calls "Cablinasian," is often used to illustrate the extent to which U.S. society has become multiracial.

5 Table 2.1 does not report these multi-ethnic Asians, who are 223,593 in number (Barnes and Bennett 2002, table 4).

6 A recent study illustrated this, finding different patterns of cancer in different Asian American subgroups. Patterns varied by where individuals had grown up – including for those who were born in the U.S. (Grady 2007).

7 Another common measure is household income. Median family income is higher than median household income, because there can be single-person households, but there cannot be single-person families. Asian American median household income is also larger than median household income for Hispanics and other racial groups.

8 Asian Americans are not as well off as suggested by median family income for another reason: high living cost for areas in which many Asian Americans live. New York, California, and Hawai'i are states where housing and commodity prices are particularly high. Average annual expenditures for a consumer unit was $49,931 in New York City, $55,346 in San Francisco, $47,459 in Los Angeles, and $43,458 in Honolulu in years 2001–2. The national average was $39,518 in 2001 and $40,677 in 2002 (U.S. Bureau of Census 2005a, 438). Note that living expenditures are high in Hawai'i, where most commodities have to be imported from outside the islands.

9 "Gook" was a slur which emerged from the Vietnam War, and, strictly speaking, was meant as a racial slur toward Vietnamese.

10 According to Census 2000, 58 per cent of individuals who marked only the "American Indian and Alaskan Native" box lived in metropolitan statistical areas or consolidated metropolitan statistical areas. See Census 2000, summary file 1, tables P3 and P12C.

CHAPTER 3

1 Permanent residents who are in the military can now apply for citizenship if they have been in active duty for more than one year. Such expediting procedure existed before the 9/11 terrorist attacks, but the requirements were relaxed as the government found it imminent to win the war on terror.

2 U.S.-born respondents are citizens, by virtue of being born in the U.S. All non-citizens,

therefore, are foreign-born. The zero per cent voting rate of non-citizens is simply a reflection of current U.S. laws, which generally prohibit non-citizens from voting. In the 19th century, some states allowed non-citizens to vote in federal elections as part of their efforts to boost populations in frontier areas (Hayduk 2006, ch. 2). Asian immigrants did not benefit from these provisions because their entry to the U.S. was restricted. The U.S. constitution does not explicitly forbid non-citizens from voting in federal elections but lets each state prescribe its election rules (Article 1, Section 4).

3 Verba et al. (1995) is based on a large-scale nationwide telephone poll (with more than 15,000 respondents). Although the survey made specific efforts to include African Americans and Latinos in the sample, it excluded Asian Americans from research design. The phrase "Asian Americans" does not appear in the index of the 600-page book and is mentioned where the authors say they calculate sample population without them (Verba et al. 1995, 237 n. 13).

4 One of the authors has in fact witnessed this, observing women who had been active in children's ministry apply the same skills to encouraging church attendees to participate in a church-organized effort to emphasize the importance of children's issues to state legislators.

5 Reflecting the religious diversity of Asian Americans, the survey asked about respondents' "religious services," not simply church attendance. Using the same dataset, Lien (2003) examines the relationship between religious and political activities for Asian Americans. Asian American religion is a growing field of research that has attracted scholarly attention in the past decade. Examples of publications include Yoo (1999), Min and Kim (2002), and Carnes and Yang (2003), and Iwamura and Spickard (2003).

6 The PNAAPS study cannot deal with one other criticism of involvement in homeland politics – that those who do so are not sufficiently concerned with U.S.-based events. It is possible that the U.S. political participation is focused on international affairs. Roberto Suro has argued that Mexican immigrants tend to focus too much on a future life in Mexico, to the detriment of building a better life in the U.S. While the immigrant generation is not adversely affected, their children may suffer the consequences of living in bad neighborhoods and attending bad schools. Suro argues that the parents are willing to tolerate such conditions because they are focused on returning to Mexico, but they do not always realize that their children will not always be able to resist the negative influences (Suro 1998). Even if Suro's argument is correct, however, it probably applies less to Asian Americans, who are less likely to be enticed by the prospects of returning to their homeland in their later years.

7 Thomas P. Kim believes that parties can be quick to abandon Asian Americans, however (Kim 2007). Kim argues that because Asian Americans are perceived as foreign (a subject we address in chapter 7), parties will find it in their interest to disassociate if Asian Americans are the target of unfavorable publicity. The campaign contribution controversies in 1996 were a good demonstration of this, Kim suggests.

8 Party identification is an individual's long-term, "lasting" attachment or "psychological identification" with one political party (Campbell et al. 1960, 121).

9 Many men are also concerned about family leave policies, of course.

CHAPTER 4

1 None of this should be taken to mean that Indian immigrants remain outside of American society. As Sharmila Rudrappa has noted, South Asian American organizations and practices that appear to be distinctively "ethnic" may in fact be part of the assimilation process (Rudrappa 2004).

2 The word "SNEHA" "denotes a loving relationship" (Purkayastha, Raman, and Bhide 1997, 107).

3 The Pathet Lao were the communist forces in Laos, and were allied with the North Vietnamese against the U.S. during the Vietnam War.

4 It would seem appropriate to refer to Laos as the Hmong homeland, except that many Hmong still think of China as their homeland, even though many have never lived there, their ancestors having left China a century or more ago.

5 Migrants from Thailand usually enter as immigrants.

6 Some Americans probably did not even perceive transnationalism, only foreigners bent on harming the U.S. However, others understood that Asian Americans had some roots in America, but those roots were perceived to have much less influence than the ties to Asia.

7 Americans of Middle Eastern ancestry have recently experienced this process of being perceived as transnational and a threat. Not surprisingly, their racial definition is ambiguous, considered by the Census Bureau to be "white," but viewed as non-white by many Americans.

8 In chapter 6, we will discuss how Asian Americans have at times joined with other peoples of color to build even larger coalitions.

CHAPTER 5

1 Pitkin (1967) actually examines four forms of representation, but we only deal with two of them for the sake of simplicity, and also because these two forms have been the most widely discussed in the context of minority representation.

2 For example, see the following comment by Sharon Tomiko Santos, a Japanese American elected from Seattle to the Washington State House of Representatives:

> I am very proud to serve as the first Japanese American woman Legislator, not only in the State of Washington, but in fact on the entire United States Mainland. That distinction does play [sic] some pressure on me to ensure that I serve as one role model for other Asian Pacific Americans and other Japanese American members of my community to consider a profession in the field of public service, which is what I see this as . . . [B]eing a role model and having younger people see, "Aha! There is a Nikkei woman who is helping to change people's minds and hearts and make decisions that are fair on the half of all other constituencies, is an important part of inspiration. (Takeda ed. 2006, 101–2)

3 Another issue involved in reporting the number of Asian Americans (and minorities in general) in Congress is whether to include non-voting "delegates" in the House. "Delegates" are not allowed to cast a vote in the chamber, but can participate in committee and floor deliberation and introduce bills and resolutions. There are five such "delegates" in the House, representing Washington, D.C., Puerto Rico, Virgin Islands, American Samoa, and Guam. Some argue that these areas have been "oppressed" by the United States government, with the policy of "taxation without representation." All these areas could be characterized as having majority-minority populations, so it is not surprising that these areas are represented by members considered to be ethnoracial minorities. For example, American Samoa is represented by Eni Faleomavaega (D), a Pacific Islander who is active in the congressional Asian Pacific American Caucus. If we include such delegates in table 5.1, the percentage of minority members increases a little, although the percentage of Asian Americans does not. If we include Filipino resident commissioner in table 5.2 (the Philippines was a territory of the United States prior to 1945, and sent delegates to Congress), the list of Asian American members of Congress in history becomes much longer (Tong 2000).

4 Saund had been a U.S. citizen for seven years and sixteen days before beginning his service in January 1957 – just barely satisfying the Constitutional requirement that one must be a citizen for seven years to be a House member (Article 1, Section 2). In this regard, it was significant that Congress passed a bill in 1946 to lift bans for immigrants from India

to naturalize. Saund became naturalized in December 1949 (Saund 1960, 68–96). If Congress had waited to allow Indians to naturalize until later, just as it did for Japanese Americans (who were not allowed to naturalize until 1952), it would have been impossible for Saund to run for election in 1956.

5 The difficulty of characterizing elected officials' ethnicity applies to Van Tran, too. One North American Chinese daily paper reported that Tran's ancestors included overseas Chinese (*World News* (Los Angeles), April 23, 2005, B2). Intermarriage between Vietnamese and overseas Chinese is not uncommon in Southeast Asia. We identify Van Tran as a Vietnamese American, because that is how he is commonly identified.

6 This view is sometimes given jokingly by successful Asian American politicians who have overcome such cultural obstacles, if any. For example, Fiona Ma, an accountant who was elected to be a San Francisco Supervisor (called city council members elsewhere) and then a California State Assembly member in 2006, tells the following in an interview in a professional magazine:

> My parents were born in China, which meant that growing up, I pretty much had four choices for a profession: lawyer, engineer, accountant or doctor. My parents saw getting a good education and entering one of these professions as the American dream, and the key to success. I was always good at math, so they thought accounting would be good for me.
>
> California CPA [Interviewer]: With the many options available for CPAs – public practice, industry and education, among them – how did you end up in public office?
>
> FM [Fiona Ma]: I never thought I would be in public office – ever. Being an accountant is an honorable profession to Chinese parents, while being a politician is completely foreign to them. But it was something I fell into. (F. Ma 2007, 15)

7 Similarly, Cho and Lad (2004, 261) compiled a list of Asian Indians who ran for state legislatures.

8 However, in his study of Little Saigon in Orange County, California, Collet (2005) points out that Vietnamese Americans supported Asian candidates over white candidates, even when the Asian candidates were not Vietnamese.

CHAPTER 6

1 Information drawn from Helen Zia's accounts in *Asian American Dreams* (2000).

2 Another very important aspect of this transformation is the growth of the Latino population, now the largest "minority" group in the U.S. For most of the country's history, of course, African Americans had been the most numerous ethnoracial minority, and the rapid growth of Latinos has created numerous tensions. However, since our focus is on Asian Americans, we do not explore that change in this book.

3 The *Times* asked many of the same questions again on the tenth anniversary of the riots (2002), but, unfortunately, did not oversample Asian Americans, and so did not have enough responses to give separate results for the Asian American respondents.

4 Useful summaries of relevant surveys can be found in Lien (2001), ch. 4, and T. Lee (2000).

5 Together and in cooperation with others, the UCLA AASC has published considerable work on public policy issues affecting Asian Americans – e.g. their *State of Asian Pacific America* series.

6 They were later tried in federal court, and, on April 17, 1993, two of the four officers were found guilty of violating King's civil rights (Abelmann and Lie 1995, 181).

7 Korean American women filmmakers and professors produced a videotape entitled "Sa-I-Gu", which offers a vivid account of the impact of the death of a Korean man on his family and community.

8 The stores discussed here are sometimes referred to as "liquor stores," sometimes as "grocery stores." Neither fully captures the reality of these establishments that stock significant amounts of liquor, but also serve as important suppliers of groceries for neighborhood residents.

9 Popular culture may have told this story better than the news media. Spike Lee's critically acclaimed movie *Do the Right Thing* portrays African Americans expressing a range of complex views about an Asian-owned (presumably Korean American) grocery store in a black neighborhood, with both hostility and sympathy toward the Asian immigrants.

10 In chapter 8, we look in some detail at public policy issues, some of which present the potential for coalition-building between ethnoracial groups, and some of which might create tensions ethnoracial groups.

CHAPTER 7

1 While this article echoed a widespread bias among Americans, it should be noted that a remarkable correction was run later and placed in the online edition, noting that "The article . . . should have noted that since many U.S. citizens are of Asian descent, it is difficult to determine just what constitutes 'American facial features.' "

2 When Kristof was bureau chief of the *New York Times* Tokyo bureau, his articles were criticized as mocking and stereotyping people of Japan. Long-time Japanese residents in New York City went so far as publish a bilingual book to present his bias in his reporting. His remark about ethnic Koreans going into organized crime is obviously hyperbole, but still disturbing in light of his tendency to write in stereotypes.

3 In statistics, the mode is the most frequent (common) case.

4 Campaign finance law is complex, and changes periodically. Since 2002, a major reform known as the Bipartisan Campaign Reform Act of 2002 (BCRA) altered some of the rules regarding corporate money. However, as this chapter was being completed, the U.S. Supreme Court issued a ruling placing substantial limits on a key provision of the BCRA (*Federal Election Commission* v. *Wisconsin Right to Life, Inc.* (2007). For more information about campaign finance law, consult the Federal Elections Commission website at www.fec.gov.

5 The APAMC includes the Asian American Justice Center (AAJC — formerly known as the National Asian Pacific American Legal Center), the Center for Asian American Media (CAAM – formerly NAATA), East–West Players, Japanese American Citizens League (JACL), Media Action Network for Asian Americans (MANAA), Organization of Chinese Americans (OCA), and Visual Communications. APAMC reports can be found on the AAJC website, www.advancingequality.org.

6 In the early years of movies, African American characters were often portrayed by whites using facepaint. This came to be known as "blackface," and came to be highly criticized. Critics of the practice of non-Asian Americans portraying Asian American characters sometimes called this "yellowface."

7 The following description draws heavily on Helen Zia's excellent account in *Asian American Dreams* (2000), ch. 5.

8 As these names change, there are often different preferences. And so, some indigenous activists prefer the name "Native American," but the name "American Indian" appears to have more support among the indigenous people of the United States. Likewise, some African-ancestry individuals continue to use the term "black" (some prefer it to be capitalized, i.e. "Black"), while others prefer "African American." Among those classified by the census as "Hispanic," there are similar differences, with some preferring "Latino," while others use "Hispanic." As with Asian Americans, many use ethnic or national labels (e.g. "Mexican," "Salvadoran").

CHAPTER 8

1 Language issues are important beyond the classroom, of course. Access to emergency services such as 911 operators, interaction with police, or the ability to vote can be severely hampered for non-native English speakers (Imahara 1993).

2 As of mid-2007, any one of the following conditions would trigger the requirement for translators:

> The number of United States citizens of voting age in a single language group within the jurisdiction
> 1. Is more than 10,000, or
> 2. Is more than five per cent of all voting age citizens, or
> 3. On an Indian reservation, exceeds five per cent of all reservation residents; and
> 4. The illiteracy rate of the group is higher than the national illiteracy rate.
>
> ("About Language Minority Voting Rights" n.d.)

3 This section draws heavily on Maki et al. 1999, the most extensive study of the redress movement.

4 There is disagreement over how to label the detention of Japanese Americans. Today, many prefer the terms "imprisonment" or "incarceration." The most frequently used term, however, is probably "internment," and those who were held in the relocation centers are frequently referred to as "internees."

The vast majority of Japanese Americans who were imprisoned were held in camps run by the War Relocation Authority (established in March 1942). Internees and others often referred to the camps as "relocation camps" (or "relocation center"). But many people now prefer to call them "concentration camps," in part because they think the term "relocation center" masks the facts that the relocation was forced on those affected, that the camps were surrounded by barbed wire, and that the armed soldiers in the watchtowers faced inward (not outward).

However, the use of word "concentration camps" has invited criticism from a different perspective. Some people believe the words should be used only for the Holocaust camps where the atrocities against the Jewish people occurred. Some Jewish groups made this point when an exhibit of Japanese American "concentration camps" was traveling in the country (Sengupta 1998).

Complicating the terminology is that there were two kinds of "camps." While over 100,000 Japanese Americans were held in one of the ten camps run by the War Relocation Authority, some 10,000 to 20,000 Japanese were held in camps run by the Department of Justice (DOJ). The DOJ camps held Japanese who were considered to be dangerous for their alleged connection to Japan (as was the case for Shigeru Aoki, whom we saw in chapter 1), as well as German and Italian enemy aliens, and later Japanese Latin Americans who were forced to move from Peru and other countries and then repatriated to Japan. In legal terms, only these camps were called "internment camps," because "internment" is a legal process to apprehend enemy aliens during a war (Daniels 2005). Some scholars argue that the word "internment" and "internees" should be used for those held in these camps, and that the vast majority of Japanese Americans were "incarcerated" by an action of the government which did not even have "the color of law" (Maki et al. 1999, 5). For further discussion of the DOJ camps, see Kashima (2003).

The reality is that there is no single term which everyone finds satisfactory, and we use all terms —"detention," "imprisonment," "incarceration," and "internment" – to refer to the process where Japanese Americans were detained, whether in relocation camps or DOJ internment camps. For the camps run by the War Relocation Authority, we use all terms that have been commonly used in the past: "relocation camp," "internment camp," "concentration camp," and, following the usage of many former detainees, simply "camp."

5 Japanese Americans, and to a lesser degree, Korean Americans, are unusual in giving distinct names to each generation. The names are derivations of Japanese numbers. "Ichi" is number one, and the first generation were known as "Issei." "Ni" is the Japanese word for "two," and the second generation (the first one born in the United States) are known as "Nisei." "San" is the Japanese word for "three," and the third generation is known as the "Sansei." In all cases, the second syllable is pronounced "say." For "issei" and "nisei", the vowel sound in the first syllable is a long "e," as in "tree."

6 Although a presidential veto can be overridden with a two-thirds vote in each house of Congress, it rarely happens. Usually, a veto means that the bill is dead.

7 "Rescission" today usually refers to a budgetary process (which changed significantly in 1974). In this case, though, it meant declaring that the Filipino veterans had never served in the U.S. armed forces, despite the fact that many had.

8 This can be seen easily when meeting Japanese Americans. Most third-generation (Sanseis) can quickly tell you the camp(s) their parents were in, even though the interment experience often had ended a decade or more before they were born.

Works Cited

"AACRE 2007 Legislative Agenda." n.d. Asian Americans for Civil Rights and Equality. Available at http://www.aacre.org/agenda/2007legagenda/.

AALDEF. See Asian American Legal Defense and Education Fund.

Abelmann, Nancy and John Lie. 1995. *Blue Dreams: Korean Americans and the Los Angeles Riots*. Cambridge, Mass.: Harvard University Press.

"About Language Minority Voting Rights." n.d. U.S. Department of Justice, Civil Rights Division, Voting Section Home Page. Available at http://www.usdoj.gov/crt/voting/sec_203/activ_203.htm.

Alba, Richard D. 1990. *Ethnic Identity: The Transformation of White America*. New Haven: Yale University Press.

Alba, Richard and Victor Nee. 2003. *Remaking the American Mainstream: Assimilation and Contemporary Immigration*. Cambridge, Mass.: Harvard University Press.

Allport, Gordon. 1954. *The Nature of Prejudice*. Cambridge, Mass.: Addison-Wesley.

American Coalition for Filipino Veterans (ACFV). n.d., <http://usfilvets.tripod.com/> (accessed April 9, 2007).

American National Election Study. 2004. Pre- and Post-Election Survey [Computer file]. ICPSR04245-v1. University of Michigan, Center for Political Studies, American National Election Study. Ann Arbor: University of Michigan, Center for Political Studies, American National Election Study [producer], 2004. Ann Arbor, Mich.: Inter-university Consortium for Political and Social Research [distributor], 2006-02-17.

Aoki, Andrew L. and Don T. Nakanishi. 2001. "Asian Pacific Americans and the New Minority Politics." *PS: Political Science & Politics* 34(3): 605–10.

Asian American Legal Defense and Education Fund (AALDEF). 2005a. Asian American Access to Democracy in the 2004 Elections: Local compliance with the Voting Rights Act and Help America Vote Act (HAVA) in NY, NJ, MA, RI, MI, IL, PA, VA. Released on August 18. <http://www.aaldef.org/articles/2005-08-18_189_AsianAmericanA.pdf> (downloaded March 5, 2007).

—. 2005b. The Asian American Vote: A Report on the AALDEF Multilingual Exit Poll in the 2004 Presidential Election. Released on April 20. <http://www.aaldef.org/articles/2005-04-20_67_TheAsianAmeric.pdf> (accessed March 5, 2007).

"Asian Americans and the Voting Rights Act: The Case for Reauthorization." 2006. A report of the Asian American Legal Defense and Educational Fund. Available at http://www.aaldef.org/docs/AALDEF-VRAReauthorization-2006.pdf.

Asian Pacific American Legal Center (APALC). 2006. Asian Americans at the Ballot Box: The 2004 General Election: Growing Voter Participation in Southern California. Released on June 2nd. <http://apalc.org/demographics/wp-content/uploads/2006/09/ballot-box-060916.pdf> (accessed March 6, 2007).

Avakian, Monique. 2002. *Atlas of Asian-American History.* New York: Facts on File.

Banfield, Edward C. 1970. *The Unheavenly City.* Boston: Little, Brown.

Barnes, Jessica E. and Claudette E. Bennett. 2002. The Asian Population: 2000. Census 2000 Brief. (C2KBR/01-16). Washington. U.S. Bureau of Census. http://www.census.gov/prod/2002pubs/c2kbr01-16.pdf

Basch, Linda, Nina Glick Schiller, and Cristina Szanton Blanc.1993. *Nations Unbound: Transnational Projects, Postcolonial Predicaments, and Deterritorialized Nation-states.* New York: Routledge.

Bauman, Kurt J. and Nikki L. Graf. 2003. Educational Attainment: 2000. Census 2000 Brief (C2KBR-24). Washington. U.S. Bureau of Census. http://www.census.gov/prod/2003pubs/c2kbr-24.pdf

Bean, Frank and Gillian Stevens. 2003. *America's Newcomers and the Dynamics of Diversity.* New York: Russell Sage Foundation.

Bell, David. 1985. "The Triumph of Asian-American: America's Greatest Success Story." *New Republic.* July 15: 24-31.

Bishaw, Alemayehu and John Iceland. 2003. Poverty: 1999. Census 2000 Brief (C2KBR-19). Washington. U.S. Bureau of Census. http://www.census.gov/prod/2003pubs/c2kbr-19.pdf.

Blum, Lawrence. 2002. *'I'm not a racist, but . . .' The Moral Quandry of Race.* Ithaca, NY: Cornell University Press.

Blumer, Herbert. 1958. "Race Prejudice as a Sense of Group Position." *Pacific Sociological Review* 1(1): 3-7.

Bobo, Lawrence and Vincent L. Hutchings. 1996. "Perceptions of Racial Group Competition: Extending Blumer's Theory of Group Position to a Multiracial Social Context." *American Sociological Review* 61(6): 951-72.

Bobo, Lawrence D. and Susan A. Suh. 2000. "Surveying Racial Discrimination: Analyses from a Multiethnic Labor Market." In Lawrence D. Bobo, Melvin L. Oliver, James H. Johnson Jr., and Abel Valenzuela Jr., eds., *Prismatic Metropolis: Inequality in Los Angeles.* New York: Russell Sage Foundation, 523-60.

Bobo, Lawrence et al. 2000. *Multi-City Study of Urban Inequality, 1992-1994.* UCLA/Inter-university Consortium for Social Research.

Brackman, Harold and Steven P. Erie. 1995. "Beyond 'Politics by Other Means'? Empowerment Strategies for Los Angeles' Asian Pacific Community." In Michael Peter Smith and Joe R. Feagin, eds., *The Bubbling Cauldron: Race, Ethnicity, and the Urban Crisis.* Minneapolis: University of Minnesota Press. 282-303.

Brown, Curt. 2007. "The Arrest of Gen. Vang Pao." *Star Tribune* (June 6): 1.A. Available at www.startribune.com.

Browning, Rufus P., Dale Rogers Marshall, and David H. Tabb. 2003. "Mobilization, Incorporation, and Policy in 10 California Cities." In Rufus P. Browning, Dale Rogers Marshall, and David H. Tabb, eds., *Racial Politics in American Cities*, 3rd edn. New York: Longman, 17-48.

Butterfield, Fox. 1986. "Why Asians Are Going to the Head of the Class." *New York Times Magazine* (November 30): 75-6, 89-90, 92.

California Secretary of State. various years. *Statement of Vote.* Available at http://www.sos.ca.gov/elections/elections_elections.htm>.

California State Assembly. 2007. *Member Directory* http://www.assembly.ca.gov/acs/acsframeset7text.htm> (accessed August 11, 2007).

"Campaign Finance Key Player: John Huang." 1998. *Washington Post* (September 4). Available at http://www.washingtonpost.com/wp-srv/politics/special/campfin/players/huang.htm

Campaign for Justice. n.d. Campaign for Justice: Redress Now for Japanese Latin American Internees! Action Packet <http://www.campaignforjusticejla.org/resources/pdf/cfjactionpacket.pdf> (accessed March 31, 2007).

Campbell, Angus, Philip E. Converse, Warren E. Miller, and Donald E. Stokes. 1960. *The American Voter*. New York: Wiley.

Carnes, Tony and Fenggang Yang, eds. 2003. *Asian American Religions: The Making and Remaking of Borders and Boundaries*. New York: New York University Press.

Cervantes, Roy. 2007. "Asian Americans in the New American Labor and Immigrant Rights Movements: An Interview with Kent Wong, Director of the UCLA Center for Labor Research and Education." *Asian American Policy Review* 16: 9–17.

Chan, Kenyon S. 2001. "U.S.-Born, Immigrant, Refugee, or Indigenous Status: Public Policy Implications for Asian Pacific American Families." In Gordon H. Chang, ed., *Asian Americans and Politics: Perspectives, Experiences, Prospects*. Washington: Woodrow Wilson Center Press: 197–229.

Chan, Sucheng. 1991. *Asian Americans: An Interpretive History*. London: Twayne.

Chang, Edward T. and Jeannette Diaz-Veizades. 1999. *Ethnic Peace in the American City: Building Community in Los Angeles and Beyond*. New York: New York University Press.

"Changes to the Hmong Veterans' Naturalization Act of 2000." 2001. Immigration and Naturalization Service. Available at http://www.ailc.com/publicaffairs/factsheets/Hmong.htm.

"Changing Faiths: Latinos and the Transformation of American Religion." 2007. Pew Research Center. Available at http://pewforum.org/surveys/hispanic/hispanics-religion-07.pdf.

Cho, Wendy K. Tam. 2002. "Tapping Motives and Dynamics Behind Campaign Contributions: Insights from the Asian American Case." *American Politics Research* 30(4): 347–83.

Cho, Wendy K. Tam and Suneet P. Lad 2004. "Subcontinental Divide: Asian Indians and Asian American Politics." *American Politics Research* 32(3): 239–63.

Chuman, Frank F. 1976. *The Bamboo People: The Law and Japanese-Americans*. Del Mar, Calif.: Publishers Inc.

Collet, Chris. 2005. "Bloc Voting, Polarization and the Panethnic Hypothesis: The Case of Little Saigon." *Journal of Politics* 67(3): 907–33.

Commission on Wartime Relocation and Internment of Civilians (CWRIC). 1983 [1997]. Personal Justice Denied: Report of the Commission on Wartime Relocation and Internment of Civilians. Washington: U.S. Government Printing Office. Reprint, Washington: The Civil Liberties Education Fund; Seattle: University of Washington Press.

A Community of Contrasts: Asian Americans and Pacific Islanders in the United States. Demographic Profile. 2006. Asian American Justice Center and Asian Pacific American Legal Center.

Congressional Quarterly. 1995. *Presidential Elections 1789–1992*. Washington. D.C.: Congressional Quarterly Inc.

Congressional Quarterly. 2007. "Women and Minorities in the 110th Congress" *CQ Weekly* Feb. 26: 607.

Cook, Thomas D. and Donald T. Campbell. 1979. *Quasi-Experimentation: Design and Analysis Issues for Field Settings*. Boston: Houghton Mifflin.

Dahl, Robert. 1961: *Who Governs? Democracy and Power in an American City*. New Haven: Yale University Press.

Daniels, Roger. 2005. "Words Do Matter: A Note on Inappropriate Terminology and the Incarceration of the Japanese Americans." In Louis Fiset and Gail M. Nomura, eds., *Nikkei in the Pacific Northwest: Japanese Americans and Japanese Canadians in the Twentieth Century*. Seattle: University of Washington Press, 190–214.

—.1988. *Asian America: Chinese and Japanese in the United States since 1850*. Seattle and London: University of Washington Press.

—.1981. *Concentration Camps: North America Japanese in the United States and Canada During World War II*. Malabar, Fla.: Robert E. Krieger Publishing Company.

Das Gupta, Monisha. 2006. *Unruly Immigrants: Rights, Activism, and Transnational South Asian Politics in the United States*. Durham, NC: Duke University Press.

David Wu for Congress. n.d. "Background/Experience." <http://wuforcongress.com/background.htm> (accessed September 22, 1998).

Dawson, Michael C. 2001. *Black Visions: The Roots of Contemporary African-American Political Ideologies*. Chicago: University of Chicago Press.

de la Cruz, C. Patricia and Angela Brittingham. 2003. The Arab Population: 2000. Census 2000 Brief (C2KBR-23). Washington: U.S. Bureau of Census. <http://www.census.gov/prod/2003pubs/c2kbr-23.pdf>

de la Garza, Rodolfo O. et al. 1992. *Latino Voices: Mexican, Puerto Rican, and Cuban Perspectives on American Politics*. Boulder, Colo.: Westview.

Diaz, Vicente M. 2004. " 'To "P" or Not to "P"?': Marking the Territory between Pacific Islander and Asian American Studies." *Journal of Asian American Studies* 7(3): 183–208.

Dovi, Susanne. 2002. "Preferable Descriptive Representatives: Will Just Any Woman, Black, or Latino Do?" *American Political Science Review* 96(4): 729–43.

"A Drive to Excel." 1984. *Newsweek-on-Campus* (April): 4–8, 12–13.

D'Souza, Dinesh. 1995. "Separation of Race and State." *Wall Street Journal* (September 12): A26.

DuBois, W. E. B. 1903. *The Souls of Black Folk*. Chicago: A. C. McClurg & Co.

Edmunds, R. David, ed. 2001. *The New Warriors: Native American Leaders since 1990*. Lincoln: University of Nebraska Press.

Edsall, Thomas B. and Edward Walsh. 2002. "FEC Issues Record Fines In Democrats' Scandals" *Washington Post* (September 21): A5

Edwards, George C., Martin P. Wattenberg, and Robert L. Lineberry. 2006. *Government in America: People, Politics, and Policy* 12th edn. New York: Pearson.

Endo, Russell and William Wei. 1988. "On the Development of Asian American Studies Programs." In Gary Y. Okihiro, Shirley Hune, Arthur A. Hansen, and John M. Liu, eds, *Reflections on Shattered Windows: Promises and Prospects for Asian American Studies*. Pullman: Washington State University Press: 5–15.

Erie, Steven P. 1988. *Rainbow's End. Irish-Americans and the Dilemmas of Urban Political Machines, 1840-1985*. Berkeley: University of California Press.

Espenshade, Thomas J. and Chang Y. Chung. 2005. "The Opportunity Cost of Admission Preferences at Elite Universities." *Social Science Quarterly* 86(2): 293–305.

Espenshade, Thomas J., Chang Y. Chung, and Joan L. Walling. 2004. "Admission Preferences for Minority Students, Athletes, and Legacies at Elite Universities." *Social Science Quarterly* 85(5): 1422–46.

Espina, Marina E. 1988. *Filipinos in Louisiana*. New Orleans: A. F. Laborde & Sons.

Espiritu, Yen Le. 2004. "Asian American Panethnicity: National and Transnational Possibilities." In Nancy M. Foner and George M. Fredrickson, eds, *Not Just Black and White: Historical and Contemporary Perspectives on Immigration, Race, and Ethnicity in the United States*. New York: Russell Sage Foundation: 217–34.

—. 2001. "Possibility of a Multiracial Asian America". In Teresa Williams-León and Cynthia L. Nakashima, eds, *The Sum of Our Parts: Mixed-Heritage Asian Americans*. Philadelphia: Temple University Press: 25–33.

—. 1997. *Asian American Women and Men: Labor, Laws, and Love*. Thousand Oaks, Calif.: Sage Publications.

—. 1992. *Asian American Panethnicity: Bridging Institutions and Identities*. Philadelphia: Temple University Press.

Espiritu, Yen Le and Michael Omi. 2000. " 'Who Are You Calling Asian?': Shifting Identity Claims, Racial Classifications, and the Census." In Paul M. Ong, ed., *The State of Asian Pacific America: Transforming Race Relations. A Public Policy Report*. Los Angeles: LEAP Asia Pacific American Public Policy Institute and UCLA Asian American Studies Center: 43–101.

Feagin, Joe R. and Clairece Booher Feagin. 1996. *Racial and Ethnic Relations*. 5th edn. Upper Saddle River, NJ: Prentice Hall.

Federal Election Commission. 2003. Report of Receipts and Disbursements for an Authorized Committee. Available online at http://www.fec.gov/pdf/forms/fecfrm3i.pdf

Fix, Michael and Ron Haskins. 2002. "Welfare Benefits for Non-citizens." WR &B Brief #15. Washington: Brookings Institution. Available at http://www.brook.edu/es/research/projects/wrb/publications/pb/pb15.htm.

Foner, Nancy. 2001. "Transnationalism Then and Now: New York Immigrants Today and at the Turn of the Twentieth Century." in Héctor R. Cordero-Guzmán, Robert C. Smith, and Ramón Grosfoguel, eds, *Migration, Transnationalization, and Race in a Changing New York*. Philadelphia: Temple University Press: 35–57.

Fong, Matt. 1999. "Silence is Not Golden: Speak Out Against Insinuations of Disloyalty." *Asian Week* May 20.

Fong, Timothy P. 2002. *The Contemporary Asian American Experience: Beyond the Model Minority*. Upper Saddle River, NJ: Prentice Hall.

—. 1994. *The First Suburban Chinatown: The Remaking of Monterey Park, California*. Philadelphia: Temple University Press.

Fossett, Mark A. and K. Jill Kiecolt. 1989. "The Relative Size of Minority Populations and White Racial Attitudes." *Social Science Quarterly* 70(5): 51–61.

Fragomen, Austin T., Jr. 1996. "Welfare Bill Severely Curtails Public Assistance to Noncitizens." *International Migration Review* 30(4): 1087–95.

Freer, Regina. 1994. "Black–Korean Conflict." In Mark Baldassare, ed., *The Los Angeles Riots: Lessons for the Urban Future*. Boulder, Colo.: Westview Press: 175–203.

Fremstad, Shawn. 2004. "The Impact of the Seven-Year Limit on Refugees' Eligibility for Supplemental Security Income." Center on Budget and Policy Priorities. Available at http://www.cbpp.org/5-17-04imm.pdf.

—. 2002. "Immigrants and Welfare Reauthorization." Center on Budget and Policy Priorities. Available at http://www.cbpp.org/1-22-02tanf4.htm.

Fugita, Stephen S. and David J. O'Brien, 1991. *Japanese American Ethnicity: The Persistence of Community*. Seattle: University of Washington Press.

—. 1977. "Economics, Ideology, and Ethnicity: The Struggle between the United Farm Workers Union and the Nisei Farmers League." *Social Problems* 25(2): 146–56.

Fujiwara, Lynn H. 1998. "The Impact of Welfare Reform on Asian Immigrant Communities." *Social Justice* 25(1): 82–94.

Gamm, Gerald. 1989. *The Making of New Deal Democrats: Voting Behavior and Realignment in Boston, 1920-1940*. Chicago: University of Chicago Press.

Gans, Herbert J. 1979. "Symbolic Ethnicity: The Future of Ethnic Groups and Cultures in America." *Ethnic and Racial Studies* 2: 1–20

Geron, Kim, Enrique de la Cruz, Leland T. Saito, and Jaideep Singh. 2001. "Asian Pacific Americans' Social Movements and Interest Groups." *PS: Political Science & Politics* 34(3): 619–24.

Glazer, Nathan and Daniel Patrick Moynihan. 1970/1963. *Beyond the Melting Pot: The Negroes, Puerto Ricans, Jews, Italians, and Irish of New York City*, 2nd edn. Cambridge, Mass.: MIT Press

Golden, Daniel. 2006. "Is Admissions Bar Higher for Asians at Elite Schools? School Standards Are Probed Even as Enrollment Increases." *Wall Street Journal* (November 11): A1.

Gooding-Williams, Robert. 1993. "Introduction: On Being Stuck." In Robert Gooding-Williams, ed., *Reading Rodney King/Reading Urban Uprising*. New York & London: Routledge: 1–12.

Grady, Denise. 2007. "Researchers Find Distinctive Patterns of Cancer in 5 Groups of Asian-Americans." *New York Times* (July 11): A12.

Graham, Barbara L. 2004. "Toward an Understanding of Judicial Diversity in American Courts." *Michigan Journal Race and Law* 10(1): 153–93.

Grieco, Elizabeth M. and Rachel C. Cassidy. 2001. Overview of Race and Hispanic Origin: Census 2000 Brief (C2kBR/01-1). Washington. U.S. Bureau of Census. http://www.census.gov/prod/2001pubs/c2kbr01-1.pdf

Grofman, Barnard and Chandler Davidson eds. 1992. *Controversies in Minority Voting: The Voting Rights Act in Perspective*. Washington. Brookings Institution.

Gyory, Andrew. 1998. *Closing the Gates: Race, Politics, and the Chinese Exclusion Act.* Chapel Hill: University of North Carolina Press.

Haney López, Ian. 1996. *White by Law: The Legal Construction of Race*. New York: New York University Press.

Harlan, Heather. 2006. "Grace Meng Drops Out of Race." *Asian Week: Voice of Asian America* (August 25).

Harper, Charles L. 1998. *Exploring Social Change: America and the World*, 3rd edn. Upper Saddle River, NJ: Prentice Hall.

Harris, John F. 1997. "White House Unswayed by China Allegations." *Washington Post* (July 20): A1.

Hatamiya, Leslie. 1993. *Righting a Wrong: Japanese Americans and the Passage of the Civil Liberties Act of 1988*. Stanford, Calif.: Stanford University Press.

Hayashi, Mary Chung. 2003. *Far from Home: Shattering the Myth of the Model Minority*. Arlington, Tex.: Tapestry Press.

Hayduk, Ron. 2006. *Democracy for All: Restoring Immigrant Voting Rights in the United States*. New York: Routledge.

Hein, Jeremy. 2006. *Ethnic Origins: The Adaptation of Cambodian and Hmong Refugees in Four American Cities*. New York: Russell Sage Foundation.

Hing, Bill Ong. 2001. "Asians without Blacks and Latinos in San Francisco: Missed Lessons of the Common Good." *Amerasia Journal* 27(2): 19–27.

—. 1993. *Making and Remaking Asian America through Immigration Policy, 1850–1990*. Stanford, Calif.: Stanford University Press.

Horn, Wade F. 2006. Testimony before the Committee on Ways and Means, U.S. House of Representatives. July 26. Available at http://www.hhs.gov/asl/testify/t060726.html.

Horton, John. 1995. *The Politics of Diversity: Immigration, Resistance, and Change in Monterey Park, California*. Philadelphia: Temple University Press.

Hum, Tarry. 2004. "Asian Immigrant Settlements in New York City: Defining 'Community of Interest'" *AAPI Nexus* 2(2): 20–48.

Hune, Shirley. 1995. "Rethinking Race: Paradigms and Policy Formation." *Amerasia Journal* 21(1&2): 29–40.

Hutchings, Vincent and Cara Wong. 2006. "Whose Side Are You On? Explaining Perceptions of Competitive Threat in a Multi-racial and Multi-ethnic National Sample." Paper presented at the annual meeting of the American Political Science Association, Philadelphia, Pennsylvania.

Ignatiev, Noel. 1995. *How the Irish became White*. London: Verso.

Imahara, Kathryn K. 1993. "Language Rights Issues to the Year 2020 and Beyond: Language Rights Policy." In *The State of Asian Pacific America: A Public Policy Report. Policy Issues to the Year 2020*. Los Angeles: LEAP Asian Pacific American Public Policy Institute and UCLA Asian American Studies Center: 233–51.

"Information Sharing Could Help Institutions Identify and Address Challenges that Some Asian American and Pacific Islander Students Face." 2007. United States Government Accountability Office Report to Congressional Requesters. GAO-07-925. Available at http://www.gao.gov/new.items/d07925.pdf.

Irons, Peter. 1989a. "Introduction: Righting a Great Wrong." In Peter Irons, ed., *Justice Delayed: The Record of the Japanese American Internment Cases*. Middletown, Conn.: Wesleyan University Press: 3–46.

—, ed. 1989b. *Justice Delayed: The Record of the Japanese American Internment Cases*. Middletown: Conn.: Wesleyan University Press.

—. 1983. *Justice at War: The Story of the Japanese American Internment Cases*. New York: Oxford University Press.

Iwamura, Jane Naomi, and Paul Spickard. 2003. *Revealing the Sacred in Asian and Pacific America*. New York: Routledge.

Jackson, Robert L. 2000. "Democratic Fund-Raiser Convicted of 5 Felonies." *Los Angeles Times* (March 3): 1.

Jacobs, Jane. 1961. *The Death and Life of Great American Cities*. New York: Random House.

Jacobson, Matthew Frye. 1998. *Whiteness of a Different Color: European Immigrants and the Alchemy of Race*. Cambridge, Mass.: Harvard University Press.

Jacoby, Tamar. 2000. "In Asian America." *Commentary* (July–August): 21–8.

Jeung, Russell. 2005. *Faithful Generations: Race and New Asian American Churches*. New Brunswick, NJ: Rutgers University Press.

Jindal, Bobby. n.d. "Biography." http://jindal.house.gov/biography/.

Johnson, James H., Jr. and Melvin L. Oliver. 1989. "Interethnic Minority Conflict in Urban America: The Effects of Economic and Social Dislocations." *Urban Geography* 10(5): 449–63.

Johnston, David. 1999. "Friend of President Admits to Violating Fund-Raising Laws." *New York Times* (May 22): A1.

Jones-Correa, Michael. 2002. "The Study of Transnationalism among the Children of Immigrants: Where We Are and Where We Should be Headed." In Peggy Levitt and Mary C. Waters, eds, *The Changing Face of Home: The Transnational Lives of the Second Generation*. New York: Russell Sage Foundation: 221–52.

Kamen, Al. 2001. "The Honeymoon Sinks in the East." *Washington Post* (May 25): A37.

Kang, Cecilla. 2004. "Political Group Aiming Higher: Club Focuses on Assembly Race after Successful Local Efforts." *San Jose Mercury News* (Jan. 25).

Kashima, Tetsuden. 2003. *Judgment without Trial: Japanese American Imprisonment During World War II*. Seattle: University of Washington Press.

Kennedy, Tony and Paul McEnroe. 2005. "The Covert Wars of Vang Pao." *Star Tribune* (July 5): 1.A. Available at www.startribune.com

Kernell, Samuel and Gary C. Jacobson. 2006. *The Logic of American Politics*, 3rd edn. Washington: CQ Press.

Key, V. O. 1949. *Southern Politics in State and Nation*. Knoxville: University of Tennessee Press.

Khagram, Sanjeev, Manish Desai, and Jason Varughese. 2001. "Seen, Rich, but Unheard? The Politics of Asian Indians in the United States." In Gordon H. Chang, ed., *Asian Americans and Politics: Perspectives, Experiences, Prospects*. Washington: Woodrow Wilson Press: 258–84.

Khandelwal, Madhulika S. 2002. *Becoming American, Being Indian: An Immigrant Community in New York City*. Ithaca, N.Y. & London: Cornell University Press.

Kiang, Peter N. and Vivian Wai-Fun Lee. 1993. "Exclusion or Contribution? Education K-12 Policy." In *The State of Asian Pacific America: A Public Policy Report. Policy Issues to the Year 2020*. Los Angeles: LEAP Asian Pacific American Public Policy Institute and UCLA Asian American Studies Center: 25–48.

Kiang, Peter Nien-chu, and Shirley Suet-ling Tang. 2006. "Electoral Politics and the Contexts of Empowerment, Displacement, and Diaspora for Boston's Vietnamese and Cambodian American Communities." *Asian American Policy Review* 15: 13–29.

Kibria, Nazli. 2002. *Becoming Asian American: Second-Generation Chinese and Korean American Identities*. Baltimore: Johns Hopkins University Press.

Kim, Claire Jean. 2004. "Asian Americans are People of Color, Too . . . Aren't They? Cross-Racial Alliances and the Question of Asian American Political Identity" *AAPI Nexus* 2(1): 19–47.

—. 2000. *Bitter Fruit: The Politics of Black–Korean Conflict in New York City*. New Haven: Yale University Press.

—. 1999. "The Racial Triangulation of Asian Americans." *Politics and Society* 27 (1): 105–38.

Kim, Elaine. 1993. "Meditations on the Year 2020: Policy for Women." *In The State of Asian Pacific America: A Public Policy Report. Policy Issues to the Year 2020*. Los Angeles:

LEAP Asian Pacific American Public Policy Institute and UCLA Asian American Studies Center: 253–61.

Kim, Hyung-chan. 1994. *A Legal History of Asian Americans, 1790–1990*. Westport, Conn.: Greenwood Press.

Kim, Thomas P. 2007. *The Racial Logic of Politics: Asian Americans and Party Competition*. Philadelphia: Temple University Press.

Kitano, Harry H. L. 1976. *Japanese Americans: The Evolution of a Subculture*. Englewood Cliffs, NJ: Prentice Hall.

Knecht, B. Bruce. 2002. "Vietnam's 'Dust Children' Seek Visas, but Appearance Stands in the Way." *Wall Street Journal* (April 8). Available at http://online.wsj.com.

Kobayashi, Audrey. 1992. "The Japanese-Canadian Redress Settlement and its Implications for 'Race Relations.'" *Canadian Ethnic Studies* 24(1): 1-19.

Kristof, Nicholas D. 2006. "The Model Student." *New York Times* (May 14): Sec. 4, p. 13.

Kwong, Peter. 1996/1987. *The New Chinatown* rev. edn. New York: Hill and Wang.

Lachica, Eric. 1999. " 'The Filipino Veterans SSI Extension Act,' H.R. 26." Prepared Statement before a hearing of the Human Resources Subcommittee of the House of Ways and Means Committee. February 3.

Lai, Eric and Dennis Arguelles, eds. 2003. *The New Face of Asian Pacific America: Numbers, Diversity and Change in the 21st Century*. San Francisco: Asian Week.

Lai, James S. forthcoming. *Suburban Transformations and Immigrant Incorporation: The Political Mobilization of Asian Americans in Ten U.S. Suburbs*.

—. 2005. "The Suburbanization of Asian American Politics." In Don T. Nakanishi, James S. Lai, and Daphne Kwok eds, *National Asian Pacific American Political Almanac*, 12th edn. Los Angeles: UCLA Asian American Studies Center and Washington: Asian Pacific American Institute for Congressional Studies.

—. 2000. "Asian Americans and the Pan-Ethnic Question." In Richard A. Keiser and Katherine Underwood, eds, *Minority Politics at the Millennium*. New York: Garland Publishing, 203–26.

—. 1998-9. "Racially Polarized Voting and its Effects on the Formation of a Viable Latino–Asian Pacific Political Coalition." In Don T. Nakanishi and James S. Lai, eds, *National Asian Pacific American Political Almanac*, 8th edn. Los Angeles: UCLA Asian American Studies Center: 156–83.

Lai, James S. and Kim Geron. 2006. "When Asian Americans Run: The Suburban and Urban Dimensions of Asian American Candidates in California Local Politics." *California Politics and Policy* (June): 62–88.

Lai, James, Wendy K. Tam Cho, Thomas P. Kim, and Okiyoshi Takeda. 2001. "Asian Pacific-American Campaigns, Elections, and Elected Officials." *PS: Political Science & Politics* 34(3): 611–17.

"Language Access Publications and Materials." n.d. Asian American Justice Center. Available at http://www.advancingequality.org/.

Lawless, Jennifer L. and Richard L. Fox. 2005. *It Takes a Candidate: Why Women Don't Run for Office*. New York: Cambridge University Press.

Lee, Robert G. 1999. *Orientals: Asian Americans in Popular Culture*. Philadelphia: Temple University Press.

Lee, Sharon M. and Barry Edmonston. 2005. "New Marriages, New Families: U.S. Racial and Hispanic Intermarriage." *Population Bulletin* 60(2).

Lee, Taeku. 2000. "Racial Attitudes and the Color Line(s) at the Close of the Twentieth Century. In Paul M. Ong, ed., *The State of Asian Pacific America: Transforming Race Relations*. Los Angeles: LEAP Asian Pacific American Public Policy Institute and UCLA Asian American Studies Center: 103–58.

Levitt, Peggy and Mary C. Waters. 2002. "Introduction." In Peggy Levitt and Mary C. Waters, eds, *The Changing Face of Home: The Transnational Lives of the Second Generation*. New York: Russell Sage Foundation: 1–30.

Lewis, Neil A. 2000a. "Jury Deliberations to Begin in Gore Fund-Raiser's Trial." *New York Times* (February 29): A19.

—. 2000b. "Longtime Fund-Raiser for Gore Convicted in Donation Scheme." *New York Times* (March 3): A1.

(Joint Committee on Printing, U.S. Congress), *Biographical Directory of the United States Congress* <http://bioguide.congress.gov/biosearch/biosearch.asp>

Lie, John. 2004. "The Black–Asian Conflict?" In Nancy Foner and George M. Fredrickson, eds, *Not Just Black and White: Historical and Contemporary Perspectives on Immigration, Race, and Ethnicity in the United States*. New York: Russell Sage Foundation: 301–14.

Lien Pei-te. 2006. "Transnational Homeland Concerns and Participation in U.S. Politics: A Comparison among Immigrants from China, Taiwan, and Hong Kong." *Journal of Chinese Overseas* 2(1): 269–98.

—. 2003. "Religion and Political Adaptation among Asian Americans: An Empirical Assessment from the Pilot National Asian American Political Survey" in Carnes and Yang (2003): 263–84.

—. 2001. *The Making of Asian America through Political Participation*. Philadelphia: Temple University Press.

—. 1998. "Does the Gender Gap in Political Attitudes and Behavior Vary Across Racial Groups?" *Political Research Quarterly* 51(4): 869–94.

Lien, Pei-te, Christian Collet, Janelle Wong, and S. Karthick Ramakrishnan. 2001. "Asian Pacific American Public Opinion and Political Participation" *PS: Political & Politics* 34(3): 625–30.

Lien, Pei-te, M. Margaret Conway, and Janelle Wong. 2004. *The Politics of Asian Americans: Diversity & Community*. New York: Routledge.

Lin, Lynda. 2007. "The Count Me In! Campaign Strives to Shed Light on the Plight of Smaller APA Ethnic Groups. A Calif. Assembly Bill Seeks to Do the Same for State Agencies." *Pacific Citizen* June 15. Available at http://www.pacificcitizen.org/content/2007/national/june15-lin-countmein. htm.

Link, Michael and Robert Oldenick. 1996. "Social Construction and White Attitudes toward Equal Opportunity and Multiculturalism." *Journal of Politics* 58(1): 149–68.

Lippmann, Walter. 1922/1945. *Public Opinion*. New York: Macmillan.

Liu, Eric. 1998. *The Accidental Asian: Notes of a Native Speaker*. New York: Vintage Books.

Los Angeles Times Poll. 2004. National and California Exit Poll, Study #513. November 4.

Los Angeles Times Poll. 2000. Exit Poll: The Nation and California, Study #449. November 9.

Los Angeles Times Poll 1997a. #395.

Los Angeles Times Poll 1997b. #396.

Lott, Juanita Tamayo. 1998. *Asian Americans: From Racial Category to Multiple Identities*. Walnut Creek, Calif.: AltaMira Press.

Louie, Miriam Ching. 1997. "Breaking the Cycle: Women Workers Confront Corporate Greed Globally." In Sonia Shah, ed., *Dragon Ladies: Asian American Feminists Breathe Fire*. Boston: South End Press: 121–31.

Lowe, Lisa. 1991. "Heterogeneity, Hybridity, Multiplicity: Marking Asian American Differences." *Diaspora* 1(1): 24–44.

Ma, Fiona. 2007. "Q plus A with Assembly Member Fiona Ma." *California CPA* (June): 14–17.

Ma, Jason. 2000. "Straight from the Church: How Korean American Churches in California Rallied against Gay Rights." *Asian Week* (January 20). Available at http://www.asianweek.com/2000_01_20/feature_church.html.

Ma, L. Eve Armentrout. 1991. "Chinatown Organizations and the Anti-Chinese Movement, 1882–1914." In Sucheng Chan, ed., *Exclusion and the Chinese American Community in America*. Philadelphia: Temple University Press. 147–69.

McClain, Charles J. 1994. *In Search of Equality: The Chinese Struggle against Discrimination in Nineteenth-Century America*. Berkeley: University of California Press.

Magpantay, Glenn D. 2006. "The Ambivalence of Queer Asian Pacific Americans toward Same-Sex Marriage." *Amerasia Journal* 32(1): 109–17.

—. 2004. "Ensuring Asian American Access to Democracy in New York City." *AAPI Nexus* 2(2): 87–113.

Maki, Mitchell T., Harry H. L. Kitano, and S. Megan Berthold. 1999. *Achieving the Impossible Dream: How Japanese Americans Obtained Redress*. Urbana: University of Illinois Press.

Mansbridge, Jane. 1999. "Should Blacks Represent Blacks and Women Represent Women? A Contingent 'Yes.'" *Journal of Politics* 61(3): 628–57.

Massey, Douglas S. and Nancy A. Denton. 1993. *American Apartheid: Segregation and the Making of the Underclass*. Cambridge, Mass.: Harvard University Press.

—. 1988. "The Dimensions of Residential Segregation." *Social Forces* 67(2): 281–315.

Melendy, H. Brett. 1984. *Chinese & Japanese Americans*. rev. edn. New York: Hippocrene Books.

Mills, Karen M. 2001. Congressional Apportionment. Census 2000 Brief (C2KBR/01-7). <http://www.census.gov/prod/2001pubs/c2kbr01-7.pdf>

Min, Pyong Gap. 2006. "Settlement Pattern and Diversity." In Pyong Gap Min, ed., *Asian Americans: Contemporary Trends and Issues*, 2nd edn., Thousand Oaks, Calif.: Pine Forge Press: 32–53.

—. 2002. *Second Generation: Ethnic Identity among Asian Americans*. Walnut Creek, Calif.: AltaMira Press.

—. 1995. "Korean Americans." In Pyong Gap Min, ed. *Asian Americans: Contemporary Trends and Issues*. Thousand Oaks, Calif.: Sage: 199–231.

Min, Pyong Gap, and Jung Ha Kim, eds. 2002. *Religions in Asian America: Building Faith Communities*. Walnut Creek, Calif.: AltaMira Press.

Mink, Gwendolyn. 1986. *Old Labor and New Immigrants in American Political Development: Union, Party, and State, 1875–1920*. Ithaca, NY: Cornell University Press.

Minnesota Secretary of State. n.d. "2002 Election Results" http://www.sos.state.mn.us/home/index.asp?page=285> (accessed August 18, 2007).

Moore, Thomas and Vicky Selkowe. 1999. "The Impact of Welfare Reform on Wisconsin's Hmong Aid Recipients." A Report by the Institute for Wisconsin's

Future. Available at http://www.wisconsinsfuture.org/publications/workingfamilies/Hmong.pdf.

Moss, Philip and Chris Tilly. 2001. *Stories Employers Tell: Race, Skill, and Hiring in America*. New York: Russell Sage.

Nagel, Joane. 1996. *American Indian Ethnic Renewal: Red Power and the Resurgence of Identity and Culture*. New York: Oxford University Press.

Nakanishi, Don T. 1991. "The Next Swing Vote? Asian Pacific Americans and California Politics." In Byran O. Jackson and Michael B. Preston, eds., *Racial and Ethnic Politics in California*. Berkeley, Calif.: IGS Press. 25–54.

—.1998. "When Numbers Do Not Add Up: Asian Pacific Americans and California Politics." In Michael B. Preston, Bruce E. Cain and Sandra Bass, eds, *Racial and Ethnic Politics in California*, vol. 2. Berkeley, Calif.: Institute of Governmental Studies: 3–43.

—.1986. "Asian American Politics: An Agenda for Research." *Amerasia Journal* 12(2): 1–27.

Nakanishi, Don T. and James S. Lai, eds. 2003. *National Asian Pacific American Political Almanac*, 11th edn. Los Angeles: UCLA Asian American Studies Center.

—.2001 *National Asian Pacific American Political Almanac*, 10th edn. Los Angeles: UCLA Asian American Studies Center.

—.2000–1. *National Asian Pacific American Political Almanac*, 9th edn, Special Election edn. Los Angeles: UCLA Asian American Studies Center.

—.1998–9. *National Asian Pacific American Political Almanac*, 8th edn. Los Angeles: UCLA Asian American Studies Center.

—.1996. *National Asian Pacific American Political Almanac*, 7th edn. Los Angeles: UCLA Asian American Studies Center.

—.1995. *National Asian Pacific American Political Almanac*, 6th edn. Los Angeles: UCLA Asian American Studies Center.

Nakanishi, Don T., James S. Lai, and Daphne Kwok, eds. 2005. *National Asian Pacific American Political Almanac*, 12th edn. Los Angeles: UCLA Asian American Studies Center and Washington, D.C.: Asian Pacific American Institute for Congressional Studies.

Nakano, Satoshi. 2000. "Nation, Nationalism and Citizenship in the Filipino World War II Veterans Equity Movement, 1945–1999." *Hitotsubashi Journal of Social Studies* (Hitotsubashi University, Tokyo) 32: 33–53. Available at the homepage of American Coalition for Filipino Veterans http://usfilvets.tripod.com/id10.html> (accessed May 11, 2007).

Nash, Phil Tajitsu and Frank Wu. 1997. "Asian-Americans under Glass: Where the Furor over the President's Fundraising Has Gone Awry—and Racist." *The Nation* (March 31): 15–16.

National Election Pool Poll #2004. 2004. Edison Media Research/Mitofsky International.

Newman, David M. 2000. *Sociology: Exploring the Architecture of Everyday Life*, 3rd edn. Thousand Oaks, Calif.: Pine Forge Press.

Niiya, Brian, ed. 2001. *Encyclopedia of Japanese American History: An A-to-Z Reference from 1868 to the Present*, updated edn. New York: Checkmark Books.

"OCA Demands Apology from Rosie O'Donnell and 'The View.' " n.d. OCA press release, available at http://www.ocanational.org (accessed on July 5, 2007).

Okihiro, Gary. 1994. *Margins and Mainstreams: Asians in American History and Culture.* Seattle: University of Washington Press.

Oliver, J. Eric and Janelle Wong. 2003. "Intergroup Prejudice in Multiethnic Settings." *American Journal of Political Science* 47(4): 567–82.

Omi, Michael. 1993. "Out of the Melting Pot and into the Fire: Race Relations Policy." In *The State of Asian Pacific America: Policy Issues to the Year 2020.* Los Angeles: LEAP Asian Pacific American Public Policy Institute and UCLA Asian American Studies Center.

Omi, Michael and Howard Winant. 1994. *Racial Formation in the United States: From the 1960s to the 1990s,* 2nd edn. New York: Routledge.

Ong, Paul M. 2000. "The Affirmative Action Divide." In Paul M. Ong, ed., *The State of Asian Pacific America: Transforming Race Relations. A Public Policy Report.* Los Angeles: LEAP Asian Pacific American Public Policy Institute and UCLA Asian American Studies Center.

Ong, Paul, Edna Bonacich, and Lucie Cheng. 1994. "The Political Economy of Capitalist Restructuring and the New Asian Immigration." In Paul Ong, Edna Bonacich, and Lucie Cheng, eds., *The New Asian Immigration in Los Angeles and Global Restructuring.* Philadelphia: Temple University Press: 3–35.

Ong, Paul and Don T. Nakanishi. 1996. "Becoming Citizens, Becoming Voters: The Naturalization and Political Participation of Asian American Immigrants." In Bill Ong Hing and Ronald Lee, eds, *The State of Asian America: Reframing Immigration Debate.* Los Angeles: LEAP Asian American Public Policy Institute and UCLA Asian American Studies Center: 275–305.

"Organizations Call for Historic National APA Mobilization for Just and Humane Immigration Reform." 2007. National Mobilization of Asian Pacific Americans for Just and Humane Immigration Reform. Available at http://www.searac.org/pr-searac3-27-07.html.

Padilla, Felix M. 1985. *Latino Ethnic Consciousness: The Case of Mexican Americans and Puerto Ricans in Chicago.* Notre Dame, Ind.: University of Notre Dame Press.

Park, Edward J. W. and John S.W. Park. 2005. *Probationary Americans: Contemporary Immigration Policies and the Shaping of Asian American Communities.* New York: Routledge.

Passel, Jeffrey S. 2005. "Unauthorized Migrants: Numbers and Characteristics." Pew Hispanic Center. Available at http://pewhispanic.org/files/ reports/46.pdf.

PBS. n.d. "Searching for Asian America: Asian American Politicians: Swati Dandekar." http://www.pbs.org/searching/aap_sdandekar.html> (accessed August 17, 2007).

Petersen, William. 1971. *Japanese Americans: Oppression and Success.* New York: Random House.

—. 1966. "Success Story, Japanese-American Style." *New York Times Magazine* (January 9): 20–1, 33, 36, 38, 40–1, 43.

Pilot National Asian American Political Survey (PNAAPS). 2000–1. ICPSR version. Pei-te Lien [principal investigator], Van Nuys, Calif.: Interviewing Service of America, Inc. [producer], 2001. Ann Arbor, Mich.: Inter-university Consortium for Political and Social Research [distributor], 2004.

Pinderhughes, Dianne M. 2003. "Chicago Politics: Political Incorporation and Restoration." In Rufus P. Browning, Dale Rogers Marshall, and David H. Tabb, eds, *Racial Politics in American Cities,* 3rd edn. New York: Longman: 143–66.

Piore, Michael J. 1979. *Birds of Passage: Migrant Labor and Industrial Societies*. Cambridge: Cambridge University Press.

Pitkin, Hanna Fenichel. 1967. *The Concept of Representation*. Berkeley: University of California Press.

Portes, Alejandro and Rubén G. Rumbaut. 2001. *Legacies: The Story of the Immigrant Second Generation*. Berkeley: University of California Press.

Portes, Alejandro and Richard Schauffler. 1996. "Language and the Second Generation: Bilingualism Yesterday and Today." In Alejandro Portes, ed., *The New Second Generation*. New York: Russell Sage Foundation: 8–29.

Public Papers of the Presidents of the United States: Lyndon B. Johnson, 1965. 1966. Vol.2, entry 301. Washington: Government Printing Office: 635–40.

Purkayastha, Bandana, Shyamala Raman, and Kshiteeja Bhide. 1997. "Empowering Women: SNEHA's Multifaceted Activism." In Sonia Shah, ed., *Dragon Ladies: Asian American Feminists Breathe Fire*. Boston: South End Press: 100–7.

Putnam, Robert D. 2000. *Bowling Alone: The Collapse and Revival of American Community*. New York: Touchstone.

Quillian, Lincoln. 1996. "Group Threat and Regional Change in Attitudes toward African-Americans." *American Journal of Sociology* 102(3): 816–60.

Ramirez, Roberto R. 2004. We the People: Hispanics in the United States. Census 2000 Special Reports (CENSR-18). Washington: U.S. Bureau of Census. <http://www.census.gov/prod/2004pubs/censr-18.pdf>

"The Rebellion in Los Angeles: The Context of a Proletarian Uprising." 1992. *Aufheben* 1(summer). Available online http://www.geocities.com/aufheben2/1.html. Accessed on July 20, 2007.

Reeves, Terrance J. and Claudette E. Bennett. 2004. "We the People: Asians in the United States". *Census 2000 Special Reports* (CENSR-17). Washington, D.C.: U.S. Bureau of Census. <http://www.census.gov/prod/2004pubs/censr-17.pdf>

Reimers, David M. 2005. *Other Immigrants: The Global Origins of the American People*. New York: New York University Press.

Rhee, Margaret. 2006. "Towards Community: KoreAm Journal and Korean American Cultural Attitudes on Same-Sex Marriage." *Amerasia Journal* 32(1): 75–88.

Rodríguez, Clara E. 2000. *Changing Race: Latinos, the Census, and the History of Ethnicity in the United States*. New York: New York University Press.

Rohrabacher, Dana. 1989. "College Admission Quotas against Asian-Americans: Why is the Civil Rights Community Silent?" Speech given at the Heritage Foundation, September 19. Available at http://www.heritage.org. Accessed on July 7, 2007.

Romano, Lois, "Hill Demographic Goes Slightly More Female." *Washington Post* (Nov. 9, 2007), A39.

Rosenzweig, David. 1998. "Reno, Democrats Criticized by Judge" *Los Angeles Times* (December 15): A1.

Rudrappa, Sharmila. 2004. *Ethnic Routes to Becoming American: Indian Immigrants and the Cultures of Citizenship*. New Brunswick, NJ: Rutgers University Press.

Rumbaut, Rubén G. 2002. "Severed or Sustained Attachments? Language, Identity, and Imagined Communities in the Post-Immigrant Generation." In Peggy Levitt and Mary C. Waters, eds, *The Changing Face of Home: The Transnational Lives of the Second Generation*. New York: Russell Sage Foundation: 43–95.

Saito, Leland T. 2006. "The Political Significance of Race: Asian American and Latino Redistricting Debates in California and New York." In Nicholas De Genova, ed., *Racial Transformations: Latinos and Asians Remaking the United State*. Durham, NC: Duke University Press, 120–43.

—. 2001. "Asian Americans and Multiracial Political Coalitions: New York City's Chinatown and Redistricting, 1990–1991." In Gordon H. Chang, ed., *Asian Americans and Politics: Perspectives, Experiences, Prospects*. Stanford, Calif.: Stanford University Press.

—. 1998. *Race and Politics: Asian Americans, Latinos, and Whites in a Los Angeles Suburb*. Urbana: University of Illinois Press.

Saito, Leland T. and Edward J. W. Park. 2000. "Multiracial Coalitions and Collaborations." In Paul M. Ong, ed., *The State of Asian Pacific America: Transforming Race Relations*. Los Angeles: LEAP Asian Pacific American Public Policy Institute and UCLA Asian American Studies Center: 435–74.

Sakamoto, Arthur and Yu Xie. 2006. "The Socioeconomic Attainments of Asian Americans." In Pyong Gap Min, ed., *Asian Americans: Contemporary Trends and Issues*, 2nd edn., Thousand Oaks, Calif.: Pine Forge Press: 54–77.

Saliba, Therese. 1999. "Resisting Invisibility: Arab Americans in Academia and Activism". In Michael W. Suleiman, ed., *Arabs in America: Building a New Future*. Philadelphia: Temple University Press: 304–19

Samhan, Helen Hatab. 1999. "Not Quite White: Race Classification and the Arab-America Experience". In Michael W. Suleiman, ed., *Arabs in America: Building a New Future*. Philadelphia: Temple University Press: 209–26.

Sanjek, Roger. 1998. *The Future of Us All: Race and Neighborhood Politics in New York City*. Ithaca, NY: Cornell University Press.

Sassen, Saskia. 1990. "Economic Restructuring and the American City." *Annual Review of Sociology* 16(1): 465–90.

Saund, Dalip Singh. 1960. *Congressman from India*. New York: E. P. Dutton.

Saxton, Alexander. 1990. *The Rise and Fall of the White Republic: Class Politics and Mass Culture in Nineteenth-Century America*. London: Verso.

—. 1971. *The Indispensable Enemy: Labor and the Anti-Chinese Movement in California*. Berkeley: University of California Press.

Schmidt, Ronald, Sr. 2000. *Language Policy and Identity Politics in the United States*. Philadelphia: Temple University Press.

Schultz, Jefferey, Andrew Aoki, Kerry L. Haynie, and Anne M. McCulloch. 2000a. *Encyclopedia of Minorities in American Politics, vol. 1: African Americans and Asian Americans*. Phoenix, Ariz.: Oryx Press.

—. 2000b. *Encyclopedia of Minorities in American Politics, vol. 2: Hispanic Americans and Native Americans*. Phoenix, Ariz: Oryx Press.

Sears, David O. 1994. "Urban Rioting in Los Angeles: A Comparison of 1965 with 1992." In Mark Baldassare, ed., *The Los Angeles Riots: Lessons for the Urban Future*. Boulder, Colo.: Westview Press: 237–54.

Secretary of the State of California. Various Years. *Roster: California State, County, City and Township Officials, State Officials of the United States*. Sacramento, Calif.: California Office of State Printing.

Sengupta, Somini. 1998. "What Is a Concentration Camp? Ellis Island Exhibit Prompts a Debate." *New York Times* (March 8).

Seper, Jerry. 2000. "Thai Women to Plead Guilty in False Statements to FEC." *Washington Times* (June 22): A3.

Shah, Sonia. 1997. "Introduction: Slaying the Dragon Lady. Toward an Asian American Feminism." In S. Shah, ed., *Dragon Ladies: Asian American Feminists Breathe Fire*. Boston: South End Press: xii–xxi.

Shore, Elena. 2004. "Ethnic Communities Speak Out Against Gay Marriage." *Pacific News Service* (June 8). Available at http://www.alternet.org/story/18901/.

Shukla, Sandhya. 1999/2000. "New Immigrants, New Forms of Transnational Community: Post-1965 Indian Migrations." *Amerasia Journal* 25 (3): 18–36.

—. 2003. "New Immigrants, New Forms of Transnational Community: Post-1965 Indian Migrations." In Don T. Nakanishi and James S. Lai, eds., *Asian American Politics: Law, Participation, and Policy*. Lanham, Md.: Rowman & Littlefield: 181–92.

—. 2003. "New Immigrants, New Forms of Transnational Community: Post-1965 Indian Migrations." In Don T. Nakanishi and James S. Lai, eds., *Asian American Politics: Law, Participation, and Policy*. Lanham, Md.: Rowman & Littlefield: 181–92.

Sigelman, Lee and Susan Welch. 1993. "The Contact Hypothesis Revisited: Black–White Interaction and Positive Social Attitudes." *Social Forces*. 71(3). 781–95.

Smith, Rogers. 1997. *Civic Ideals: Conflicting Visions of Citizenship in U.S. History*. New Haven: Yale University Press.

Smith, Robert C., Héctor R. Cordero-Guzmán, and Ramón Grosfoguel. 2001. "Introduction: Migration, Transnationalization, and Ethnic and Racial Dynamics in a Changing New York." In Héctor R. Cordero-Guzmán, Robert C. Smith, and Ramón Grosfoguel, eds. *Migration, Transnationalization, & Race in a Changing New York*. Philadelphia: Temple University Press: 1–32.

Sonenshein, Raphael J. 2003. "The Prospects for Multiracial Coalitions: Lessons from America's Three Largest Cities." In Rufus P. Browning, Dale Rogers Marshall, and David H. Tabb, eds., *Racial Politics in American Cities*, 3rd edn., New York: Longman: 333–56.

Soo, Julie D. 2004. "We Asked, They Told: Chinese Americans Unsettled on Same-Sex Marriage. *AsianWeek* (May 21). Available online at http://news.asianweek.com.

Spilerman, Seymour. 1970. "The Costs of Racial Disturbances: A Comparison of Alternative Explanations." *American Sociological Review* 35(4): 627–49.

Srikanth, Rajini. 1998. "Ram Yoshino Uppuluri's Campaign: The Implications for Panethnicity in Asian America." In Lavina Dhingra Shankar and Rajini Srikanth, eds., *A Part, Yet Apart: South Asians in Asian America*. Philadelphia: Temple University Press.

State of California. 1975. California Blue Book. Sacramento, Calif.: California Office of State Printing.

Sterngold, James. 2000. "Nuclear Scientist Set Free after Plea in Secrets Case; Judge Attacks U.S. Conduct." *New York Times* (September 14). Available at www.nytimes.com.

Stober, Dan and Ian Hoffman. 2001. *A Convenient Spy: Wen Ho Lee and the Politics of Nuclear Espionage*. New York: Simon & Schuster.

"Success Story of One Minority Group in U.S." 1966. *U.S. News & World Report* (December 26): 73–6.

Suro, Roberto. 1998. *Strangers Among Us: How Latino Immigration is Transforming America*. New York: Alfred A. Knopf.

Swain, Carol M. 1993. *Black Faces, Black Interests: The Representation of African Americans in Congress*. Cambridge, Mass.: Harvard University Press.

Sweatshop Slaves: Asian Americans in the Garment Industry 2006. Los Angeles: UCLA Labor Center.

Tajima, Renee E. 1989. "Lotus Blossoms Don't Bleed: Images of Asian Women." In Asian Women United of California, ed., *Making Waves: An Anthology of Writings by and about Asian American Women*. Boston: Beacon Press: 308–17.

Takagi, Dana Y. 1998/1992. *The Retreat from Race: Asian-American Admissions and Racial Politics*. New Brunswick, NJ: Rutgers University Press.

Takaki, Ronald. 1998. *Strangers from a Different Shore: A History of Asian Americans*, updated and revised edn. Boston: Little, Brown.

Takeda, Okiyoshi, ed. 2006. Public Symposium Report: Japanese American Leadership Delegation "From Art to Business: Japanese Americans in the Professional Arena." Tokyo: Japan Foundation Center for Global Partnership.

—. 2001. "The Representation of Asian Americans in the U.S. Political System." In Charles E. Menifield, ed., *Representation of Minority Groups in the U.S.: Implications for the Twenty-First Century*. Lanham, Md.: Austin & Weinfeld University Press of America & Winfield: 77–109.

Takezawa, Yasuko. 1995. *Breaking the Silence: Redress and Japanese American Ethnicity*. Ithaca, NY: Cornell University Press.

Tam, Wendy. 1995. "Asians – A Monolithic Voting Bloc?" *Political Behavior*. 17: 223–49.

Tate, Katherine. 2003. *Black Faces in the Mirror: African Americans and Their Representatives in the U.S. Congress*. Princeton, NJ: Princeton University Press.

—. 1994. *From Protest to Politics: The New Black Voters in American Elections*, enlarged edn. Cambridge, Mass.: Harvard University Press.

Tatum, Beverly Daniel. 1997. *"Why Are All the Black Kids Sitting Together In the Cafeteria?" And Other Conversations about Race*. New York: Basic Books.

Taylor, Charles. 1992. *Multiculturalism and the "Politics of Recognition": An Essay*. Princeton, NJ: Princeton University Press.

Taylor, Marylee C. 1998. "How White Attitudes Vary with the Racial Composition of Local Populations: Numbers Count." *American Sociological Review* 63(4): 512–35.

"The *Times* and Wen Ho Lee." 2000. *New York Times* (September 26). Available online at www.nytimes.com.

Tong, Lorraine H. 2000. *Asian Pacific Americans in the United States Congress*. Congressional Research Service Report for Congress, 97–398 GOV.

Tran, My-Thuan and Christian Berthelsen. 2008. "Leaning Left in Little Saigon." *Los Angeles Times* (February 28).

Tsai, Shih-shan Henry. 1986. *The Chinese Experience in America*. Bloomington and Indianapolis: Indiana University Press.

Tuan, Mia. 2001. *Forever Foreigners or Honorary Whites? The Asian Ethnic Experience Today*. New Brunswick, NJ: Rutgers University Press.

Tucker, Clyde, Brian Kojetin, and Roderick Harrison. n.d.[1995] "A Statistical Analysis of the CPS Supplement on Race and Ethnic Origin." Bureau of Labor Statistics, Bureau of the Census. <http://www.census.gov/prod/2/gen/96arc/ ivatuck.pdf>

Umemoto, Karen. 1989. " 'On Strike!' San Francisco State College Strike, 1968–69: The Role of Asian American Students." *Amerasia Journal* 15(1): 3–41.

U.S. Bureau of Census 2005a. Summary File 2: 2000 Census of Population and Housing. Technical Documentation (SF2/06 (RV)). Washington: U.S. Bureau of Census. <http://www.census.gov/prod/cen2000/doc/sf2.pdf>

—. 2005b. *Statistical Abstract of the United States, 2004–2005.* Washington: U.S. Bureau of Census.

—. 2004. Current Population Survey (November).

—. 2001. Difference in Population by Race and Hispanic or Latino Origin, for the United States: 1990 to 2000. PHC-T-1, table 4. http://www.census.gov/population/www/cen2000/phc-t1.html>

—. Census 2000 Summary File 1. 110th Congressional District Summary File (100-per cent).

—. "Net Undercount and Undercount Rate for U.S. (1990)" http://www.census.gov/dmd/www/pdf/underus.pdf

USDA. n.d. "Non-Citizen Requirements in the Food Stamp Program." Available at http://www.fns.usda.gov/fsp/Rules/Legislation/pdfs/Non_Citizen_Guidance.pdf.

Verba, Sidney, Kay Lehman Scholzman, and Henry E. Brady. 1995. *Voice and Equality: Civic Voluntarism in American Politics.* Cambridge, Mass.. Harvard University Press.

Vergara, Vanessa B. M. 1997. "Broken Promises and Aging Patriots: An Assessment of US Veteran Benefits for Filipino World War II Veterans." *Asian American Policy Review* 7 (spring): 163–82.

Vickerman, Milton. 1999. *Crosscurrents: West Indian Immigrants and Race.* New York: Oxford University Press.

Villaroman, Rene. 2007. "Asian American Lawyers Support Same-Sex Union." *Asian Journal Online* (September 30). Available at http://www.asianjournal.com/.

Viruell-Fuentes, Edna A. 2006. " 'My Heart Is Always There': The Transnational Practices of First-Generation Mexican Immigrant and Second-Generation Mexican American Women." *Identities: Global Studies in Culture and Power* 13(3): 335–62.

Walker, Thaal. 2004. "Jobs Are Key Issue in 20th Assembly District Contest." *San Jose Mercury News* (February 5).

Wang, Ling-chi. 1995. "The Structure of Dual Domination: Toward a Paradigm for the Study of the Chinese Diaspora in the United States." *Amerasia Journal* 21(1&2): 149–69.

Watanabe, Paul Y. 2001. "Global Forces, Foreign Policy, and Asian Pacific Americans." *PS: Political Science & Politics* 34(3): 639–44.

Waters, Mary C. 1999. *Black Identities: West Indian Immigrant Dreams and American Realities.* New York: Russell Sage Foundation.

—. 1990. *Ethnic Options: Choosing Ethnic Identities in America.* Berkeley: University of California Press.

Wei, William. 1993. *The Asian American Movement.* Philadelphia: Temple University Press.

Welch, Susan, Lee Sigelman, Timothy Bledsoe, and Michael Combs. 2001. *Race and Place: Race Relations in an American City.* New York: Cambridge University Press.

Wilkes, Rima and John Iceland. 2004. "Hypersegregation in the Twenty-First Century." *Demography* 41(1): 23–36.

Wilkins, David E. 2002. *American Indian Politics and the American Political System.*

Lanham, Md.: Rowman & Littlefield.

Williams-León, Teresa and Cynthia L. Nakashima. 2001. *The Sum of Our Parts: Mixed-Heritage Asian Americans*. Philadelphia: Temple University Press.

Wolfinger, Raymond and Steven J. Rosenstone. 1980. *Who Votes*. New Haven: Yale University Press.

"Women and Minorities in the 110th Congress." *CQ Weekly* (Feb. 26, 2007), 607.

Wong, Diane Yen-mei, with Dennis Hayashi. 1989. "Behind Unmarked Doors: Developments in the Garment Industry." In Asian Women United of California, ed., *Making Waves: An Anthology of Writings by and about Asian American Women*. Boston: Beacon Press: 159–71.

Wong, Janelle S. 2006. *Democracy's Promise: Immigrants & American Civic Institutions*. Ann Arbor: University of Michigan Press.

—. 2004. "Getting Out the Vote among Asian Americans in Los Angeles County: The Effects of Phone Canvassing." *AAPI Nexus* 2(2): 49–65.

Wright, Lawrence. 1994. "One Drop of Blood." *New Yorker* (July 25): 46–55.

Wu, Frank H. and May L. Nicholson. 1997. "Have You No Decency? An Analysis of Racial Aspects of Media Coverage of the John Huang Matter." *Asian American Policy Review* 7: 1–37.

Wu, Jeremy S. and Carson K. Eoyang. 2006. Asian Pacific American Senior Executives in the Federal Government. *AAPI Nexus* 4(1): 39–50.

Yamamoto, Eric K. et al. 2001. *Race, Rights and Reparation: Law and the Japanese American Internment*. New York: Aspen.

Yancey, George. 2003. *Who Is White? Latinos, Asians, and the New Black/Nonblack Divide*. Boulder, Colo.: Lynne Rienner Publishers.

Yoo, David K., ed. 1999. *New Spiritual Homes: Religion and Asian Americans*. Honolulu: University of Hawai'i Press.

Yoon, Sam. 2006. "From Chinatown to City Council: An Interview with Sam Yoon, Boston City Councilor." Interviewed by P. J. Kim. *Asian American Policy Review* 15: 1–5.

Yoshikawa, Taeko. 2006. "From a Refugee Camp to the Minnesota State Senate: A Case Study of a Hmong American Woman's Challenge." *Hmong Studies Journal* 7. <http://hmongstudies.org/Yoshikawa.pdf> (accessed January 3, 2007).

Zia, Helen. 2000. *Asian American Dreams: The Emergence of an American People*. New York: Farrar, Straus, and Giroux.

Zolberg, Aristide. 2008. *A Nation by Design: Immigration Policy in the Fashioning of America*. New York: Russell Sage.

Index

Asian Community Development
 Corporation (ACDC), 107
Asian Immigrant Women's Advocates
 (AIAW), 173
Asian Indians
 identity and India, 82–3
 numbers, 34, 35, 36
 socioeconomics, 41
 terminology, 192
Asian Law Caucus, 87
Asian Pacific American Caucus (APAC), 90
Asian Pacific American Institute for
 Congressional Studies (APAICS),
 80, 90
Asian Pacific American Legal Center of
 California (APALC), 87, 133
Asian Pacific American Media Coalition
 (APAMC), 151–2
Asian Pacific Environmental Network
 (APEN), 88
assimilation paradigm, 84
Association for Multiethnic Americans
 (AMEA), 31
Azerbaijan, 29

Bacerra, Xaiver, 111
Bangladeshis
 education, 160
 numbers, 34, 35
Barred Zone Act, 11
Bauman, Kurt, 159
Bennett, Claudette, 158
Bhatt, Ash, 112
Biddle, Francis, 175
Black Power, 137
Boston, 107
Boxer, Barbara, 103
Brady, Henry, 67
Bruno, Dan, 148
Buffon, George-Louis, 14
Bulgarians, 5
Burling, John, 178
Bush, George H., 179
Bush, George W., 73, 114
Butterfield, Fox, 157

California
 alien land laws, 17
 Asian American population, 39–40,
 120
 Asian American Studies Center
 (AASC), 128

campaign funding, 61
Chinese electoral fundraising, 49
early Asian immigrants, 7
education statistics, 160
executive employment, 115
intergroup perceptions, 122–4
labor issues, 173
language policy, 169–70
Latinos-Asian Americans relations,
 132–3
Monterey Park and San Gabriel
 Valley Region, 131–2
political participation, 67–8
political partisanship, 72, 73–4
political representation, 99, 101,
 103–6, 111–12
taxation of Chinese residents, 8–9
Third World Strikes, 165
World War II aliens, 19, 175
Cambodians
 education, 158
 geographical clusters, 107
 numbers, 34, 35
 socioeconomics, 41–2
Campaign for Justice, 180
campaign funding, 49, 60–1, 149–51
Campbell, Ben Nighthorse, 99
Caribbeans, 28–9, 118, 137
cartoons, 49
Caucasians, 5, 14, 15
Cayetano, Benjamin, 115
Census Bureau
 Current Population Survey, 71
 ethnic categories, vii, viii, 30–1, 32, 33
 methodology, 191–5
 terminology, 195
Center for Labor Research and
 Education, 173
Central Pacific, 9
CHAMP (Chinese for Harmony in
 Monterey Park), 132
Chan, Wilma, 103
Chan is Missing, 153
Chao, Elaine, 114–15
Charlie Chan, 152, 153
Chavez, Cesar, 132
Chiang, John, 103
Chicago, 47, 126–7
Chin, Vincent, 30, 91
China
 espionage, 148
 US wartime ally, 145

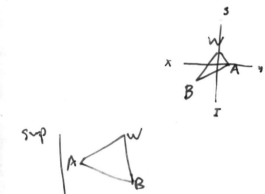

s

W

x   A   y

B

I

sup

W

A

B

inf

out   ins